# GOOD NEWS STUDIES

Consulting Editor: Robert J. Karris, O.F.M.

Volume 14

# The Sermon on the Mount

*Proclamation and Exhortation*

*by*

*Jan Lambrecht, SJ*

Michael Glazier
Wilmington, Delaware

About the Author
Jan Lambrecht, S.J., is Professor of New Testament and
Biblical Greek at the Catholic University of Leuven in Bel-
gium. His articles have appeared in many scholarly journals
and his books include: *Parables of Jesus: Insight and Challenge*; and *Once More Astonished: The Parables of Jesus
Christ*.

First published in 1985 by Michael Glazier, Inc., 1723 Delaware Avenue,
Wilmington, Delaware 19806

Library of Congress Catalog Card Number: 85-047751
International Standard Book Number:
  Good News Studies: 0-89453-290-1
  THE SERMON ON THE MOUNT: 0-89453-467-X

Printed in the United States of America

# TABLE OF CONTENTS

## Chapter Two

## Chapter Three

## Chapter Four

### *Exterior Display and Prayer*
### *(Mt 6:1-18)* .................................122

## Chapter Five

## Chapter Six

**Chapter Seven**

*The Lucan Sermon on the Plain*

# Appendix

# Indexes

# FOREWORD

The beginning of the letter to the Hebrews is famous: "In many and various ways God spoke of old to our fathers by the prophets; but in these last days he has spoken to us by a Son" (1:1-2a). This Son, Our Lord Jesus Christ, is called in v. 3 the reflection of the glory of God and the "very stamp of his nature." Jesus brought good news in the name of God, and he called people to respond. This double aspect of message and call, of proclamation and exhortation, is eminently present in Jesus' first programmatic sermon. It is for all of us, therefore, to listen to the definitive word of God and to act on it.

The programmatic sermon has been preserved in two versions: in Matthew's Sermon on the Mount (chapters 5-7) and in Luke's Sermon on the Plain (6:20-49). In the seven chapters of the present book, I examine not only both versions of the text as we have them, but also the material that was taken up in them, the older texts and traditions. This is done to understand them better, of course, but also to be able to apply them more effectively to contemporary circumstances.

As in some of my previous publications, I will present not only the results of current biblical exegesis but also the stages involved in this research. I am not writing primarily for specialists but for a broader public: students of theology, priests and religious, religion teachers, catechists, and the many non-professionals who are eager to learn. Although I have not supplied burdensome footnotes, I am aware that the occasionally detailed analyses will demand perseverance from the reader. Nevertheless, I hope this study will bring about greater familiarity with the Scriptures and thus provide insight, encouragement, and challenge.

The Bible translation is that of the Revised Standard Version unless otherwise indicated. The text is also printed synoptically in a separate fascicle for ready reference. Should the reader wish to continue his or her study in greater depth, a select bibliography is given at the end of each chapter. (A fuller bibliography with more German, French, and Dutch titles can be found in the Dutch and German editions of this work.) This study is based largely on these cited works. Most of what is in this book I have taught to young people. It is my hope that it will be of service to them and to new generations. Chapters three, four, and five are based on some of my previous publications: "Er is u gezegd ..., maar Ik zeg u ..." (Groepsgesprek van de religieuzen 110; Mechelen 1981); "Zo moet U bidden. Het Onze Vader: uitleg en vertaling (*Tijdschrift voor liturgie*, 61, 1977, pp. 185-205); "De bergrede over het gebed" and "Broodbede en menselijke inzet" (*Thuis in Gods ruimte. Over gebed en gebedsopvoeding in onze tijd*, Niké-reeks 1, Leuven 1981, pp. 121-137 and 139-157). I thank the respective publishers for their permission to use this material here.

With the completion of this English edition, I wish to express my gratitude to my student Richard Thompson, who was most helpful in editing the text and correcting the proofs. I also wish to offer my sincere thanks to Dr. Florence Morgan Gillman of Gonzaga University, Spokane, Washington, and Dr. Wilfrid Harrington, O.P., St. Mary's, Tallaght, Co Dublin, who gave the manuscript a final critical review.

Paradoxically, as some put it, the question is not whether we agree with the Sermon on the Mount but whether the Sermon on the Mount agrees with us. Do we, perhaps, consider this sermon beautiful but without any obligation for us? Christians have too often debilitated God's last word and rendered it innocuous — or forgotten it in discourgement. "Not every one who says to me, 'Lord, Lord,' shall enter the Kingdom of heaven, but he who does the will of my Father who is in heaven" (Mt 7:21). In this book, I try to link the Bible to life, the past to the present, and to do this intelligently and discreetly. Jesus' programmatic sermon obviously has a social and world-changing dynamism. Nevertheless, it seems to me, it cannot be stressed enough how Jesus touches and calls the individual in the most profound depths of his or her personality.

Jan Lambrecht, S.J.

# ABBREVIATIONS

The books of the Old and New Testaments are abbreviated as in the Revised Standard Version of the Bible.

Series and *Journals*:

*Afr. Theol. Journ.*
  African Theological Journal
An. Bibl.
  Analecta biblica
Ass. Seign. II
  Assemblées du Seigneur (second series)
*Austr. Bibl. Rev.*
  Australian Biblical Review
*Bib. Kirche*
  Bibel und Kirche
*Bib. Leb.*
  Bibel und Leben
*Bibl.*
  Biblica
Bibl. Eph. Theol. Lov.
  Bibliotheca Ephemeridum theologicarum Lovaniensium
*Bibl. Theol. Bull.*
  Biblical Theology Bulletin
*Bibl. Zeitschr.*
  Biblische Zeitschrift

Cah. Trad. Oec. Bible
    Cahiers de la traduction oecuménique de la Bible
*Cath. Bibl. Quart.*
    *The Catholic Biblical Quarterly*
Et. Bibl.
    Etudes bibliques
*Exp. Times*
    *The Expository Times*
Forsch. Bib.
    Forschung zur Bibel
*Ir. Bibl. Stud.*
    *Irish Biblical Studies*
*Journ. Bibl. Lit.*
    *Journal of Biblical Literature*
*Journ. Rel.*
    *The Journal of Religion*
*Journ. Stud. N.T.*
    *Journal for the Study of the New Testament*
*Journ. Theol. S. Afr.*
    *Journal of Theology for Southern Africa*
*Journ. Theol. Stud.*
    *Journal of Theological Studies*
*Louv. Stud.*
    *Louvain Studies*
*Neotest.*
    *Neotestamentica*
*New Test. Stud.*
    *New Testament Studies*
*Nouv. Rev. Theol.*
    *Nouvelle revue théologique*
*Nov. Test.*
    *Novum Testamentum*
*Ons Geest. Leven*
    *Ons geestelijk leven*
Quaest. Disput.
    Quaestiones disputatae
*Rev. Théol. Louv.*
    *Revue théologique de Louvain*

*Scott. Journ. Theol.*
*The Scottish Journal of Theology*
Soc. New Test. Stud. Mon. Ser.
Society for New Testament Studies. Monograph Series
Stud. A.N.T.
Studien zum Alten und Neuen Testament
*Stud. Ev.*
*Studia evangelica*
Stud. N.T. Umwelt
Studien zum Neuen Testament und seiner Umwelt
Stuttg. Bib. Stud.
Stuttgarter Bibelstudien
Suppl. Nov. Test.
Supplements to Novum Testamentum
Texte u. Unters.
Texte und Untersuchungen zur Geschichte der altchristlichen
Literatur
Theol. Büch.
Theologische Bücherei
*Theol. Evang.*
*Theologia Evangelica*
Theol. Ex. H.
Theologische Existenz heute
*Theol. Stud.*
*Theological Studies*
*Trier. Theol. Zeitschr.*
*Trierer theologische Zeitschrfit*
*Zeitschr. Neutest. Wiss.*
*Zeitschrift für die neutestamentliche Wissenschaft*
*Zeitschr. Theol. Kirche*
*Zeitschrift für Theologie und Kirche*

Other abbreviations:
ed.(s)    editor(s)
ET        English translation
Fs.       *Festschrift*
Q         *Quelle* (*Logienquelle*, sayings source)
R         Redaction (created by the evangelist himself)
S         *Sondergut* (traditions found only in one evangelist)

*Chapter One*

# THE SERMON ON THE MOUNT AND THE SERMON ON THE PLAIN (Mt 5-7; Lk 6:20-49)

Both the Gospel of Matthew and the Gospel of Luke contain an important sermon quite early in their texts: Mt 5:1-7:29 and Lk 6:20-49. Matthew's is long, consisting of three entire chapters (111 verses); Luke's is much shorter, not even a complete chapter (30 verses). So we have the Matthean Sermon on the Mount and the Lucan Sermon on the Plain — according to Luke, Jesus descended the mountain and gave this sermon on a level place (cf. Lk 6:17).

Notwithstanding the differences in length and location, the two sermons have much in common. They both begin with the beatitudes and end with the parable of the house and the storm, and almost everything that Luke writes is also found in Matthew. In both sermons, Jesus deals with the behavior of his disciples and lays great stress on love of neighbor and even of one's enemy. Both are situated at the beginning of Jesus' public life, and both are followed immediately by the cure of the servant of the centurion.

In this introductory chapter I will first consider briefly how this important sermon has been explained in the past. The second part will give an overview of Matthew's Sermon on the Mount, and the third Luke's Sermon on the Plain. In the fourth part, I will deal with the source text the two evangelists used and the question of whether or not that older sermon goes back to Jesus.

## I. The Explanations

The Matthean Sermon on the Mount has been continually the subject of re-interpretation by Christians throughout the ages. This happened much less often with the Lucan Sermon on the Plain. One can even speak of a "history of interpretation" of the Sermon on the Mount. Different explanations were favored at one time or another.

### THREE COMPETING INTERPRETATIONS

With J. Jeremias and others, one may, for the sake of convenience, distinguish three kinds of explanation that have been advocated in the course of history. They are the ethical, the pedagogical, and the eschatological interpretations.

a) According to the first and oldest interpretation, the Sermon on the Mount contains the new law for the disciples of Christ. It presents a summary of Christian morality. Jesus states precisely what he expects from his disciples, what they must do and not do, how they must live. Obviously, the commands of the Sermon on the Mount are judged to be practicable. In this discourse, Jesus is, as it were, the lawgiver par excellence. He intentionally poses an ideal of moral perfection . This is the *ethical* interpretation, which was defended in the early Church by Justin and John Chrysostom, among others.

b) The second approach to the Sermon on the Mount is associated with Martin Luther, and many Protestants have followed him. In the Middle Ages, there was talk of a double morality, one for ordinary Christians, who must abide by the commandments to be saved, and one for monks, who were to strive for perfection by following the three evangelical counsels: poverty, chastity, and obedience. The distinction made in the gospels between the people and the disciples was cited to support this. Much of what is required in the Sermon on the Mount seemed to be unattainable for ordinary Christians and, strictly speaking, applied only to those who were situated in the state of perfection. They were the ones who had to take the Sermon on the Mount seriously and realize its ideal.

In some of his writings, Luther considered the Sermon on the Mount to be intended for everybody, but he saw its demands as impracticable. Therefore, he rejected the solution that changed its commands for all into counsels for monks. According to Luther, Jesus had a very particular purpose with his radical instructions and commands. Because they could not be carried out, we are forced to accept our total sinfulness. Confronted with the Sermon on the Mount, we become aware that we are and remain sinners. We despair totally of ourselves, but this is salvific, for we can open ourselves to God's grace in authentic faith only by recognizing our pride and impotence. Righteousness, and thus also the ability to fulfill the commandments, must be given gratuitously. Luther thus explained the Sermon on the Mount in the Pauline manner! Like the law of the Old Covenant, that of the New is only a preparation for the true and authentic gospel. In this conception, Jesus is the great preacher of repentance, and he intended the Sermon on the Mount as a way of preparing people. It envisions education and conversion. This is the *pedagogical* explanation.

c) Around 1900, a third type of explanation won widespread acceptance. Biblical scholars such as J. Weiss and A. Schweitzer developed the insight that Jesus had preached the arrival of the Kingdom of God in the near future. The Kingdom of God was at hand and would appear very soon.

Only a short interval remained. The Sermon on the Mount therefore contained a morality intended for this intervening time. Its radical demands are exceptional laws that apply in a time of distress, a final crisis. One must become aware of the seriousness of this situation. One must seize the last chance and convert before the "eschaton." One must join in the penitential movement that immediately precedes God's definitive intervention. In this *eschatological* explanation, Jesus is a completely apocalyptic figure.

## IMPRACTICABLE?

Before dealing with other interpretations, I will take up the much discussed question of whether the demands of the Sermon on the Mount can be met. In a short study devoted to this Sermon, G. Schmahl distinguishes between *Gültigkeit* and *Verbindlichkeit*, which we may translate as applicability and binding character. Does the Sermon on the Mount apply to everyone and does it actually bind them? Are its demands general and are they truly demands? The three positions summarized above assume the binding character of Jesus' sermon. They consider its content to be law. But all three are obviously impressed with the number of extremely difficult prescriptions. One and the same question underlies all three: Is the Sermon on the Mount practicable? A solution is sought, a way out. The first explanation tends to assign living according to the Sermon on the Mount to specialists, to a religious elite: Jesus' prescription is "supererogation," an extra obligation not intended for all Christians. The second admits the impossibility of living up to it, and holds that Jesus had a pedagogical intention because the "impracticable" law leads to grace. The third explanation offers a new solution: the radical Sermon on the Mount must be maintained, certainly, but only during a short period, "momentarily." The extraordinary may be demanded in a crisis!

Further on in this book, I will discuss in detail the applicability and binding character of the Sermon on the Mount. But let it be said here that it has often been argued in recent years that the Sermon on the Mount does not make concrete demands and need not be taken literally. It only requires an attitude and presents an ideal toward which it is sufficient to strive. The Sermon on the Mount does envision a fundamental change of mentality, but it would be erroneous, it is argued, to attempt to find prescriptions in it that are applicable always and for everyone. What is cast in the form of a prescription merely indicates the orientation of the desired effort. Although it is presented sincerely and is well-intentioned, can one agree with such an explanation?

Many other explanations and, consequently, ways of acting have been proposed. The following summary is not intended to be exhaustive. Calvin, for example, did not want to consider Jesus a new lawgiver. In his view, Jesus had restored the honor of the Law of the Old Covenant by purifying it of erroneous Pharisaic interpretations, so there is continuity between the Law and the Gospel. Like Luther and other reformers, he opposed the anarchism and the ethical radicalism of the Anabaptists, the apocalyptic fanatics. Arguing from the Sermon on the Mount, these people refused to serve in the army, to swear oaths, and to exercise judicial functions. They demanded a sharp division between church and state, and, as true Christians, they would have nothing to do with the state and formed small communities of their own. Throughout the centuries, sectarian groups have often tried to obey the prescriptions of the Sermon (or at least some of them) literally.

Luther, too, distinguished two kingdoms, that of God and that of the world, and held that the Sermon on the Mount applies only to God's kingdom. God himself wants the secular power to exercise its authority according to its own laws. Luther, who is primarily concerned here with individual salvation, argued that Christians may participate in the secular order and occupy office in it, but that they must remain true to the Sermon on the Mount in their hearts.

Toward the end of the eighteenth century and during the nineteenth, some exegetes stressed that the Sermon on the Mount defended the most profound human values. Without doubt, Jesus wanted to have his words applied in reality, but, these exegetes argued, he was particularly concerned with the disposition of the human act. In more recent times, however, there has been a tendency to emphasize the parts of the Sermon that are critical of society. For example, the passage concerned with offering no resistance (Mt 5:39-41 = Lk 6:28-30) lends itself to citation in discussions on the arms race.

One more observation concludes this section. It used to be accepted without question that Jesus himself preached the sermon. But historical-critical exegesis teaches us that about fifty years intervened between the time when Jesus preached and the time the Synoptic Gospels were given their definitive form. Moreover, we have the Lucan Sermon on the Plain in addition to the Matthean Sermon on the Mount. Which of the two is the most Jesus-like? But is this really a useful question? In these texts, we come in contact primarily with the Matthean and the Lucan Christ and not directly with the earthly Jesus. Before we can answer the historical question, therefore, we must listen attentively to what each evangelist has to say and carefully compare the two texts.

## II. The Matthean Sermon on the Mount

With its 28 chapters, the Gospel of Matthew is much longer than Mark's. Matthew takes over the topographical and chronological scheme of Mark in large measure and used it as his basic structure. He follows its pattern very closely after 14:1, but in the first half of his gospel he is more independent in the ordering of the pericopes. He expands Mark considerably, in the beginning with the so-called Infancy Narrative (Mt 1-2) and at the end with the appearance of the Risen Jesus to the eleven on the mountain (28:16-20). He also adds a number of passages. Many exegetes hold (and I agree) that he used a separate tradition (S: the Matthean *Sondergut* that is material proper to Matthew) and the sayings source (*Quelle, Logienquelle,* which no longer exists but can be reconstructed from the material that Matthew and Luke share and that is not found in Mk). Like Mk, the Gospel of Matthew presents Jesus as active for a long period in Galilee before he goes up to Jerusalem where he will die.

In addition to this fidelity to the Marcan order, Matthew's method of compilation — combining, interweaving, and merging — is characteristic. He often brings together similar material and combines it into a new whole, for example, the two mission sermons in Mt 10 (that of Mk 6:7-13 and that from Q, cf. Lk 10:1-11). Thus, we can rightly speak of a Matthean tendency to gather, order and systematize.

## THE CONTEXT OF THE SERMON ON THE MOUNT

The Sermon on the Mount is the first of five long speeches in the Matthean Gospel. After each speech, the transition to a narrative part is always made with roughly the same formula: "And when Jesus had finished these sayings..." (7:28; cf. 11:1; 13:53; 19:1; 26:1). The Sermon on the Mount consists predominantly of material from Q, but there is also a significant amount from S.

Mt 4:12-11:1 is one of the sections in which Matthew radically altered the Marcan order. Is it still possible to determine where in the Marcan order Matthew inserted his Sermon on the Mount? After Mk 3:7-13 is often suggested. Indeed, we find at this point in Mk a summary with which Mt 4:23-25 has similarities, and there is also the mountain motif (cf. Mt 5:1) and the separate mention of the crowds of people and the disciples (cf. Mt 4:25-5:1).

But another insertion point should be preferred. One must set the two gospels next to each other and compare:

Mk 1:16-20 (call of the first four disciples)
Mt 4:18-22 (call of the first four disciples)
Mk 1:21 (teaching)
Mt 5:2 (teaching)

> Mk 1:22 ("And they were astonished at his teaching, for he taught them as one who had authority, and not as the scribes.")
>
> Mt 7:28-29 (". . . the crowds were astonished at his teaching, for he taught them as one who had authority, and not as their scribes.")
>
> Mk 1:40-45 (cleansing of the leper)
>
> Mt 8:1-4 (cleansing of the leper)

In the light of these striking agreements, we may conclude that Matthew inserted his Sermon on the Mount between Mk 1:21 (= Mt 5:2) and 22 (= Mt 7:28-29). Of course, this does not mean that he did not borrow sayings and motifs from Mk 3:7-13 (and other Marcan passages) in the redaction of his summary in 4:23-25.

Matthew intentionally placed this speech, the first of a series, at the beginning of his gospel. The Sermon on the Mount is the programmatic sermon of the Matthean Jesus. After the temptation pericope (4:1-11), Matthew formed a long introduction (4:12-25) to this important sermon by revising and rewriting what he preserved from Mk Ch. 1 (Jesus' return to Galilee, start of the preaching, call of the first four disciples, activity in Galilee).

## THE STRUCTURE OF THE SERMON ON THE MOUNT

Here in Chapter One it is not yet necessary to present the content of Mt 5-7 in detail. A global overview will suffice, since the primary question here is how Matthew structured his sermon. The opinions of scholars diverge sharply on this point. I will discuss three positions.

a) According to J. Fitzmyer, Matthew's Sermon on the Mount, unlike Luke's Sermon on the Plain, is quite well structured. The structure is simple, because the predominant thematic word is "righteousness." Fitzmyer's division, which he gives almost incidentally and without much argumentation in his commentary on Luke, is as follows:

I: Introduction (5:3-16)
  1. 5:3-12: the beatitudes
  2. 5:13-16: introductory sayings
II: Proposition (5:17-20: the three kinds of righteousness are contrasted, see v. 20)
III: The righteousness of the scribes (5,21-48: six antitheses)
IV: The righteousness of the Pharisees (6:1-18: the triad of alms, prayer, and fasting)
V: The righteousness of the disciples (6:19-7:27: a series of unrelated sayings).

In Fitzmyer's outline, Matthew's very important concept of righteousness dominates. The question, however, is whether Matthew does indeed distinguish three kinds of righteousness. One has the impression that, for Matthew, the scribes and the Pharisees belong to the same category. Further, already in the third and fourth parts (and not only in the fifth, as the classification suggests), the Matthean Jesus is certainly concerned with stating the content of Christian righteousness. Finally, Fitzmyer himself admits that a large portion of the Sermon (V: 6:19-7:27) has very little structure.

b) In a short and now rarely cited study, O. Hanssen proposed a plan in 1970 that is quite attractive at first sight: Matthew composed his sermon in part chiastically. Hanssen, too, considers 5:3-16 as an introduction and 7:13-27 as the conclusion of the sermon. The principal part, 5:17-7:12 consists of:

I: The theme (5:17-20, the greater righteousness)
II: First part: Christians and Jews (5:21-6:18)
  1. The new attitude toward *the neighbor*: 5:21-48 (five antitheses)
  2. The new attitude toward *God*: 6:1-18 (three pious practices)

III: Second part: Christians and pagans (6:19-7:12)
  1. The new attitude toward *God*: 6:19-34 (against mammon; do not be anxious)
  2. The new attitude toward *the neighbor*: 7:1-12 (Golden Rule; do not judge).

Objections can also be raised against this proposal. One wonders whether 5:17-20 is not actually an introduction only to 5:21-48 so that these verses do not, or at least not primarily, give the theme of the entire section (5:17-7:12). If Matthew contrasts the Christians to the Jews in II and to the pagans in III, then he did not mark the transition clearly. The chiastic alternation of neighbor-God and God-neighbor is also not clearly visible.

But perhaps these observations are too harsh on Fitzmyer, Hanssen, and other authors who have looked for a structure in the Sermon on the Mount. Even though one might not agree with their proposals, they do draw our attention to data and details that might otherwise often be overlooked or ignored. In addition, they help us to organize and grasp the content. The risk of exaggerations is a small price to pay for these benefits.

c) I will use the following structure as a working hypothesis:

Narrative beginning: 5:1-2
Sermon: 5:3-7:27
  I: Introduction (prologue): 5:3-16
  II: Middle part: 5:17-7:12
    1. The antitheses (5:17-48)
    2. Not before men (6:1-18)
    3. Unconcern and commitment (6:19-7:12)
  III: Conclusion (epilogue): 7:13-27
Narrative ending: 7:28-29.

Like Hanssen and many others, I consider 5:17-7:12 as the actual body of the sermon. Verse 12 of Chapter 7 is the "Golden Rule": "So whatever you wish that men would do to you, do so to them; for this is the Law and the Prophets." This generalizing verse ("whatever") rounds off and summarizes the unit: "so." Moreover, the expression "the Law and the Prophets" reminds us of 5:17, the opening verse of this section which has "the Law or the Prophets." It is also possible to see 7:13-27 as a conclusion or epilogue to the sermon; in 7:13, there is a new start, and the content of these concluding verses more or less forms a thematic unity. The beatitudes (5:3-12) and the sayings about salt and light (5:13-16) belong together and can be considered an introduction or prologue to the sermon.

The three-part division of the middle portion presents no difficulties for the first two sections: 5:17-48 (the antitheses) and 6:1-18 (not before men). I hope to be able to show below in Chapter Five that 6:19-7:12 also has a certain thematic unity. Whether Matthew the Evangelist intended this structure himself is, of course, uncertain. But I am of the opinion that this proposition does not falsify Matthew's thought development nor does it force it. As the reader will note, this structure is the basis of the division of the present book.

## THREE INCLUSIONS

Mt 5:17 and 7:12 are sometimes called "inclusions." Inclusion is a literary technique by which a text, small or large, is framed or boxed in. The framing elements correspond to each other in vocabulary and motifs. Sometimes an inclusion is merely a rounding off, the result of a stylistic habit that has little or no importance for the content of the passage. For the Sermon on the Mount, however, there are three inclusions that are significant in addition to those of 5:17 and 7:12.

a) *The Hearers*

> 5:1-2: Seeing the crowds, he went up on the mountain, and when he sat down his *disciples* came to him. And he opened his mouth and taught them saying.

> 7:28-29: And when Jesus finished these sayings, the *crowds* were astonished at his teaching, for he taught them as one who had authority, and not as their scribes.

Strictly speaking, the beginning and the end of the narrative do not form a real inclusion. Nevertheless, they are related to each other, and both mention listeners. Notwithstanding 7:28-29, one might well argue that Matthew's Sermon on the Mount was addressed only to the disciples. The arguments for this are the following: in addition to 5:1-2 (Jesus avoids the crowd, the people; he isolates himself; his disciples approach him), there are the sayings of 5:13-16 on the salt of the earth and the light of the world, which clearly refer to the disciples' obligation to give witness to other people. Further, one could reason from Matthew's pastoral insistence. The disciples for whom he is writing are his fellow Christians. The Sermon on the Mount is their life program.

Still, one should not stress this exclusivity, for the people are mentioned in 7:28-29. In addition, although "the people, the crowd" are, for Matthew, neutral in comparison with the disciples, they are rather well-disposed toward Jesus (see, for example, 9:33 and 12:23). This remains the case until the day that "all the people," incited by the chief priests and the elders, cry out "His blood be on us and on our children!" (27:25). In Matthew's conception, the listening people form a more distant circle than do the disciples, but the present and listening people are, after all, potential disciples. Thus, it is better not to invoke the introductory verses to argue that the Sermon on the Mount is not for everybody, that it does not apply to ordinary Christians but is rather a kind of supplementary course for advanced students.

b) *Word and Deed*

> 4:23: And he [Jesus] went about all Galilee, teaching in their synagogues and preaching the gospel of the kingdom and healing every disease and every infirmity among the people.

> 9:35: And Jesus went about all the cities and villages, teaching in their synagogues and preaching the gospel of the kingdom, and healing every disease and every infirmity.

With the second, more encompassing inclusion, Matthew shows that he wants to consider Chapters 5-9 as a unit. This unit consists of two parts: a long sermon (the Sermon on the Mount, Chapters 5-7) and a series of miracles (Chapters 8-9). Matthew (as is often said following J. Schniewind) thus first presented the Messiah of the word and then the Messiah of the deed. Perhaps, we may conclude from this double picture of Jesus that, in Matthew's belief, Jesus not only called men to perfection and greater righteousness but also enabled them to achieve this by his redemptive, miraculous power.

## c) *The Observance*

> 5:1-2: Seeing the crowds, he went up on the mountain, and when he sat down his disciples came to him. And he opened his mouth and taught them saying.
>
> 28:19-20: Go therefore and make disciples of all nations, baptizing them ..., teaching them to observe all that I have commanded you ....

Matthew certainly alludes to his Sermon on the Mount with the closing words of his gospel. We have a mountain scene in Galilee both at the beginning of Jesus' public life and after his resurrection (cf. 5:1 with 28:16). As Jesus' redemptive acts (Chapters 8-9) have given the disciples the power to follow him and to observe everything that he commanded (see the second inclusion), in the same way baptism after the resurrection transforms the Christian into a new person who, with God's grace, is capable of living in a Christian manner. The evangelist concludes his gospel with a Jesus who expressly orders the people to be taught to observe what he commanded. The Matthean Jesus almost obsessively stresses that it is not sufficient to hear the word: one must act according to it. This idea is present in all its clarity in the initial sermon of Matthew's gospel: see 7:21-27. We find it again in such places as the parable of the last judgment (25:31-46), in the second part of the parable of the unwilling wedding guests (22:11-14), and in the very last verse of this gospel: 28:20.

## III. The Lucan Sermon on the Plain

It is now generally accepted that the Gospel of Luke and the Acts of the Apostles were written by the same author. In the same way as for Matthew's gospel, three sources can be cited for Luke's: Mk, the author's own material (S: the Lucan "*Sondergut*"), and the sayings source (Q). But while Matthew readily compiles, Luke composes in blocks. He apparently proceeds successively from one source to the other, placing them next to each other. He juxtaposes. Luke also follows the Marcan account as a basic outline, but he omits parts of Mk (the so-called omissions: e.g., Mk 3:20-30; 9:42-10:12, and particularly 6:45-8:26), and he inserts blocks of Q and S material: see 6:20-8:3 and 9:51-18:14. Since Jesus begins the journey to Jerusalem in 9:51 and arrives in 19:45, he is on the way for ten chapters of Luke's gospel. Therefore, 9:51-19:44, the last large insertion, is called the Lucan travel narrative.

### THE CONTEXT OF THE SERMON ON THE PLAIN

The Sermon on the Plain is not as close to the beginning of Luke's gospel as the Sermon on the Mount is in Matthew's. Indeed, it is not a programmatic beginning for Luke. In Lk, Jesus appears formally for the first time in Nazareth, and there he announces his program: see 4:16-30. In 3:1-6:6, Luke follows the Marcan order quite faithfully. He places his Sermon on the Plain after the passage Mk 3:7-19 where it forms the beginning of the small insertion (Lk 6:20-8:3). It is worth investigating how Luke changed the sequence in Mk 3:7-19.

To begin with a synoptic comparison:

| Mk 3:1-6 | Lk 6:6-11 | The withered hand |
|---|---|---|
| 3:7-12 | — | Summary |
| 3:13 | 6:12 | Mountain |
| 3:14-19 | 6:13-16 | The Twelve |
| | 6:17-19 | Summary |
| | 6:20-49 | Sermon on the Plain |

This table shows clearly how Luke has transferred the summary: it now comes after the events on the mountain. In 6:17a, Jesus descends from the mountain. The sermon that follows the summary is given at the foot of the mountain on a level place.

While in Mt the mountain serves as a podium in the sermon situation, the mountain in Lk is the place of prayer during the night and the setting of the formal selection of the twelve apostles (see 6:12-16). We may assume that Luke reversed the Marcan order because he considered a flat area more suitable for a sermon directed to the crowd, and perhaps there was also a theological motive. H. Schürmann would call Luke's address the "sermon *at* the mountain" (*Predigt am Berge*) instead of the "sermon on the plain," and he sees a Moses typology that is probably intended by the evangelist: 6:12-16 parallels Ex 24 and 6:17-19 parallels Ex 32. First, as Moses and the elders climb Mount Sinai, so Jesus and the disciples climb the mountain in Galilee; second, Moses encounters God in the cloud on the mountain, and Jesus spends the night on the mountain in prayer to his Father; third, the people wait at the foot of the mountain, as do a large group of disciples and the crowd in the gospel.

## THE STRUCTURE AND THE HEARERS OF THE SERMON ON THE PLAIN

Lk 6:20-49 contains mostly Q-material. Since the seventh chapter below will be devoted entirely to this rather short sermon, our discussion of the content and structure here can be brief. As with the Matthean Sermon on the Mount, there is no unanimity among exegetes regarding the structure of the Sermon on the Plain. I would suggest the following division. Beatitudes and woes (6:20-26) form the beginning, the introduction; the parable of the house and the storm (6:46-49) is the conclusion of this sermon. What lies in between is concerned with love of enemy (6:27-36) and is more or less related to the theme of "not judging" (6:37-45). This four-part division provides us with a good initial approach to the content of the sermon.

The audience of the Sermon on the Plain also poses a problem. Some exegetes see an opposition between 6:20 and 7:1, between the disciples and the people. In 6:20a, we read: "And he lifted up his eyes on his *disciples*, and said"; in 7:1: "After he had ended all his sayings in the hearing of the *people* he entered Capernaum." For whom does Luke intend the sermon, the people or the disciples? One may accept that "his disciples" of 6:20a, a phrase that stands between two verbs in the Greek, belongs both to the first (lifted up) and to the second (said to): The disciples are indeed addressed in 6:20b: "Blessed are you poor . . ." But can one conclude from this that the people are not being addressed?

The following three facts argue against considering the group of the disciples as the only audience of the Sermon on the Plain. First, as noted above, Luke has reversed the context that precedes the sermon. The selection of the twelve apostles took place on the mountain, and the sermon is given only after the descent. One of the reasons for this inversion was most probably that Luke wanted Jesus to address the sermon also to the people from "all Judea and Jerusalem and the seacoast of Tyre and Sidon, who came to hear him" (6:18). Moreover, Luke stresses the size of the crowd: "a great multitude of people" (6:17). Second, there is a change in those addressed within the sermon. In 6:20, the disciples are explicitly indicated, but the disciples can no longer be the intended audience for "woe to you that are rich" in 6:24. Were rich people present among the listeners? Furthermore, in 6:27, there is: "But I say to you that hear . . . ." Are these people only the disciples or also the many who, according to 6:18, had come to listen to Jesus? In the light of verses 18 and 27 and particularly the change in v. 24, one may consider the audience in a very broad sense. Third, in Chapter 12 there is also a situation addressed to disciples (12:1-21) and to listening people (thousands of people, 12:1; even interrupting in 12:13). In 12:54, Jesus' words are addressed to the people.

In conclusion, the largest part of the Sermon on the Plain is addressed directly to the disciples (but not the woes:

6:24-26). This group is much larger than the small group of the twelve apostles (see 6:12-17: chosen from the larger group of disciples). And the group of listening people present must be envisioned still more broadly. Indeed, it is questionable whether Luke is being consistent with his distinction between the large group of disciples and the great crowd (cf. 6:17).

## IV. An Older Sermon?

When the Matthean Sermon on the Mount and the Lucan Sermon on the Plain are placed alongside each other, the agreements and the differences are striking. Almost everything that is in Luke's sermon is also found in Matthew's, while the Matthean sermon is much longer, and its structure is also different. Almost nothing of the two sermons is found in Mk, and no speech in Mark's gospel even resembles them. Thus, there was apparently an older Q-sermon, the common source that Matthew and Luke each reproduced or revised in their own ways.

(We need not concern ourselves with the apocryphal Gospel according to Thomas in our comparison of Matthew and Luke. Although parts of these sermons do appear in this later gospel, many details seem to indicate that these parts are secondary to the parallels in Matthew and Luke if not dependent on them.)

### COMPARISON

I will not compare the details at this point. It is best to set the smaller units of the two sermons next to each other twice.

a) On the basis of the *Lucan order*, the material can be presented in three columns: one for Lk, one for Mt 5-7, and one for the verses that are in Mt but not in the sermon (Mt 5-7).

|  | Lk 6 | Mt 5-7 | Mt |
|---|---|---|---|
| Introduction | 20a | 5:1-2 | |
| Beatitudes | 20b-23 | 5:3-12 | |
| Woes | 24-26 | | |
| Love of enemy | 27-36 | 5:38-48 | |
| Golden Rule | 31 | 7:12 | |
| Not judging | 37-38 | 7:1-2 | |
| The blind leader | 39 | | 15:14 |
| Master and disciple | 40 | | 10:24 |
| Splinter and beam | 41-42 | 7:3-5 | |
| The tree and its fruit | 43-45 | 7:16-20 | |
| Lord, Lord | 46 | 7:21 | |
| The house and the storm | 47-49 | 7:24-27 | |

It is striking that almost everything Luke has in his Sermon on the Plain has a parallel text in Mt, and specifically in the fifth and the seventh chapters. Matthew does not have the woes, and he places the sayings about the blind leader and the master and the disciple elsewhere in his gospel. Further, Matthew puts the Golden Rule in the middle of his seventh chapter and not in the fifth chapter, as one would expect from the Lucan order.

b) A survey of the two sermons with the *Matthean order* as a guide is also instructive. Again, we need three columns, one for the Sermon on the Mount, one for the Sermon on the Plain, and one for Luke's material that he situates elsewhere than in his sixth chapter.

|  | Mt 5-7 | Lk 6 | Lk |
|---|---|---|---|
| Introduction | 5:1-2 | 20a | |
| Beatitudes | 3-12 | 20b-23 | |
| Salt and light | 13,14-16 | | 14,34-35;11:33 |
| Law | 17-20 | | |
| Not one dot | 18 | | 16:17 |
| Murder | 21-26 | | |
| Going to the judge | 25-26 | | 12:57-59 |
| Adultery | 27-30 | | |

| | | | |
|---|---|---|---|
| Divorce | 31-32 | | 16:18 |
| Oath | 33-37 | | |
| Retaliation | 38-42 | 29-30 | |
| Love of enemy | 43-45,46-48 | 27-28,32-36 | |
| Alms | 6:1-4 | | |
| Praying | 5-15 | | |
| Our Father | 9-13 | | 11:2-4 |
| Fasting | 16-18 | | |
| Treasures and cares | 19-34 | | 12:22-34 |
| The eye | 22-23 | | 11:33-36 |
| Two masters | 24 | | 16:13 |
| Not judging | 7:1-2 | 37-38 | |
| Splinter and beam | 3-5 | 41-42 | |
| The holy | 6 | | |
| Hearing of prayer | 7-11 | | 11:9-13 |
| Golden Rule | 12 | 31 | |
| The narrow gate | 13-14 | | 13:23-24 |
| The tree and its fruit | 15-20 | 43-45 | |
| Lord, Lord | 21-23 | 46 | |
| Never known! | 22-23 | | 13:26-27 |
| The house and the storm | 24-27 | 47-49 | |
| Conclusion | 28-29 | | cf. 7:1 |

To judge by this table, Matthew has brought together three kinds of material in his sermon: first, the Q-material that is also present in the Lucan parallel; second, the Q-material that is dispersed elsewhere throughout Luke's gospel; and third, his own material, his *Sondergut*. One can also see how Matthew sometimes inserts particular Q-verses in the middle of smaller units (see indented verses).

## THE Q-SERMON

No exegete would suppose that Matthew or Luke copied the source text everywhere literally. We must take into account their editorial activity both as regards the rewriting of the sentences and the form of the sermon. Notwithstanding the deviations, the two evangelists are in rough agreement in the common portions for the order of the material and sometimes for the vocabulary. We must therefore conclude that their source, the Q-sermon, was already an established text in Greek, probably a translation of an earlier Aramaic version. Generally, Luke is considered to have preserved the Q-order more faithfully than Matthew. But this is only a tentative and still general observation. Is it possible to determine by careful comparison which of the two evangelists added or omitted something? Can the hypothetical Q-sermon be reconstructed with certainty? There are a number of elements that considerably complicate such a task.

In the following chapter of this book, we will have to decide whether it was Luke who composed the woes and placed them after the beatitudes. The opposing conception, namely that Matthew omitted them, is still defended by some scholars. The same problem occurs, for example, with regard to Lk 6:39-40. Further, it is not *a priori* excluded that passages from the Matthean Sermon on the Mount that are called *Sondergut* did in fact belong to the Q-sermon but were not taken up by Luke for one reason or another. Perhaps he considered that some of the antitheses (see Mt 5) or the three pious practices (giving alms, praying, fasting; see Mt 6) were too Jewish for his Gentile-Christian readers. But it is more probable that the Matthean *Sondergut* did not belong to the form of Q that Luke knew.

It is possible that there were intermediary stages between the old, short Q-form and the long Matthean Sermon on the Mount. Does not the Matthean text witness to a slow evolution so that different stages may be distinguished in the history of the tradition? Or must we rather consider that Matthew expanded the text himself? As in his other sermon complexes, Matthew would then have used much Q-material that did not originally belong to the sermon as well as much of the *Sondergut*, and he would also have composed some of the verses himself.

Although I would tend to opt for the second assumption, the data that seem to indicate a somewhat more complex transmission history are still impressive. For example, in the first half of Mt 6 it is striking that the three units, vv. 2-4 (almsgiving), vv. 5-6 (praying), and vv. 16-18 (fasting), have the same structure:

(a) "When you..."
(b) Prohibition
(c) Reward

(a') "But when you..."
(b') Commandment
(c') Reward

Did Matthew find these units already combined in his *Sondergut*? One gets that impression. Structurally they belong together, and I would hesitate to suggest that Matthew composed them himself and then interrupted their continuity by vv. 7-15. However, even if we consider vv. 2-4, 5-6, and 16-18 a pre-Matthean whole, it is still not certain that this composition already belonged to the pre-Matthean Sermon on the Mount, which then would have been larger than the original Q-sermon as Luke knew it.

It is probably best to assume that the old Q-sermon was roughly similar to the Lucan Sermon on the Plain as regards its structure and content (without the woes, the blind leader, and the master and the disciple). The author of this sermon apparently was addressing disciples of Jesus. They are first called blessed, and then immediately enjoined to practice love (even of the enemy), not to take revenge, and not to judge. The end of the sermon stresses the necessity of action, the need to bear fruit, and the theme of judgment.

## DID JESUS PREACH A SERMON ON THE MOUNT?

With the Greek sermon on the Q-level, we are approximately twenty years after the first Easter, and we have moved from Palestine. The extent to which the author of the older Aramaic Q-text himself composed this sermon with the aid of independent sayings and small parables can no longer be determined. However, it is possible that a kind of Sermon on the Mount already existed in a pre-literary stage. Did this sermon or its core go back to the earthly Jesus? It is difficult to answer such a question with confidence. In any case, one must keep in mind that much of the material of both the Matthean and the Lucan sermons derives from Jesus even though it might have originally been disseminated and transmitted outside a sermon context. But our question is: Did Jesus preach a sermon on the mount?

Since the site of the sermon on a flat area is secondary (i.e., it must be ascribed to Luke as concluded above) and since both evangelists associate the sermon with a mountain, it seems safe to assert that the sermon in Q was already a sermon on the mount. Moreover, both Luke and Matthew place the sermon more or less in the beginning of their gospels, which leads us further to conclude that it also stood at the beginning of Jesus' public life in the Q-document. Where did Q get this information? From the tradition.

An important question here is whether this tradition is historically reliable, whether it did indeed preserve something that has actually happened: Jesus delivered a sermon on a mountain at the beginning of his public life. Even while maintaining this line of reasoning as likely, we still must consider the content of the sermon. It probably had a programmatic character from the very beginning. With his messianic awareness, Jesus proclaimed with the beatitudes the great breakthrough of God's grace and then called for a response that consists primarily in love of neighbor. The Sermon on the Mount, we may justifiably presume, formed the core of Jesus' preaching of the Kingdom of God.

# Bibliography

A great deal has been and is being written about the Sermon on the Mount. Here are listed some commentaries on the Gospels of Matthew and Luke and references to a number of books and articles on the Sermon on the Mount (for the Lucan Sermon on the Plain, see also Chapter 7, p. 233). This selection was made in view of the importance of each publication and its recentness. Obviously, there are a large number of publications not mentioned here that approach the Sermon on the Mount only incidentally or from very specific points of view.

## COMMENTARIES

*The Gospel of Matthew*
Albright, W.F. and C.S. Mann (Anchor Bible), New York, 1971.
Allen, W.C. (Intern. Crit. Comm.), Edinburgh, [3]1912.
Beare, F.W., Oxford, 1981.
Bonnard, P. (Commentaire N.T.), Neuchâtel-Paris,[2]1970.
Fenton, J.C. (Pelican), Harmondsworth-Baltimore, 1963.
Filson, F.V. (Black), London, 1960.
Gundry, R.H., Grand Rapids, 1982.
Guy, H.A., London, 1971.
Hill, D. (Century Bible), London, 1972.
Lagrange, M.-J. (Et. Bibl.), Paris, [8]1948.
M'Neile, A.H., London-New York, 1915.
Meier, J.P. (N.T. Message), Dublin, 1980.
Plummer, A., London, 1909.
Radermakers, J., Brussels, [2]1974.
Robinson, T.H. (Moffatt), London, 1928.

Schweizer, E. (Das N.T. Deutsch), Göttingen, ³1981 (ET by
D.E. Green: Atlanta, 1975).
Senior, D., Garden City, 1977.

*The Gospel of Luke*
Bossuyt, J. and J. Radermakers, Brussels, 1981.
Caird, G.B. (Pelican), Harmondsworth-Baltimore, 1963.
Danker, E.W., St. Louis, 1976.
Ellis, E.E. (Century Bible), London, 1966.
Fitzmyer, J.A. (Anchor Bible), New York, 1981.
Geldenhuys, N. (New Intern. Comm. N.T.), Grand Rapids,
1975.
Lagrange, M.-J. (Et. Bibl.), Paris, ⁴1948.
LaVerdière, E. (N.T. Message), Dublin, 1980.
Leaney, A.R.C. (Black), London, ²1966.
Manson, W. (Moffatt), London, 1930.
Marshall, I.H. (New Intern. Greek Test. Comm.), Exeter,
1978.
Plummer, A. (Intern. Crit. Comm.), Edinburgh, ⁴1901.
Schürmann, H. (Herders Theologischer Kommentar N.T.),
Freiburg, 1969.
Schweizer, E. (Das N.T. Deutsch), Göttingen, 1982 (ET by
D.E. Green: Atlanta, 1984).

STUDIES

Betz, H., "The Hermeneutical Principles of the Sermon on
the Mount," *Journ. Theol. S. Afr.* 42 (1983) 17-28.
Betz, H.D., "The Sermon on the Mount: Its Literary Genre
and Function," *Journ. Rel.* 59 (1979) 285-297.
Bligh, J., *The Sermon on the Mount. A Discussion on Mt.
5-7*, Slough, 1975.
Bornkamm, G., "Der Aufbau der Bergpredigt," *New Test.
Stud.* 24 (1977-78) 419-432.
Carson, D.A., *The Sermon on the Mount*, Grand Rapids, 1978.
Catchpole, D., "The Sermon on the Mount in Today's World,"
*Theol. Evang.* 14 (1981) 4-11.
Davies, W.D., *The Sermon on the Mount*, Cambridge, 1966.
Davies, W.D., *The Setting of the Sermon on the Mount*,
Cambridge, 1964.

Descamps, A.-L., "Le discours sur la montagne. Esquisse de théologie biblique," *Rev. Théol. Louv.* 12 (1981) 5-39.

Dibelius, M., "Die Bergpredigt," in: Dibelius, *Botschaft und Geschichte. Gesammelte Aufsätze I*, Tübingen, 1953, pp. 79-174.

Dupont, J., *Les Béatitudes. I: Le problème littéraire. Les deux versions du Sermon sur la montagne et des Béatitudes* (Et. Bibl.), Paris, ²1969.

Giesen, H., *Christliches Handeln. Eine redaktionsgeschichtliche Untersuchung zum "dikaiosynē"-Begriff im Matthäus-Evangelium* (Europäische Hochschulschriften XXIII: Theologie 181), Freiburg-Bern, 1982.

Grant, R.M., "The Sermon on the Mount in Early Christianity," *Semeia* (1978), no. 12, pp. 215-223.

Guelich, R.A., *The Sermon on the Mount. A Foundation for Understanding*, Waco, Texas, 1982.

Häring, B., "The Normative Value of the Sermon on the Mount," *Cath. Bibl. Quart.* 29 (1967) 375-385.

Hanssen, O., "Zum Verständnis der Bergpredigt. Eine missionstheologische Studie zu Mt. 5,17-18," in: E. Lohse (ed.), *Der Ruf Jesu und die Antwort der Gemeinde. Fs. J. Jeremias*, Göttingen, 1970, pp. 94-111.

Hendrickx, H., *Sermon on the Mount*, Manila, 1970.

Hickling, C.J.A., "Conflicting Motives in the Redaction of Matthew: Some Considerations on the Sermon on the Mount and Matthew 18:15-20," in: *Stud. Ev. VII* (Texte u. Unters. 126), Berlin, 1982, pp. 247-260.

Hill, D., "The Meaning on the Sermon on the Mount in Matthew's Gospel," *Ir. Bibl. Stud.* 6 (1984) 120-133.

Hoffmann, P., "Die Stellung der Bergpredigt im Matthäusevangelium. Auslegung der Bergpredigt I," *Bib. Leb.* 10 (1969) 57-65.

Jeremias, J., *The Sermon on the Mount* (Facet Books, Bibl. Ser.), ET by N. Perrin, Philadelphia, 1963.

Keegan, T.J., "Introductory Formulae for Matthean Discourses," *Cath. Bibl. Quart.* 44 (1982) 415-430.

Kissinger, W.S., *The Sermon on the Mount: A History of*

*Interpretation and Bibliography* (ATLA Bibliography Series 3), Metuchen, 1975.

McArthur, H.K., *Understanding the Sermon on the Mount*, Westport, [2]1978.

McEleney, N.J., "The Principles of the Sermon on the Mount," *Cath. Bibl. Quart.* 41 (1979) 552-570.

Neirynck, F., "The Sermon on the Mount in the Gospel Synopsis," *Eph. Theol. Lov.* 53 (1976) 350-357; also in: Neirynck, *Evangelica* (Bibl. Eph. Theol. Lov. 60), Leuven, 1982, pp. 729-736.

Roberts, J.H., "The Sermon on the Mount and the Idea of Liberty," *Neotest.* 1(1967) 9-15.

Sand, A., "Die Polemik gegen 'Gesetzlosigkeit' im Evangelium nach Mätthaus und bei Paulus. Ein Beitrag zur neutestamentlichen Überlieferungsgeschichte," *Bibl. Zeitschr.* 14 (1970) 112-125.

Schmahl, G., "Gültigkeit und Verbindlichkeit der Bergpredigt," *Bib. Leb.* 14 (1973) 180-187.

Schnackenburg, R., "The Sermon on the Mount and Modern Man," in Schnackenburg, *Christian Existence in the New Testament I*, Notre Dame, 1968, pp. 128-157.

Schneider, G., *Botschaft der Bergpredigt* (Der Christ in der Welt. VI: Das Buch der Bücher 8a), Leipzig, [2]1973.

Strecker, G., *Die Bergpredigt. Ein exegetischer Kommentar*, Göttingen, 1984.

Thielicke, H., *Life Can Begin Again. Sermons on the Sermon on the Mount*. ET by J.W. Doberstein, Philadelphia, 1963.

For the reconstruction of the text of the Q-sermon carried out in the following chapters, I refer to, among others:

Polag, A., *Fragmenta Q. Textheft zur Logienquelle*, Neukirchen, 1979.

Schulz, S., *Q. Die Spruchquelle der Evangelisten*, Zürich, 1972.

*Chapter Two*

# THE BEATITUDES: JESUS AND Q-TEXT (Mt 5:3-16; Lk 6:20b-26)

Ever since antiquity, the sayings at the beginning of the Sermon on the Mount and the Sermon on the Plain have been called the "beatitudes." Who has not heard of the "eight beatitudes" of the Gospel according to Matthew? Matthew first introduces the speaker of the Sermon on the Mount in 5:1-2: "Seeing the crowds, he went up on the mountain, and when he sat down his disciples came to him. And he opened his mouth and taught them, saying" (see also, 4:23-25). Luke is more restrained in 6:20a: "And he lifted up his eyes on his disciples, and said" (see, however, 6:17-19). But both evangelists begin Jesus' sermon very formally with the beatitudes. Indeed, the beatitudes have been likened to the pillars of the formal entrance to a building.

Blessedness is glory and joy, a situation of supreme happiness or salvation. one speaks of acquiring eternal blessedness. Beatitude is blessedness. However, the gospel expression, "blessed is" encompasses more than a particular situation. It is an active expression that refers to the conditions necessary for happiness and that, of itself, produces happiness. The English term "beatitude" comes from the Latin *beatus*.

Originally, a beatitude was clearly distinguished from a formal blessing, as was a woe saying from a curse. The content of blessing and beatitude is often the same in the Old Testament: having many children, good harvests, and herds and conquering one's enemy. Thus, Ps 144:12-15 functions as a beatitude:

> May our sons in their youth be like plants full grown,
> our daughters like corner pillars cut for the structure of a palace;
> may our garners be full, providing all manner of store;
> may our sheep bring forth thousands and ten thousands in our fields;
> may our cattle be heavy with young, suffering no mischance or failure in bearing;
> may there be no cry of distress in our streets!
> Happy (= blessed) the people to whom such blessings fall!
> Happy the people whose God is the LORD!

A blessing is actually accomplished by God: it comes from above. God's blessing word creates the blessing. His word is powerful and effective, charged with strength. The people, parents, priests, kings, and officials bless in the name of God. A beatitude, however, is spoken by a human being "upwards": one notices and praises in another person something that is worthy of honor and offers congratulations for something desirable. For example, Ps 1:1:

> Blessed is the man
> who walks not in the counsel of the wicked,
> nor stands in the way of sinners,
> nor sits in the seat of scoffers;
> but his delight is in the law of the Lord
> and on his law he meditates day and night.

In Deut 27-28, the blessings and curses are juxtaposed, and in the Gospel of Luke, the four beatitudes are followed by four woes. However, the juxtaposition of beatitudes and woes and the linking of them into sayings in series do not seem to go back very far in pre-Christian times.

Still another development occurred. In the wisdom sayings, profane or religious congratulations initially referred
to a happy condition that the praised individual already had
achieved. Under the influence of prophetic preaching, beatitudes also began to praise future happiness. In the still later
apocalyptic literature, the beatitudes focused on the judgment and salvation that is expected in the eschaton. These
shifts are important, because the distinction between the
present and the future made it possible to consider someone
blessed in the present in view of a future happiness, even
though the present condition might well be unhappy. Such
eschatological beatitudes are no longer purely objective
observations or congratulations, but, by being pronounced,
they themselves, in a sense, generate blessedness in those
addressed.

Matthew in 5:3-12 presents nine sayings introduced by
"blessed"; Luke has only four such sayings (6:20b-23), but
immediately thereafter he has four woes (vv. 24-26). It is
generally accepted that the four common beatitudes were
present in the Q-source, but there is no unanimity about
another question. Can one, by means of literary analysis,
derive or postulate traditional stages between Q and the
gospels, that is to say, further developed and divergent
forms of Q? Sometimes the existence of a Matthean or
Lucan Q (QMt, QLc) is suggested, one that would have
contained more than the first Q-source. The question is thus
whether the evangelists Matthew and Luke themselves were
or were not active authors, rewriting and expanding extensively. As noted in the first chapter, I am inclined to attrib-
ute a great deal to the editorial activity of the evangelists.

For the sake of clarity, I will divide my argument into
three parts on the basis of the three versions: the Q, Matthean, and Lucan beatitudes. Obviously, this rather simplified arrangement is not intended to prejudice the discussion
on the origin and the development of the beatitudes. Thus,
in the first part, I will treat questions of which beatitudes
Jesus spoke and what his intention was. The Lucan woes
and what Matthew adds to his beatitudes in 5:13-16 also

belong in this chapter. I will conclude this chapter by posing a hermeneutic question: What do the beatitudes mean for the contemporary world?

Anyone who writes about this material will gladly acknowledge his debt to the Belgian exegete J. Dupont who like no other wrote about the Sermon on the Mount and particularly the beatitudes often, extensively, and with great soundness.

## I. The Beatitudes: Jesus and Q-Text

In order to speak about the beatitudes from Jesus, we must first try to reconstruct the oldest text by comparing Mt and Lk. This is the only chance we have to go back to Jesus' words. In the second part of this chapter, the five sayings that occur only in the Sermon on the Mount are shown to have been added by Matthew. Presumably, he created them himself. Is it possible to determine the Q-text of the four common beatitudes?

### THE Q-TEXT

A Q-reconstruction of the first three sayings is given here and placed between the Matthean and Lucan versions:

| *Mt 5* | *Q-Reconstruction* | *Lk 6* |
|---|---|---|
| 3 Blessed are the poor in spirit, for *theirs* is the Kingdom of heaven. | *a* Blessed are the poor, for theirs is the Kingdom of God. | 20b Blessed are you poor, for yours is the Kingdom of God. |
| 6 Blessed are those who hunger and thirst for righteousness for *they* shall be satisfied. | *b* Blessed are those who who hunger for they will be satisfied. | 21a Blessed are you that hunger now, for you shall be satisfied. |
| 5 Blessed are those who mourn, for *they* shall be comforted. | *c* Blessed are those who mourn, for they shall be comforted. | 21b Blessed are you that weep now, for you shall laugh. |

How is such a reconstruction arrived at? Since Matthew probably wanted to round off the first strophe of the four beatitudes with the added "righteousness" in v. 6, as he also does at the end of the second strophe in v. 10, he probably altered the Q-sequence of the sayings (poor, hungry, mourning). The fourth beatitude of Q (= *d*, Mt 5:11-12 = Lk 6:22-23) certainly was in the second person plural, which we can conclude from the agreement of Mt and Lk. Did Luke adapt the first three beatitudes to the fourth by rewriting them in the second person? Since Luke also introduced the second person form elsewhere in his gospel, it is more probable that Matthew has the original version here. However, many exegetes are of the opinion that the Matthean text here is secondary. Matthew, they contend, has rewritten the second person form into a general third person, and thus converted Jesus' beatitudes into traditional wisdom sayings, more like the Old Testament, more like exhortations.

Matthew expanded both *a* ("in spirit") and *b* ("and thirst for righteousness") and interiorized them. The examination of the five beatitudes he added will make this even more credible. There is also no convincing reason to suppose that the pronoun stressed by Matthew (*theirs, they*) already belonged to Q. On the other hand, it is generally agreed that Luke added the "now" to *b* and *c*. It is more difficult to decide what vocabulary of *c* was in Q. It is not without hesitation that I select "mourn-be comforted" instead of "weep-laugh." The first two terms do have a Matthean spiritual ring to them (in 9:15, Matthew wrote "mourn" where Mk 2:19 has "fasting") but from Lk 6:25b ("Woe to you that laugh now, for you shall *mourn* and weep") and from 6:24b ("for you have received your *consolation*") it would seem that Luke encountered both themes, mourning and consolation, in his Q-source. Moreover, many exegetes assume that the first beatitude alludes to Isaiah 61:1-3, where the verb "to mourn" occurs three times, and thus also the third beatitude could well have been influenced by the same passage in Isaiah.

The reconstruction of the fourth beatitude in Q is even more difficult as regards the wording. First the texts:

| *Mt 5* | | *Q-Reconstruction* | *Lk 6* |
|---|---|---|---|
| 11 Blessed are you | d | Blessed are you | 22 Blessed are you |
| when they | | when they hate | when people hate |
| (RSV: men) | | you | you, and when they |
| | | | exclude you |
| revile you | | and revile you | and revile you, |
| and persecute you | | | |
| and utter all kinds | | and utter | and cast out your |
| of evil against you | | evil of you | name as evil, |
| falsely on my ac- | | on account of the | on account of the |
| count. | | Son of Man. | Son of Man! |
| 12 Rejoice | | Rejoice | 23 Rejoice in that day, |
| and be glad, | | and be glad, | and leap for joy, |
| for your reward | | for your reward | for behold, your re- |
| is great in heaven, | | is great in heaven, | ward is great in |
| for so | | for so | heaven; for in the |
| they persecuted | | they did | same way their |
| the prophets | | to the prophets. | fathers did to the |
| who were before | | | prophets. |
| you. | | | |

All the details need not be mentioned here, and some parts of the reconstruction will always be very uncertain. Luke probably added the subject "people" in v. 22 and the subject "their fathers" in v. 23. If so, the verbs would have been in the indefinite plural in Q, as they still are in Mt ("they"). Also, "in that day," "leap for joy," and "behold" in v. 23 are almost certainly Lucan additions. Matthew, at the end of v. 11, spontaneously replaced the older "Son of Man" by "me" (cf. "on my account" and the same change in Mt 16:21; Mk 8:31 has "Son of Man").

In the first half of this long beatitude, only two of the

words for what the Christians will endure coincide: "revile" and "evil." There is no reason to think that Luke added "hate," but we do know that Matthew seems to have a tendency to use "persecute": twice here in vv. 11-12, already in v. 10, and also elsewhere in his gospel. Probably, therefore, the "persecute" in v. 11 is a concretizing and intensifying substitution for the original "hate." Because Luke in the corresponding woe, 6:26, speaks about "speaking well of" (praise, flattery), the best reconstruction of the phrase in which "evil" appears is probably "utter evil of you." In Mt 5:11, "all kinds of," "against you," and "falsely" are thus secondary generalizations or further specifications. If Luke changed "utter evil of you" in 6:22 to "cast out your name as evil," then he probably also added "exclude you" in the same verse. We shall see in the third part that Luke, here and in the woes, has in mind antagonistic Jews who vilify and ostracize the Jewish-Christians. All these considerations taken together give the three terms "hate," "revile," and "utter evil" for the first half of this beatitude. This takes care of the principal elements, but again, the Q-text thus recovered is inevitably very conjectural.

One final question regarding the woes. Were they in Q and did Matthew purposely omit them? H. Frankemölle has recently put forth several arguments in support of this position: Matthew would have replaced the woes with his five additional beatitudes; the woes do not fit into his programmatic Sermon on the Mount; and by way of compensation he put a woe sermon in Chapter 23 at the end of his gospel. He would have found in the woes of Q the emphasis that he gives to his sayings by *theirs* and *they*: woe unto *you*. Frankemölle also discerns in the Matthean sermon "linguistic reminiscences" of these woes: "mourning" and "be comforted" would be rooted in the woes (cf. Lk 6:25b and 24).

This last argument is not convincing. One could just as well argue the other way around: Luke used these two terms to compose the woes, which are reminiscences of the Q-beatitudes in which they were originally situated. The other arguments cited by Frankemölle are also unconvincing.

Moreover, there is evidence to indicate that the woes were indeed composed by Luke, for they betray Lucan vocabulary and thought. This position is held by the majority of exegetes.

## TWO KINDS OF BEATITUDES

A strictly scientific study would have to provide still more support for the many assertions and assumptions of the last section. But the demonstration offered there is amply sufficient to give the reader a good idea of the delicate methodology involved in such a reconstruction. Inevitably, many details must remain uncertain, and decisions about them are often based on personal preferences and guesswork. Still, the method as such is sound. It is also necessary, because only in this way — a way that is justifiable in terms of literary criticism — can we obtain access to the old Q-source and, perhaps, from there move to the earthly Jesus.

What does the form of the reconstructed Q-source look like now? The first three beatitudes (*a, b, c*) look very much alike: they are short, set in the third person plural, and have two parts. The first part points to an existing situation of human misery; the second promises a future reversal and compensation: the "will" in *b* and *c*, and one can understand the "theirs is" of *a* in this same way. The second part contains the reason ("for") why the poor and mourning can now already be called blessed. How or on what basis the speaker dares to form such a connection is not indicated by the formulation. The passive form in which the second and third beatitudes are cast is a Semitic device to avoid pronouncing the name of God: thus it is God who will comfort and satisfy. Finally, like an intentional dissonance, beatitude is first paradoxically pronounced over misery, and only thereafter is the reason presented. The three-fold repetition of this scheme reinforces the emphasis.

The fourth beatitude (*d*) differs from the first three (1) by its length (it is longer than the first three together), (2) by the person addressed (second person), (3) by the orientation of the first phrase to the future (an eventual condition), (4) by the content (persecution because of the Son of Man), (5) by the urging to rejoice and be glad (imperatives), (6) by the mention of the great reward in heaven, and (7) by the comparison with the prophets of the past.

Obviously what we have here are two kinds of beatitudes. The first three are short and in verse form: the fourth is long and in prose. The seven differences in *d* in relation to the others constitute sufficient reason to treat the two kinds separately. We begin with the fourth, *d* in Q.

## THE FOURTH BEATITUDE (*d*): ENCOURAGEMENT

After the text and the form, we finally come now to the content. How did the first Christians, who knew and used the Q-version, understand this beatitude? How did they live it? In order to give structure to my exposition, the same four questions will be posed in this and the following sections.

a) *Who is intended?* The disciples are addressed in this beatitude. They are the ones who will have to endure the hatred, the reviling, and the slander. The opposition is christological: "on account of the Son of Man." The "blessed..." together with the call to joy and the mention of the reward form a complete whole. The added comparison with the prophets probably indicates that the beatitude does not intend merely the disciples in general but more specifically those who will suffer the prophets' fate because they preach.

b) *Why blessed?* The great reward in heaven provides an eschatological motive. At the same time, there is a reference to salvation history, perhaps as consolation: in the past the prophets did not have it any better! The past and the future are thus linked in the salvific plan of God. Jesus recalls the persecuted prophets and predicts the destiny of the Christians who will be reviled because of him. And it applies no less to the present. Being hated and reviled on account of the Son of Man is in itself already a profound reason for joy and provides a foundation for beatitude.

c) *What is this blessedness?* With the metaphor of "reward" and the specification "in heaven," a future salvific state is indicated, but the possession of this hope can cause happiness now in the midst of misfortune. Certainly, the suffering does not disappear, but it is illuminated and transformed because one knows the outcome. Consequently, one is rightly exhorted to rejoice now with a visible, religious, eschatological joy.

d) *Spoken by Jesus?* A number of exegetes who advocate a Q-reconstruction for this beatitude in which the term "exclude" is used (cf. Lk 6:22) stress its Jewish disciplinary tone. It expresses excommunication. But Jesus, the argument continues, did not predict this exclusion so concretely; rather, the formulation comes from the time after Easter, when Jewish Christians were excluded from the synagogue and the temple cult. The fourth beatitude, therefore, would be a "community formation" or "formulation" (*Gemeindebildung*), a word of comfort created by the primitive Church after Easter. Such is the conclusion of this line of reasoning. Nonetheless, one must still ask whether the root of this beatitude does not go back to actual predictions by Jesus of his own suffering and that of his disciples, perhaps in different words. If so, it can then be situated toward the end of his public life.

This reconstruction of the Q-text does not mention exclusion explicitly, only hatred, revilement, and slander. This reduces the strength of an objection against its historicity. But in view of its orientation to the future, I would still hesitate to consider this beatitude, which certainly functioned as an encouragement for the "Q-Christians," as going back word-for-word to Jesus. The motivating expression "on account of the Son of Man" seems almost certainly to have been formulated after Easter.

## THE FIRST THREE BEATITUDES (*a, b, c*): PROCLAMATION

Here we have three short, two-part sayings. Their structures are identical, and so I will examine them together. Again, the same four questions will be asked.

a) *Who is intended?* It is generally accepted that it is not the speaker's intention to present three distinct groups of people (the poor, the hungry, and those who mourn). Three examples are cited of a broad category that contains all the poor and alienated of society. The poor Lazarus of Lk 16:19-31 is sometimes presented as a type, someone who is poor, who hungers, and who mourns, the type of those who simply need help.

We in our society consider "poor" primarily those who have little or nothing. The Greek word that is used in the first beatitude, *ptōchos*, means "needy," but this term does not mean the same thing as *penēs*, "poor": a *penēs* works, a *ptōchos* begs. If the theme of Isaiah 61:1-2 has been intentionally taken up in the three beatitudes, a question arises. The Hebrew term for "poor" is *anaw*, which can be literally translated as "bent" and also as "socially undistinguished, oppressed." Is this sense still carried over completely in the Greek text? In every culture, the terms "being poor, being hungry, mourning" can also be religious metaphors. But there are no indications that this happens in the beatitudes of Q. As the three terms stand next to each other, the Q-text takes on the most obvious meaning of being poor, being hungry, and mourning, a meaning that implies misery and neglect. Thus, there is no spiritualization of the concepts, nor is there anything that would indicate that they are metaphors for a national disaster such as the fall of Jerusalem. All poor people are meant.

b) *Why blessed?* A beatitude in its simplest, one-part form (e.g., happy is the good man) bears its motivation in itself: the present quality is the reason for calling someone blessed. When a two-part saying gives future happiness as the reason, then it is still possible that the present situation has a true connection with that future happiness. This is the case in the fourth beatitude: "on account of the Son of Man" indicates the unity, already in the present, of the disciples with Christ. But what relationship is there between such contrasting realities as the misery of the present situation and the promised Kingdom, the future satisfaction and comfort? One must be on guard against uncritically finding the same relationship in the first three and in the fourth.

In the fourth beatitude, the Christian is blessed: the one who suffers and encounters misfortune, who freely and totally commits himself or herself to the Son of Man, will be rewarded. The Christian is blessed because of the future reward and because of the destiny shared with the prophets, and also because of his or her religious, meritorious position, the personal unity with Christ. This does not appear in the first three beatitudes. Thus, it is better not to say that the poor are blessed because of their poverty or because of their internal disposition or virtue. This idea is not totally absent, perhaps, but the stress is certainly elsewhere. The first three beatitudes are not concerned with our attitude but with God's!

What is primary in these beatitudes is God's free gift, his grace, which is always present even before any human action. Jesus proclaims and reveals this breakthrough of divine mercy, God's new initiative. Jesus' attitude toward children (see Mk 10:13-16; cf. Mt 11:25-26) and sinners (see Mk 2:17; Lk 19:10; Lk 15, etc.) permits no doubt in this regard. God is there before we do anything. The indicative (announcement) comes before the imperative (command): "The indicative is always at the center of the Gospel" (Hoffmann, *Jesus*, p. 56). God's anticipatory grace is, therefore, not dependent on a moral quality or on religious receptivity. "There is no added 'on account of me,' and the reasons why people are called blessed are not at all moral or religious. Jesus reaches out to those who are poor, who are hungry, who are sorrowful, three concrete variations on the same theme. People who, in one way or another, are miserable are pronounced blessed by Jesus, not because of any possible virtue, or their internal disposition, or their openness to the Kingdom of God, but simply because they are in situations of poverty, want of food, and sorrow" (Schreiner, p. 275).

In addition to their revelatory function, these beatitudes also have a demonstrative function. The words and actions of Jesus fulfill what the prophets of the Old Testament had foretold regarding those who were unhappy:

The spirit of the Lord God is upon me,
because the Lord has anointed me
to bring good tidings to the afflicted;
he has sent me to bind up the brokenhearted,
to proclaim liberty to the captives,
and the opening of the prison to those who are bound;
to proclaim the year of the Lord's favor,
and the day of vengeance of our God;
to comfort all who mourn;
(Is 61:1-2; cf. also the Q-text Mt 11:4-5 = Lk 7:22).

The Kingdom of God is present and the proof is that the poor have the good news preached to them, that they are called blessed. Thus, the beatitudes are rightly called "proclamations." Jesus, in his earthly life, approached people with exorcism, healing, and the forgiveness of sins, actions that completely legitimated his paradoxical proclamation.

In the first beatitude, it is stated that the Kingdom of God will belong to the poor. J. Dupont calls our attention to the fact that God, as king *par excellence*, must act for all the oppressed and the weak, for "the poor, the widows, and the orphans." A good, earthly king protects them against exploiters. How much better will God fulfill these royal obligations!

c) *What is this blessedness?* Possession of the Kingdom of God, satisfaction, and comfort are offered. These three expressions are only different images for the same reality. And, like the fourth beatitude, they must be understood eschatologically. Happiness is promised for the near future, at the end of time. And this promise is already able to divest present human misery of its tragic dimension and to invest it with blessedness.

d) *Spoken by Jesus?* There is hardly any doubt that these three beatitudes go back to Jesus. They fit into the historically reliable picture that we have of the earthly Jesus. Jesus probably began his public life with just such a "revolutionary" message. There is something triumphant about this proclamation, for the tone is joyful. Jesus proclaims God's grace-full initiative, which is radical because the unhappy can now be called happy. Something has happened, and more things will happen.

Although it is not explicit, there is a christological and salvation historical background to the first three beatitudes. For only by means of the actions of Jesus in Galilee at that particular time did the beatitudes become possible. Christ himself belongs to the fulfillment of the promises. By his authority as the messenger of God he proclaims the beatitudes. What is announced to us, poor and miserable as we are, is unearned, gratuitous, divine happiness. "The beatitude is itself an evangelical message, a piece of good news, the first concrete application of the proclamation that the Kingdom is at hand. And because this nearness of God is related in essence to the fact that Jesus now acts, these beatitudes are also, in fact, christological, though in a more hidden and indirect manner than the later beatitudes of the persecuted" (Schreiner, p. 277). W. Trilling calls this "introductory proclamation of Jesus" an "unconditional promise of salvation," an "epochal revelation of God." P. Hoffmann characterizes these beatitudes as the "proclamation of the new order of God to all the world." and J. Dupont returns again and again in his writings to this concept: "The beatitudes are above all a revelation of the mercy and the justice that must mark the Kingdom of God."

## THE SERIES OF FOUR IN Q

In the light of this analysis, we may safely assume that the series of four beatitudes in Q did not come about all at once. At one time, the first three sayings of Jesus (the proclamation) were not linked to the fourth beatitude of encouragement, which, as noted above, probably rose from a situation in which the Church was being persecuted.

That the primitive Church attached this fourth beatitude to the first three can be accounted for to some extent by the wording. Similar sayings, like the beatitudes, tended to be joined together. For this to happen, exegesis must already have been at work. The first three were now read in the light of the fourth and vice versa. To be poor and hungry and to mourn are now associated with the persecution about which the fourth beatitude speaks. One would be inclined to think that poverty, hunger, and sorrow are the results of oppression "on account of the Son of Man." The first three are, thus, "christianized" to a certain degree and interiorized.

Already in Q it is apparent how, after Easter, Jesus' message was spontaneously adapted, re-interpreted, and actualized. It could not be otherwise, for the situation had changed. To what new interpretations the transmission process led will become still clearer in the Matthean and Lucan beatitudes.

## II. The Beatitudes in the Matthean Gospel

For the second (Matthean) and the third (Lucan) parts of this chapter, the same order will be followed. First, the texts will be discussed: by comparing them with Q, and listing the differences, we will arrive at a better understanding of the redaction of the evangelists. Then I will try to specify the particular accents of each version as regards content. Finally, the difficulties of each of the beatitudes will be explained, and the intention of the evangelists summarized. And for Matthew, the small unit of 5:13-16, which belongs thematically to his beatitudes, will be briefly analyzed in the fourth section.

### DISCUSSION OF Mt 5:3-12

3 Blessed are the poor in spirit,
  for *theirs* is the Kingdom of heaven.
4 Blessed are those who mourn,
  for *they* shall be comforted.
5 Blessed are the meek,
  for *they* shall inherit the earth.
6 Blessed are those who hunger and thirst for righteousness,
  for *they* shall be satisfied.
7 Blessed are the merciful,
  for *they* shall obtain mercy.

8 Blessed are the pure in heart,
  for *they* shall see God.

9 Blessed are the peacemakers,
  for *they* shall be called sons of God.

10 Blessed are those who are persecuted for righteousness' sake,
   for *theirs* is the Kingdom of heaven.

11 Blessed are you when they revile you and persecute you and utter
   all kinds of evil against you falsely on my account.

12 Rejoice and be glad, for your reward is great in heaven, for so
   they persecuted the prophets before you.

It is possible that Matthew simply took one or another of the beatitudes he adds (or vv. 7-9 as a unit) from an existing tradition or source, or that he is dependent for one or more changes on what was present in his church community. In my opinion, however, there is much to indicate that Matthew is directly responsible for the form the series of beatitudes has in his gospel. Comparison with the Q-version shows that there are seven principal differences.

a) Matthew altered the sequence of Q (*a, b, c*). He begins with *a* (the poor), but *b* (the hungry) comes only fourth after *c* (those who mourn) because of the addition of "the meek." I have already explained that Matthew, in my opinion, wanted to conclude the first strophe of four beatitudes with the term righteousness.

b) Moreover, Matthew made two additions to the Q-beatitudes: "(the poor) in spirit" (*a*, Mt 5:3) and "thirst for righteousness" (*b*, Mt 5:6).

c) The most striking difference, however, is the addition of the five beatitudes .proper to Matthew. Almost everyone assumes that the eighth beatitude (5:10) is a Matthean creation, namely, a duplication of his ninth (*d* in Q). Therefore, as far as content is concerned, one can continue to speak of the eight different beatitudes of the Sermon on the Mount. For the first part of this doubling, Matthew takes the term "persecute" from the ninth, and he also inserts his favorite theme of "righteousness" into v. 10a. The second part literally repeats the motivation of the first (5:3b).

Whether the beatitude of the meek in 5:5 is also a duplication of the first, as J. Dupont would have it, seems to be less certain. Ps 37:11a, "the meek shall possess the land" (thus in the Septuagint), was transformed into a beatitude. It is true that the Hebrew text of Is 61:1, to which the first beatitude alludes, and that of Ps 37:11a have the same word, *anaw* (bowed down, oppressed, lowly). But did Matthew and his readers understand the same basic meaning in the two different Greek terms, *ptōchos* and *prays* (poor and meek)? This cannot simply be assumed, and, indeed, the beatitude of the meek does not follow the first in the best manuscripts. In Mt, it comes in the third place.

The remaining three supplementary sayings are in vv. 7-9: the merciful, the pure, and the peacemakers. As Matthew writes "poor *in spirit*" in v. 3, so in v. 8 he has "pure *of heart*."

d) The first eight beatitudes are, apparently intentionally, enclosed by vv. 3b and 10b: both end with the phrase "for theirs is the Kingdom of heaven." Whether Matthew intended two strophes of four is somewhat less certain, but still probable. As already pointed out, the first part of the fourth and the eighth beatitudes end with the term "righteousness" (see vv. 6a and 10a); these two parts are also somewhat longer. The first four beatitudes, moreover, display alliteration: *ptōchoi, penthountes, praeis, peinōntes*.

e) The reference of "merciful" and "peacemakers" to people with prestige and who can make creative contributions reinforces the position that the supplementary beatitudes have been added later. The original four from Q are concerned with poor or persecuted people who endure their misfortunes passively.

f) In the second part of six beatitudes (vv. 4-9), Matthew uses as subject the pronoun *autoi* (in the nominative). *Autoi* is stressed, meaning *they*, and they alone. Thus, the genitive of the same word (*autōn*) in vv. 3b and 10b must be read analogously: for *theirs*, for theirs alone. Whether this emphasis betrays Matthew's knowledge of the woes where a comparable emphasis is present (woe to *you*) seems to me to be very uncertain. From such a hypothesis, some have concluded further that these woes were already present in Q but were omitted by Matthew as not suitable for the Sermon on the Mount and replaced by his additional beatitudes. But, as noted, the basis for this conclusion seems weak.

g) The ninth beatitude (vv. 11-12) contrasts with the preceding eight by its prose style and length and by the direct addressing of the disciples in the second person. It forms a transition to vv. 13-16, which are also sayings directed to the disciples. I think that Luke adapted the first three beatitudes to the second person of the fourth and that Matthew performed a similar adaptation with the sayings about the salt and the light that follow the last beatitude: they, too, were rewritten in the second person (see below, pp. 67-68. The first part of the beatitude itself (v. 11) was extensively rewritten by Matthew: "hate" was omitted, "persecute, *all kinds* of evil things, falsely, *against* you, on *my* account" were added. In the second part (v. 12), we also have "persecute," and further the Matthean addition, "the prophets *before you.*"

At the end of this inventory, one may well be astonished at the extent and the thoroughness of Matthew's redaction. What we have now is a long series of eight beatitudes, with similar structure, still rather short and rhythmic, cast in the emphatic third person, bracketed by the concept of "the Kingdom of heaven," and probably divided by Matthew into two strophes. The ninth beatitude clearly has another style: second person, long phrases, prose. It concludes the series very nicely; it is the high point of this series but also a transition to the following part of the Sermon on the Mount. But there is, of course, a great deal more than structure and form.

## SHIFTS OF ACCENT

The Matthean rewriting is not purely stylistic or materially expansive. It witnesses to a changed mentality. The beatitudes, in the conception of the evangelist, fulfill a significantly different function than they had in the preaching of Jesus or even in the Q-community. (1) Matthew stresses the internal disposition. Expressions such as "of spirit" and "of heart," "thirsting for righteousness," "meek," and "merciful" no longer point primarily to a social group but to a disposition, a particular spiritual attitude, a way of life to be striven for, a moral attitude. (2) What is given after the "blessed" in the first part of each beatitude is not simply an observation or a naming. For Matthew it is a necessary condition that has to be fufilled — one might almost say by human effort — before one can have a share in the promises of salvation. Those who are intended, therefore, are not the paradoxically privileged, but the virtuous, the morally committed. (3) Many of the beatitudes are certainly related to Matthew's striving for completeness. In this way, the series of beatitudes forms an almost exhaustive list of Christian virtues. (4) Not only the poor or those persecuted for religion are blessed. Matthew appears to be so concerned with the "spirit" that he, perhaps unintentionally, virtually ignores the material level, particularly in the beatitudes he adds. The meek, the merciful, the pure of heart, the peacemakers are also to be found among prosperous Christians, among those who are not hungry. (5) These eight beatitudes fit perfectly into the Matthean Sermon on the Mount. Whoever is the salt of the earth and the light of the world (5:13-14) has to let his or her good works be seen (5:16); his or her righteousness must exceed that of the scribes and the Pharisees (5:20); righteousness must not be practiced in order to attract the attention of others (6:1). The Christian must be perfect, as the Father in heaven is perfect (5:48). For Matthew, the beatitudes present not only different kinds of people but also the virtues that everyone must practice. (6) Originally, the first three beatitudes were not directed to people who were already disciples of Christ. But one has the strong impression that Matthew was encouraging and exhorting his fellow Christians.

Naturally, Matthew meant eight separate virtues. But those addressed are always the same: all Christians must (as much as possible) possess all these qualities, or better still, a Christian who is not poor in spirit, not meek, not merciful, etc. will not possess the Kingdom of heaven. The images of the second part are only variants on the theme of the great eschatological reality. Perhaps it is permissible in "for *theirs* is the Kingdom of heaven" (vv. 3 and 10) to consider an already present possession of the Kingdom. But the future tense used in the other beatitudes is, as I see it, a true future: it refers to the end-time.

Like the form study, the listing of these numerous shifts of accent ought to surprise us. Matthew also changes the content. As W. Weren correctly notes, Matthew transformed the negative life situation of Q into positive attitudes toward life. Weren here is typifying the first part of the beatitudes. Matthew's beatitudes, the first and second parts together, are no longer proclamations like the three from Q: they have become exhortations, encouragements, ethical demands. The aspect of moral-religious encouragement predominates in this version. The gift from Jesus for everyone becomes, in Mt, the task of the Christian.

## MATTHEAN ENCOURAGEMENT

Several terms and phrases in Mt 5:3-12 require some explanation. What does Matthew mean by "poor of spirit"? Three senses have been advocated. (1) The *economic* explanation refers either to people who are simultaneously actually poor and interiorly detached, or to people who are interiorly detached whatever their material situation. (2) The *religious* explanation sometimes appeals to the Jewish expression "the people of the earth." In early Judaism, this meant the religious pariahs, those who are poor in spiritual goods and who are disdained because they do not know the Law. Whether or not they still live "on the land," i.e., in the countryside, or whether or not they are in fact poor, they are, according to this explanation, the little people, the religiously inferior who, in the awareness of their misery, can only place their trust in God. (3) The third explanation can be called the *Hebrew* explanation. The phrase "poor in spirit" occurs in Qumran and there means "humble, faithful to the Law, obedient to God," and thus has roughly the same connotation as "meek" (v. 5). The Greek Fathers also understood the expression in this sense of "humble." This explanation is defended by J. Dupont and others. Rightly? I do not think so. Matthew wanted to specify the Q-term "poor" and probably based himself on the Greek *ptōchos* with the meaning of "poor, needy" (see p. 55). One may not too readily assume that Matthew and his readers understood the Greek phrase in the Hebrew sense. Since the second explanation also seems forced, I prefer the first economic explanation with its double reference.

Thus, Matthew spiritualizes and interiorizes the meaning of "poor" in v. 3a and of "being hungry" in v. 6a. One may accept that he does the same thing with "mourning" in v. 4 and probably is already alluding to the persecution mentioned in the last two beatitudes. The term "earth" in v. 5 inevitably evoked the Promised Land for Jews. In the context of the Sermon on the Mount, this is one of the many metaphors that refer to the Kingdom of heaven. "Pure in heart" in v. 8 must not be interpreted as chaste. The one who is pure in heart shall see God because he or she is sincere and straightforward and shuns all duplicity, ambiguity, and deceit. Matthew intends an ethical, total, and particularly internal authenticity, cf. 23:23-28. With the beatitude of the peacemakers (v. 9), Matthew emphasizes active involvement more than in the others and not purely passive suffering or subjective disposition (but see the beatitude on the merciful, v. 7). In his recent study entitled *Die Seligpreisung der Friedensstifter*, R. Schnackenburg suggests that the term "peacemaker" is probably intentionally vague and that peace had to be established among the Christians themselves as well as between the persecutors and the persecuted.

By the doubling of v. 10, Matthew shows how much he is concerned with persecution. Grammatically, v. 10 refers to past persecutions; in v. 11, the persecution is in the future. Because not all of the accusations made in his church were without grounds (cf. 24:12: wickedness multiplies; love grows cold), Matthew adds the qualification of "falsely." It is noteworthy that, in v. 10, the "on my account" of v. 11 is replaced by the parallel expression "for righteousness' sake." Righteous is the person who does the will of God. It is obvious here that, for Matthew, morality and faithfulness to Christ imply each other.

With my last comment, I was concerned about the relationship between ethics and Christology in Matthew the evangelist. I have repeatedly said that Matthew changed this or that or meant this or that. But it is the Matthean Jesus who begins his Sermon on the Mount with the beatitudes. One wonders if Matthew, with this series of eight, wanted only to formulate the conditions for admission to the Kingdom of heaven, the urgent and necessary virtues or modes of behavior. Nor is it sufficient simply to add here that Matthew also painted the ideal image of the church by listing the *notae ecclesiae*. In fact, the Matthean Jesus paints here, as it were unintentionally, a full-length portrait of himself. He is the paradigm, the great model; he will completely accomplish his "Christian" program. The Matthean Jesus is everything the beatitudes describe. We need only recall a few texts: "He took our infirmities and bore our diseases" (8:17); "Come to me, all who labor and are heavy laden, and I will give you rest. Take my yoke upon you, and learn from me; for I am gentle and lowly in heart, and you will find rest for your souls. For my yoke is easy, and my burden is light" (11:28-30); "Behold, [said God,] my servant whom I have chosen, my beloved with whom my soul is well pleased. I will put my Spirit upon him, and he shall proclaim justice to the Gentiles. He will not wrangle or cry aloud, nor will any one hear his voice in the streets; he will not break a bruised reed or quench a smoldering wick, till he brings justice to victory; and in his name will the Gentiles hope" (12:18-21); "Tell the daughter of Zion, [commands the prophet] Behold, your king is coming to you, humble, and mounted on an ass, and on a colt, the foal of an ass" (21:5). Moreover, Jesus is the Son of Man who is present in the anonymous hungry and thirsty person, the stranger, the naked, the sick, the prisoner (cf. 25:31-46). Thus, we must also understand the Matthean beatitudes christologically. Matthew has rewritten them with an eye to the person and the work of his Lord. Encouragement and Christology are here interwoven.

The Matthean Jesus makes demands on the Christians. I have pointed out the shifts of accent in comparison with the Jesus of Q (first three); from proclamation to exhortation, from gift to command, from God's grace to human response, and from universal message to ecclesiastical exhortation. A. Descamps and others correctly warn against exaggeration, against a too radical position: in the Matthean beatitudes, we still hear the wonderful good news of a God who confirms his lordship without our first having earned it!

## THE GOOD WORKS (Mt 5:13-16)

> 13 You are the salt of the earth; but if salt has lost its taste, how shall its saltness be restored? It is no longer good for anything except to be thrown out and trodden under foot by men.
> 14 You are the light of the world. A city on a hill cannot be hid.
> 15 Nor do men light a lamp and put it under a bushel, but on a stand, and it gives light to all in the house.
> 16 Let your light so shine before men, that they may see your good works and give glory to your Father who is in heaven.

This small unit is composed in the second person plural and thus is addressed directly to the disciples. It thereby ties in very well with the last beatitude. Twice, in v. 13 and in v. 14, the second person is stressed. This is the first element of symmetry between the salt and light logia: "You are the salt of the earth; you are the light of the world." The terms are, of course, metaphors. After each logion, Jesus speaks further about the neglect of the particular function: not being salt (v. 13bc); not giving light (vv. 14b-15). V. 16 falls outside of this parallelism; thematically, it still belongs to the light logion: it is the application. But while the two developed metaphors come from both Mk and Q (for v. 13, cf. Mk

9:49-50 and Lk 14:34-35; for vv. 14-15, cf. Mk 4:21 and Lk
11:33) and are rewritten by Matthew for his Sermon, v. 16
was created completely by the evangelist. This verse contains the principal idea of the unit.

I will not go any further into how Matthew edited vv.
13-15 from his sources, but will now consider the function
and the content of the entire unit. "Can that which is tasteless be eaten without salt?" (Job 6:6a). For the non-
Christian world, Christians must be flavoring, preservative
salt and clearly visible, shining light. They will become these
things by doing the "good works" that are given in the first
part of each beatitude. It is certain that 5:13-16 functions as
the conclusion of the Matthean beatitudes. We have here
the same ethical encouragement and, more particularly, the
expression of how Matthew wants his fellow Christians to
understand what they are — salt and light — and what they
must mean for the world. By living as Christians, they will
be shining light for all people. Moreover, this missionary
passage ends on a very beautiful theological note: the good
works of the Christians will bring people to glorify God.

### III. The Beatitudes and Woes in the Lucan Gospel

In my opinion, the woes (Lk 6:24-26) probably do not
belong to the Q-version; I consider them a Lucan addition,
and so include them in our discussion here.

### DISCUSSION OF Lk 6:20b-26

20b Blessed are you poor,
   for yours is the Kingdom of God.
21a Blessed are you that hunger now,
   for you shall be satisfied.
21b Blessed are you that weep now,
   for you shall laugh.
22 Blessed are you when people hate you, and when they
   exclude you and revile you, and cast out your name as
   evil, on account of the Son of Man!

23　Rejoice in that day and leap for joy, for behold, your reward is great in heaven; for so their fathers did to the prophets.

24　But woe to you that are rich,
　　for you have received your consolation.

25a　Woe to you that are full now,
　　for you shall hunger.

25b　Woe to you that laugh now,
　　for you shall mourn and weep.

26　Woe to you, when all men speak well of you, for so their fathers did to the false prophets.

Luke has preserved the number and the sequence of the beatitudes in Q, and the short form of the first three is also better respected. In a comparison of the Lucan text with Q, four things are particularly striking.

a) The first three beatitudes are cast in the second person plural and were thus probably adapted by Luke to match the fourth. The woes, too, use "you," although, as already pointed out, it is not immediately clear if Luke considered the people he was addressing as being among the listeners. Perhaps a solution to this apparent difficulty will be found further on.

b) In v. 21, Luke inserted "now" twice, in the second and third beatitudes. "Now" also occurs twice in the corresponding woes in v. 25. This fourfold emphasis is certainly not the result of chance.

c) In the third beatitude (v. 21b), Luke prefers the more realistic terms of "weep" and "laugh," as he also did in the woe of v. 25b. In this woe, however, "mourn" comes before "weep," which seems to indicate that Luke had read this "mourn" in Q. I have applied an analogous line of reasoning above to the term "consolation" in the first woe, v. 24. The rewriting of the fourth beatitude (vv. 22-23) is still more radical: (1) "exclude" is added; (2) "utter evil against you" is replaced by "cast out your name as evil"; (3) "in that day" is added; (4) "be glad" has become "leap for joy," a verb that

Luke also used in 1:41 and 43; (5) "behold" is added; (6) twice Luke supplied subjects to verbs: "people" (v. 21) and "their fathers" (v. 22).

d) The great difference with respect to Q (and Mt) is, of course, the presence of the four woes. The first three are, as it were, formed in the pattern of the corresponding beatitudes. The fourth woe is much shorter: there is only one verb in v. 26a; there is no mention of the Son of Man, which would be impossible in this context, or of a punishment; and there is a reference to the past.

Thus the Lucan pericope in 6:20b-26 also differs considerably in form, style, and length from the Q-source, particularly due to the two-part division, the contrast between beatitude and woe, and the form of address throughout. Another opposition was already present in Q, but it is very much heightened by Luke, namely, that between now (on earth) and later (in heaven). Each of the two parts, the beatitudes (vv. 20b-23) and the woes (vv. 24-26), ends on a longer saying that differs in sentence structure from the preceding three beatitudes and woes.

## SHIFTS OF ACCENT

a) *The Lucan "now."* As throughout the New Testament, the concept that Christ has fulfilled the Old Testament expectations also occurs in Lk. The time of promises is past. Thanks to the coming of Christ, the time of salvation is now. Thus, the present time is sometimes presented in opposition to the past, with Christ being the point of division. Luke has Jesus appear in the synagogue of Nazareth at the beginning of his gospel. After reading Is 61:1-2: "The Spirit of the Lord is upon me, because he has anointed me to preach good news to the poor. He has sent me to proclaim release to the captives and recovering of sight to the blind, to set at liberty those who are oppressed, to proclaim the acceptable year of the Lord," Jesus said, "Today this scripture has been fulfilled in your hearing." (cf. Lk 4:18-21). This is the day, the present, the "now" of the *messianic* fulfillment.

The "now" of the Lucan beatitudes and woes is of another kind. The time of the present life — the time of suffering or foolish, short-lived happiness — is set in opposition to what will follow upon death: reward or punishment. The "now" is here not opposed to the past but to the future. The two periods are separated by death; the situation will be totally reversed. This second opposition appears often in profane and religious wisdom literature. The wise meditate on the meaning of human existence and the outcome of life. Therefore, this "now" is often called the *sapiential* "now." By the stress of this opposition, a shift of emphasis has occurred almost unnoticed. In Q, Jesus still proclaimed God's eschatological breakthrough; in the Lucan gospel, the emphasis is more on instruction, the fruit of reflection.

b) *"Woe to you that are rich!"* Luke did not spiritualize and interiorize the beatitudes as Matthew did by his additions. Luke's choice of words in v. 21b (weep, laugh) and especially in the woes clearly expresses one of his favorite concepts. Luke decries wealth and possessions, luxury and earthly extravagance. The poor receive his special attention. This theme is encountered very often in the Gospel of Luke and the Acts of the Apostles. Following J. Dupont and other exegetes, I offer three considerations to support this.

(1) Complete detachment is demanded of the disciples: "And when they had brought their boats to land, they left *everything* [different in Mk and Mt] and followed him" (5:11); "And he [Levi] left *everything* [different in Mk and Mt], and rose and followed him" (5:28). Cf. also 14:26 and 33, and the ideal portrait of the first Christian community as Acts 2:44-45 and 4:32, 34-36 depict it.

(2) One must, Luke says, make good use of one's possessions by giving alms. The Sermon on the Plain, which continues the beatitudes, stresses this demand. A comparison of another passage with the parallel Matthean text is instructive:

| *Mt 5:42* | *Lk 6:30* |
|---|---|
| Give to him | Give (always) to *every* one |
| who begs from you, | who begs from you; |
| and do not refuse him | and of him who *takes away your* |
| who would borrow from you. | *goods do not ask them again.* |

Cf. also 12:33-34 and the parable of the sly steward in 16:1-13: "make friends for yourself by means of unrighteous mammon" (v. 9).

(3) For Luke, the rich are lamentable *a priori*. The reason for this negative judgment is situated partially in Luke's notion that rich people may often lead morally evil lives and that they are all too often cruel and callous, that they do not help the poor, the widows, and the orphans. But Luke also considers them unfortunate because their wealth makes them captive and closed people, blind to the primary purpose of life. The rich have already received their consolation (6:24); they do not think about God and eternal life! Mammon is their idol. The small parable of the rich man who laid up provisions to be able to enjoy his wealth for many years, resting and eating and drinking, illustrates very well what Luke means: "Fool! This night your soul is required of you" (12:20a). The closing verse reads with resignation: "So is he who lays up treasure for himself, and is not rich toward God" (12:21).

With these three arguments in mind, it is not surprising that we conclude that Luke gave his beatitudes and woes a special, typically Lucan cast.

c) *Threat.* The Greek *ouai* is probably a transcription of a Hebrew or Aramaic lament and occurs often in the Greek Bible, the Septuagint. The Lucan woes lament the rich, the satisfied, the laughers, the people who are praised by everyone. For them, they proclaim pain, sorrow, and regret. Who are these rich? Only rich Jews from the time of Jesus? Also non-Christians of Luke's time? Or did Luke also mean the materially privileged, the successful Christians? From the woes, there also sounds a threat. It seems that the Lucan Jesus not only accuses and complains of the rich who are not

Christians but also warns all Christians of the danger of wealth and earthly fulfillment of life.

None of the three Lucan stresses is to be found in the Q-version in so pronounced or so clear a manner. Like Matthew, therefore, Luke also rewrote and expanded the beatitudes, and his redaction is his pastoral response to the needs of his time.

## LUCAN INSTRUCTION

The Lucan Jesus first of all addresses the poor and persecuted Christians in 6:20b-26. V. 22 is concerned with their exclusion: hate culminates in ostracism. Luke here has in mind what happened to the Jewish Christians before and during his time. Their name, probably that of "Christian" (cf. Acts 11:26), is rejected as evil. This is worse than simply "uttering evil," which presumably was the term used in Q. When Luke wrote in v. 23 that their fathers treated the prophets in the same way, he must have thought of the other Q-texts that complained about the persecution and murder of the prophets (cf. 11:47-51 and 13:33-34).

The Lucan Jesus calls in 6:23 for rejoicing "in that day." This is the day in which Luke and his fellow Christians live. The acute expectation of a speedy end has disappeared, which is indicated by the sharpened opposition between now and then. Not Jesus' return but death is imminent. So the original proclamation became reflection and instruction in Lk. With the woes Jesus informs his persecuted disciples regarding the hostility of the Jews in the past, the present, and the future.

In 6:20b-26, the Lucan Jesus decidedly expresses his preference for the poor Christians, as he does often in this gospel: consider, for example, the poor Lazarus (16:19-31). It would therefore run counter to Luke's most profound intention to consider the first pericope of his Sermon on the Plain merely as sapiential instruction. He certainly also intended the beatitudes and woes to be an indirect encouragement to actual love for the poor. Behind the public — the disciples, the chance listeners, the poor and the rich — are

Luke's readers. The poor Christians are called blessed by the Lucan Jesus; he invites the rich Christians to free themselves from their wealth and to join the poor in solidarity.

## IV. The Beatitudes and Christians Today

In "The Meaning of the Bible" (*Theology Digest* 28, 1980, pp. 305-320), Raymond E. Brown discussed the various meanings of the Scriptures. To my mind, he correctly distinguishes a threefold meaning. First, there is the literal meaning, that which the author intended and which the first readers presumably understood. There is then the meaning that arises because a text belongs to the Bible: the canonical sense, as Brown called it. With the entirety of the Scriptures in mind, the Christians must, for example, reconcile what Paul said about the Law with what Matthew wrote about it. Finally, there is also the "Church interpretation," the particular meaning that the later Church and thus also contemporary Christians discover in the Scriptures from the viewpoint of their changed circumstances. This third sense I would also call application, transposition, actualization, and it is to this third sense that I now turn.

B. van Iersel has written: "It is uncommonly fascinating to see how the same words of Jesus could be understood in different ways in the different versions. I do not mean, of course, that the interpretations contradict or exclude each other, but when we place them next to each other, there still arises just enough contrast to reveal perspectives. Are we now bound to one of the two interpretations? In any case, both are present, and they have both become Holy Scripture" (p. 9). Van Iersel has the Matthean and the Lucan versions in mind here. But we must also include Jesus (and Q) along with the evangelists in this conclusion. Is there unity in the diversity? How do modern Christians stand with respect to Luke's concept of wealth? Must we, in our lives, in our catechesis, and in our preaching give priority to one particular version?

## LEGITIMATE DIVERSITY

There is no point in glossing over the major differences of the three versions. (1) In the *source*, the first three beatitudes were *messianic proclamations*. It is easy to imagine the situation in the beginning of Jesus' earthly life in which such a proclamation took place. The public are the disciples and the people who happen to be present; Jesus' message is intended for all the disinherited. (2) For *Matthew*, a *parenetic preoccupation* determined his rewriting: the emphasis is on the conditions necessary to participate in the eschatological happiness. He seems to be thinking about the situation in the church, and he writes for Christian readers, his believing contemporaries. (3) *Luke* moderates the proclamatory character of Jesus' beatitudes in another way by converting the beatitudes into *sapiential instruction*, with the stress on the finiteness of this earthly life and the just reward hereafter. Luke has Jesus address the disciples; the woes presumably envision the rich unconverted Jews who hate the disciples and persecute them.

Jesus proclaims God's initiative; the evangelists emphasize the human response: Matthew by pointing out the necessary interior disposition, Luke by advocating real detachment. "Only when the word of Jesus is accepted by the poor man interiorly and personally is there place for an ultimate blessing, a definitive beatitude" (Schreiner, p. 281). This apparent diversity must not cause us to lose sight of the continuity between Jesus' proclamation and the later redactions. Each of the two evangelists (and already Q) shifts the accents and changes the point of view, but they do not betray the total message of Jesus or falsify its original sense. Indeed, not only do both bring in ideas that are present elsewhere in Jesus' preaching, but both Matthew's call for righteousness and Luke's love for the poor are situated in the text of the source and in the words of Jesus.

## POOR AND RICH

The poor (the unhappy!) are blessed for the happiness that will be theirs after this life and that is already offered to them in this life by Christ. In the Lucan gospel, moreover, the rich are pitied because it is very hard for them to open themselves up to this future happiness. Their decision is complicated by their possessions, and they fail to see the importance of the love of neighbor. The Lucan and Christian standpoint in this question is not primarily that of social justice, of demands or rights on the profane human level, but that of the transitoriness of all that is earthly and the permanence of the heavenly Kingdom of God. One cannot possess both the earthly and the heavenly simultaneously. A choice must be made now. The distribution of possessions or the giving of alms is seen as a means of detachment.

Obviously, this detachment will take on other forms depending on the awareness of social emancipation and economic responsibility, and that it now must also be experienced by most people through a very real and positive commitment to an earthly task. The parousia is yet to come: life goes on and demands that the necessary measures be taken, including the material and the social. But one must ultimately not forget that "also the Lucan interpretation stands under the charisma of inspiration and is in this sense truly the word of Christ. We must thus submit in obedience to this word and listen to what it has to say to us. Anyone who enjoys earthly possessions and prosperity must ask himself how far he is letting himself be preoccupied by his possessions. For to the degree that the world does in fact draw us from God", to this degree does the Lucan 'woe to you that are rich' apply to us. Whoever commits himself to transitory values has already received his consolation here. At the end, he has only hunger and tears left over" (Schreiner, p. 279). The advice that we read in the First Letter to Timothy retains its full value today: "We brought nothing into the world, and we cannot take anything out of the world; but if we have food and clothing, with these we shall be content. But those who desire to be rich fall into temptation, into a snare, into many senseless and hurtful desires that plunge men into ruin and destruction. For the love of money is the root of all evils; it is through this craving that some have wandered away from the faith and pierced their hearts with many pangs" (6:7-10).

## ACTUALIZATION

The example of the evangelists shows the way to the Christian and the pastor. He or she, guided by the Scriptures, will also adapt, transpose, and actualize. Much will depend on the concrete situation in which the modern individual finds himself. In principle, we have a wide choice, which must, moreover, vary with the times and the needs. We can listen to Jesus' message about God and proclaim it further ourselves: the messianic good news! God turns to us before we can accomplish anything. God gives freely without our earning anything. But in another day, in another situation, the same Christian will let this theological aspect rest and stress the anthropological. God's gift demands a human response, and this answer is neatly set out by Matthew in his version.

We can speak of God's definitive breakthrough: we are now already blessed; we no longer live in the time of the promises but in the messianic days of the fulfillment. But, with Luke, we can also speak of the transitory, the passing "now" with its misery and persecution, with its false certitudes and its rich self-satisfaction, and we can confront this "now" with the future of eternal life.

These are all authentically Christian, traditional data, and they all concur with Jesus' message. Everything cannot always and simultaneously be considered or said. Blessed are the Christians who work out their application, apostolically and for themselves, in freedom and with resourcefulness. And blessed is the Church with such Christians.

## Bibliography

See also the general works listed on pp. 47-44 above.

Betz, H.D., "Die Markarismen der Bergpredigt (Matthäus 5:3-12). Beobachtungen zur literarischen Form und theologischen Bedeutung," *Zeitschr. Theol. Kirche* 75 (1978) 3-19.

Böckmann, A., "What Does the New Testament Say about the Church's Attitude to the Poor?" in: *Concilium* (1977), no. 104, pp. 36-95.

Campbell, K.M., "The New Jerusalem in Matthew 5.14," *Scott. Journ. Theol.* 31 (1978) 335-363.

De Fraine, J., *Praying with the Bible. The Biblical Bases of Great Christian Prayers*, ET by J.W. Saul, New York-Tournai-Paris-Rome, 1964, pp. 127-182.

Dodd, C.H., "The Beatitudes: A Form-Critical Study," in: Dodd, *More New Testament Studies*, Manchester, 1968, pp. 1-10.

Dumbrell, W.J., "The Logic of the Role of the Law in Matthew V 1-20," *Nov. Test.* 23 (1981) 1-21.

Dupont, J., *Les Béatitudes. II: La Bonne Nouvelle* (Et. Bibl.), Paris, 1969; *III: Les évangélistes* (Et. Bibl.), Paris, ²1973.

Dupont, J., "Introduction aux Béatitudes," *Nouv. Rev. Théol.* 98 (1976) 97-108.

Dupont, J., *Le message des Béatitudes* (Cahiers Evangile 24), Paris, 1978.

Frankemölle, H., "Die Makarismen (Mt 5,1-12; Lk 6,20-23). Motive und Umfang der redaktionellen Komposition," *Bibl. Zeitschr.* 15 (1971) 52-75.

Guelich, R.A., "The Matthean Beatitudes: 'Entrance-Requirements' or Eschatological Blessings," *Journ. Bibl. Lit.* 95 (1976) 415-434.

Hoffmann, P., in: Hoffmann and V. Eid, *Jesus von Nazareth und eine christliche Moral* (Quaest. Disp. 66), Freiburg-Basel-Vienna, 1975, pp. 27-58.

Hoffmann, P., "Selig sind die Armen...." Auslegung der Bergpredigt II," *Bib. Leb.* 10 (1969) 111-122.

McEleney, N. J., "The Beatitudes of the Sermon on the Mount/Plain," *Cath. Bibl. Quart.* 43 (1981) 1-13.

Merklein, H., *Die Gottesherrschaft als Handlungsprinzip. Untersuchung zur Ethik Jesu* (Forsch. Bib. 34), Würzburg, 1978, pp. 48-55.

Schnackenburg, R., "Die Seligpreisung der Friedensstifter (Mt 5,9) im mattäischen Kontext," *Bibl. Zeitschr.* 26 (1982) 161-178.

Schreiner, G., "De acht Zaligheden," *Verbum* 32 (1965) 271-285.

Schweizer, E., "Formgeschichtliches zu den Seligpreisungen Jesu," *New Test. Stud.* 19 (1972-73) 121-126.

Strecker, G. "Die Makarismen der Bergpredigt," *New Test. Stud.* 17 (1970-71) 255-275.

Trilling, W., *Christusverkündigung in den synoptischen Evangelien. Beispiele gattungsgemässer Auslegung*, Munich, 1969, pp. 64-85.

Tuckett, C.M., "The Beatitudes: A Source-Critical Study. With a Reply by M.D. Goulder," *Nov. Test.* 25 (1983) 193-216.

Van Iersel, B. M. F., "Zalig de armen (van geest)," *Het Heilig Land* 19 (1966) 6-9.

Weren, W., "Het bestaansrecht van de zwakste. De samenhang tussen Mt 5,3-12 en Mt 25,31-46," *Ons Geest. Leven* 59 (1982) 28-36.

# Chapter Three

# THE ANTITHESES
(Mt 5:17-48)

In Mt 5:48, we read: "You, therefore, must be perfect, as your heavenly Father is perfect." There is no doubt that this verse concludes a unit; it refers back to 5:20: "For I tell you, unless your righteousness exceeds that of the scribes and Pharisees, you will never enter the Kingdom of heaven." Mt 5:20 in its turn is the concluding verse of the small passage of 5:17-20. This unit functions as an introduction to 5:21-48, a pericope that is generally called the "antitheses." In this chapter, we will therefore examine Mt 5:17-48.

The name "antitheses" refers to the opposition "You have heard that it was said ... but I say to you ... " that occurs six times in vv. 21-48 with roughly the same wording. In v. 20, Jesus places his disciples in opposition to the scribes and Pharisees. And although in vv. 17-19 Jesus stresses the continuing applicability of the Law, in the antitheses new kinds of behavior are clearly presented in opposition to the former way of living. Those who speak of a "new Law" of Christianity justify, correctly or incorrectly, this view of Jesus' moral program primarily in terms of Mt 5:17-48. Therefore, the importance of this pericope for Christian morality can hardly be overestimated.

Luke in his Sermon on the Plain presents material that parallels two Matthean antitheses: see Lk 6:27-36 and Mt 5:38-48. Mt will be compared to Lk to reconstruct the

Q-source. There are still other Q-parallels in Mt 5:17-48, but they are not in the Lucan Sermon on the Plain. Here the Lucan version will be dealt with only in passing since the parallel passages of the Sermon on the Plain will be treated in detail in Chapter Seven.

This discussion of Mt. 5:17-48 will be divided into four parts. First, the formal introduction, 5:17-20, will be analyzed. Second, the form and the composition of the antitheses, 5:21-48, will be examined, and then the content of the antitheses will be discussed: what did Jesus and Matthew mean by more abundant or better righteousness? In the fourth part, finally, we will be concerned with the important question of whether this biblical righteousness has anything to do with contemporary Christians, who all too often find themselves in an unjust society.

## *I. Jesus and the Law*

In Mt 5:17-20, the Matthean Jesus gives what we could call an outline of principles. With the introductory words of v. 17, "Think not that I have come ...", a new line of thought is clearly begun after vv. 13-16. The four verses of the introduction to the antitheses are very solemn. Not only the tension that many exegetes feel between the outline of principles (the applicability of the Law) and the antitheses (the surpassing or abolition of the Law) but also what is contained in the individual sentences themselves of vv. 17-20 make this pericope a very controverted text. The numerous explanations have grown, as W. Trilling put it, "into an almost impenetrable jungle." What does Matthew the evangelist wish to say precisely, and does this concur with Jesus' thought? But first, the text of 5:17-20:

> 17 Think not that I have come to abolish the Law or the Prophets; I have come not to abolish them but to fulfill them.
> 18 For truly, I say to you, till heaven and earth pass away, not an iota, not a dot, will pass from the Law until all is accomplished.

19 Whoever then relaxes one of the least of these commandments and teaches men so, shall be called least in
the Kingdom of heaven; but he who does them and
teaches them shall be called great in the Kingdom of
heaven.

20 For I tell you, unless your righteousness exceeds that
of the scribes and Pharisees, you will never enter the
Kingdom of heaven.

Unmistakably the first person singular predominates: in v.
17 (twice "I have come," *ēlthon*) and in vv. 18 and 20 (twice
"I say to you"). When we leave aside v. 18a, it is striking that
in the rest of v. 18 and in v. 19, Jesus uses the third person
and talks *about* things and individuals, while he uses the
second person in the framing vv. 17 and 20 (and also in 18a),
and addresses himself *to* the disciples. In addition to this
framing second person, the unity of this passage is also
strongly reinforced by the linking words: "for" (v. 18),
"then" (v. 19), and again "for" (v. 20). Only v. 18 has a
Q-parallel, namely Lk 16:17: "But it is easier for heaven and
earth to pass away, than for one dot of the Law to become
void."

I will discuss this passage verse by verse, first giving the
form and the origin and then the content of the passage and
an explanation of it.


## I HAVE COME TO FULFILL

a) The "I-word" of v. 17 belongs to the *ēlthon* (I have come)
group that contains sayings in which Jesus looks back over
his life's work and/or presents the meaning of his mission.
Did Matthew find this saying in his source (S, *Sondergut*)
and rewrite it to a certain extent, or did he create it completely himself (R, redaction)?

There are three things, particularly when taken together,
that argue for ascribing v. 17 completely to Matthew. First,
the rhetorical introduction, "do not think that I have come,"
also occurs in 10:34. Very probably the opening words in
this logion come from Matthew (cf. the other formulation in

Lk 12:51). Second, "Law and Prophets" (= the entire Scriptures) is a phrase that Matthew added in 7:12 (= Q, cf Lk 6:31, where the expression does not occur) and in 22:40 (a verse that was added by Matthew, cf. Mk 12:31). Compare also 11:13: "For all the prophets and the Law prophesied," Q; in Lk 16:16 there is "the Law and the Prophets." "The Law *or* the Prophets" in Mt 5:17 hardly differs from this Matthean phrase. Third, "fulfill" is a favorite Matthean word; it occurs in his gospel sixteen times.

Nevertheless, we must be careful in drawing our conclusion. It is not excluded that Matthew had a pre-Matthean, perhaps authentic, logion from Jesus for v. 17 as we now read it. Some authors reconstruct this postulated S-logion roughly as follows: "I have not come to abrogate the Law but to maintain it." It is quite conceivable, they say, that Jesus would have defended himself with such a saying on one or another occasion. Matthew would then have expanded and rewritten this logion for his Sermon on the Mount. In my opinion, however, v. 17 may be considered as R (redaction).

b) If account is taken only of the term "fulfill," one would tend to see this Matthean saying in terms of "salvation history." Jesus, by his coming, already fulfilled what was proclaimed in the Law and the Prophets; he fulfills the promises; he achieves what the prophets proclaimed.

But this explanation is not entirely satisfactory. "To abrogate the Law or the Prophets" means in fact to abolish them. It also means explaining that they no longer need to be obeyed. Further, both in 7:12: "So whatever you wish that men would do to you, do so to them; for this is the Law and the Prophets" (the Golden Rule) and in 22:40: "On these two commandments depend all the Law and the Prophets," the phrase added by Matthew, "the Law and the Prophets," is used in an ethical statement about love of neighbor (and of God). The normative character of the Scriptures is thus clearly placed in the forefront. By "Prophets," therefore, we must not think primarily of prophecies; the prophets were those who interpreted, defended, and actualized the Law.

Finally, there is also the context. 5:18 postulates the continuing applicability of the Law; 5:19-20 and 5:21-48 are concerned with what must be done.

More specifically, the antitheses suggest a meaning for "fulfilling" that can perhaps best be defined as follows. Jesus came in order to make known the original will of God by his teaching and, of course, also by his example. This explanation combines the salvation historical aspect (Jesus' coming) with the ethical (God's will). In this explicitly christological formulation, Jesus' fulfilling does not then mean, or at least not primarily, that he, by his life and actions, fulfills or accomplishes the Law, or that only by his pious life faithfully lives up to or fulfills it, but rather that he explains and interprets the Law and the Prophets according to God's original intention.

V. 17 is of itself a solemn declaration of principle. With the "think not," the saying is directed to the disciples as a warning. It stands at the beginning of a passage that is an introduction to the antitheses. Apparently, the Matthean Jesus is concerned that the antitheses could be misunderstood by the disciples, for they do not abolish the Law but, on the contrary, fulfill it.

## THE LAW WILL NOT PASS AWAY

a) In terms of form criticism, v. 18 can be called a "prophetic word." In order to determine its Matthean redactional content, we must compare it with Lk 16:17. It belongs to the Q-document.

| *Mt 5:18* | *Lk 16:17* |
|---|---|
| a For truly, I say to you, | It is easier for heaven and earth |
| b till heaven and earth pass away, | to pass away, |
| c not an iota, not a dot, will pass from the Law | than for one dot of the Law to become void. |
| d until all is accomplished. | |

No one doubts that v. 18bc and Lk 16:17 are very similar in content. Supposedly — not everyone would agree — both verses go back to one single Q-logion. For reasons I need not go into here, it seems to me that Luke's text is closer to the original Q-version, although he did omit "one iota" because this letter in the Greek alphabet is not particularly small as in the case in Aramaic. By "dot" is probably meant a decorative line or curl of a written letter. Thus in Q, it was said that the Law will not soon pass away; heaven and earth would pass away sooner.

Matthew has expanded this saying by adding parts a and d. This addition also caused the change in the construction of bc: the comparison "easier than" was dropped and replaced by the "till" clause. The correctness of this point of view of the Matthean redaction is confirmed by the following consideration. In Mt 24:34-35 (a slight revision of Mk 13:30-31) we read: "Truly, I say to you, this generation will not pass away till all these things take place. Heaven and earth will pass away, but my words will not pass away." It is difficult to suppose otherwise than that Matthew rewrote his Q-logion of v. 18bc and expanded it with v. 18ad under the influence of 24:34-35 (or Mk 13:30-31): v. 18 has the same construction as 24:34; the additions v. 18a and v. 18d also occur almost literally in 24:34; as in 24:35, v. 18bc has twice the same verb "to pass away" (*parerchomai*: only once in Q).

b) Unlike his contemporaries, Jesus used the word *amēn* (truly) not only as a response (a confirmation of what precedes) but also as a beginning and as a replacement for an oath formula (confirmation of what follows). Matthew has added v. 18a: the Matthean Jesus now formally introduces the statement of v. 18bcd with "for truly, I say to you." The "for" tells us that Matthew intends this saying as a concretizing explanation and confirmation of v. 17.

Q stated that the Law remains applicable to its smallest detail: it would be easier for heaven and earth to pass away! Many are convinced that this saying could not come from

Jesus because it is difficult to reconcile it with his attitude toward the Law. Indeed, this Q-logion presumably arose among conservative Jewish-Christians who thus gave expression to their opposition to a tendency in their church to neglect rigorous adherence to the Law. Matthew preserved this saying quite faithfully. His rewriting of Q resulted in a time-specifying phrase in v. 18b as also in v. 18d, which therefore became an inelegant repetition of v. 18b. Since we know from 24:35 that Matthew was convinced of the passing away of heaven and earth, we may well suppose that, in v. 18b ("till . . . "), he was thinking of the end-time, a time limit for the applicability of the Law. But must we not conclude from v. 18d that Matthew nevertheless understood v. 18bc other than did Q?

About the precise meaning of the vague v. 18d, "until all is accomplished," there is, unfortunately, still disagreement. Opinions diverge, but they can be simplified somewhat here.

First, the abundant use of "be accomplished, happen, occur" elsewhere in Mt (about 70 times: see, for example, 21:4; 24:34, and 26:56) could argue for a salvation historical meaning: everything that is announced in the Law will be accomplished "to the smallest detail." The Law in v. 18c is thus not to be understood as a collection of prescriptions but as salvation prophecy. Does "all" in this explanation then refer to the end events as in 24:34 or to the prophecies regarding Christ?

Second, because the term Law has primarily a moral reference — it contains prescriptions that must be obeyed —many exegetes opt for an "ethical" explanation: until "all," i.e., all the commandments, are obeyed. The "to be done" of 6:10 ("Thy will be done": cf. 26:42) comes to mind for this meaning as well as the immediate context of vv. 19-20, where doing is mentioned in terms of greater righteousness.

Third, J. De Vriese, along with others, proposes a synthesis model. He takes account of the explanation in v. 17. The two oppositions, that between the salvation historical events and the ethical performance (for the verb "to be accomplished," *ginomai*) and that between prophecies and prescriptions (for "everything," *panta*), are reconciled "christologically." By "all" Matthew refers to what the Law and Prophets commanded and prophesied; by "be accomplished" he means the obeying of commandments that are "fulfilled" by Jesus' teaching and example, i.e., brought back to God's actual will. The Law thus has a prophetic and ethical dimension. Fulfillment in salvation history and fulfillment through moral acts belong together. P. Hoffmann writes aptly: "Jesus fulfilled the prophetic promise in such a way that the Law's command for righteousness is fulfilled" (*Gerechtigkeit*, p. 178), and J. De Vriese: "Concretely, what this all comes down to is that Jesus fulfills the Law in salvation history insofar as he expounds this Law on the basis of the commandment to love and thus reveals the will of God. Moreover, the fulfillment is accomplished because Jesus as the Messiah also obeys this Law in his life" (pp. 75-76).

By adding "until all is accomplished" (v. 18d), which is to be understood christologically, and by having Jesus come "to fulfill" (v. 17b) the Law and the Prophets, Matthew has made the Q-logion (v. 18bc), which was difficult also for him, more acceptable.


## THE LEAST COMMANDMENTS

a) V. 19 is a "casuistic legal saying," constructed in two parts, antithetically. This double logion has many rabbinic characteristics: the distinction between large and small, between greatest and least commandments, the concept that the reward will match the performance and that the least commandment must be maintained as well as the greatest. "One of the least of these commandments" alludes to "an iota, a dot" of the Law. It is not obvious that such a saying about scrupulous faithfulness to the Law can come from Jesus, particularly when one considers v. 19 in itself, free of the context. Is it then a Matthean creation? Is it a part of the *Sondergut*? Here, too, there are no conclusive arguments.

It is quite possible that this verse was already present in the Matthean Q-source and linked with v. 18. This seems to be confirmed by the "then" (but this is a typically Matthean conjunction) and also the expression "the least of these commandments." It is difficult to determine the extent to which Matthew rewrote the saying. The phrase "one of the least. . . " also occurs in 25:40, 45 (cf. 10:42; 18:10, 14). Does the entire positive second part come from the evangelist? Did he add the verb "to teach" twice? Matthew almost always writes the "Kingdom of *heaven.*" Further, is there not a slight tension between "to relax" in v. 19a and "to do" in v. 19b as a result of the rewriting, or does "to relax" here mean simply "not to do"? But these are all less important details.

b) The important question is this: How is it that Matthew has preserved this "literary fossil," as v. 19 is sometimes called? The following hypothesis can perhaps explain the presence of this verse in Matthew's gospel. The saying would have originated in a Jewish-Christian milieu and would have been intended to oppose what was considered a too lax attitude toward the Law. Verses 18 and 19 would have existed already in a pre-Matthean Q-stage, their content being related. The second logion (v. 19) looks like a conclusion of the first (v. 18), but it is also a softening of the absolute position on the endurance of the Law. Matthew took over both verses. The insertion of v. 17 and the rewriting of v. 18 show sufficiently that he did not simply accept the most obvious meaning. V. 19 must be interpreted in the light of vv. 17 and 18. A literal understanding would run counter to Matthew's redactional purpose. J. Dupont is of the opinion that Matthew's intention with v. 19 was to soften the radicality of v. 20 ("will never enter"). In the Kingdom of heaven there is also a place, though of lower rank, for those who abolish a rigid prescription and teach people so. One perceives in v. 19 "the concern to nuance very absolute affirmations" (*Béatitudes I*, p. 138).

Still, v. 19 within the passage of vv. 17-20 looks very much like "an unabsorbed remnant." In vv. 17-18, the Matthean Jesus was talking about himself and the Law. In v. 19, the disciples and especially the teachers of the Law move to the foreground. But Matthew, in the writing of this verse, was probably thinking not only about the Jewish Law of the past but also about Jesus' actual commandments (cf. "one of the least of these commandments"). If this is true, then v. 19 must have had a very acceptable meaning for the evangelist's co-believers!

## MORE ABUNDANT RIGHTEOUSNESS

a) V. 20 is an admission saying, a saying about the conditions for being allowed into the Kingdom. Most probably this verse is genuinely Matthean (= R). This is indicated by the Matthean phrase "scribes and Pharisees" and the Matthean "For I tell you"; further, it contains Matthew's typical concept of righteousness. The verse is cast in the second person plural. We can thus accept that vv. 17 and 20 form the Matthean frame for vv. 18 and 19, which he took from the tradition.

b) "Righteousness," according to Matthew, characterizes the conduct of life that pleases God, that does God's will. However, it would be completely erroneous, using v. 19, to explain the righteousness that exceeds that of the scribes and the Pharisees as a fidelity to the Law that would maintain even more scrupulously the smallest prescriptions. No, v. 19 (like v. 18) is "neutralized" precisely by the Matthean framing. What the greater righteousness means in the concrete, moreover, is clearly illustrated by the antitheses of 5:21-48. In these antitheses, Jesus teaches with full authority how the Law must be understood and obeyed.

In fact, a shift is in process with v. 20. The "for" is not truly motivational: a new horizon is opening. Perhaps the term "great" in v. 19b gave Matthew the idea of "exceeding." But instead of talking about the Law, he now speaks of a Christian righteousness. V. 19 was concerned with the teachers; now the subject is all the disciples, and they are set in opposition to the scribes and Pharisees. For the second time, Matthew has Jesus begin with the solemn "For I tell you." V. 20 is a new beginning and as such is the immediate introduction to the antitheses that follow. It can be considered the title verse of the entire antitheses passage.

## TWO FRONTS AND A DOUBLE LEVEL

So we have tradition and redaction in Mt 5:17-20. Matthew has succeeded in presenting this small passage as a unity. It functions as an impressive "antechamber" for the antitheses. The primary idea that Matthew stresses is the enduring validity of the Law. Jesus did not abolish the Law but exposed its actual meaning. Thus, the Christians may not be lax; by the practice of their righteousness, they must be more faithful to the Law than the scribes and Pharisees or they will never enter the Kingdom of heaven!

It is often pointed out that Matthew is here fighting on two fronts. In v. 20, the Matthean Jesus distances himself from Judaism: his concept of the Law is fundamentally different from that of the scribes and Pharisees. Vv. 17-19, however, oppose the disciples who threaten to disregard the Law; it is an argument against antinomianism.

In order better to situate these two fronts, Matthew's double level must be kept in mind. Matthew certainly wants to provide information about the earthly Jesus and how, so many years before, this Jesus had taught his disciples his concept of the Law, his position with respect to the legalism of the Jews. But Matthew is also concerned with his fellow believers. He thinks along with them about the relationship of Christians to Judaism and to the Law, and with his hidden parenesis in 5:17-20 he also wants to guard these Christians against a lawlessness and an antinomian mentality.

## II. The Composition of the Antitheses

With the antitheses of Mt 5:21-48, the Matthean Jesus himself proceeds to "teach" (v. 19) how he "fulfills" the Law and the Prophets (v. 17) and how righteousness must be abundantly practiced by his disciples (cf. v. 20). Although form and content influence each other, this second part will be limited to the study of the structure and origin of vv. 21-48. The content of these verses obviously forms a structured unit. How did Matthew compose them? What sources did he use? What is the result of his redaction?

V. 48 is the concluding verse that, with v. 20 (and vv. 17-19), frames the antitheses. Vv. 21-47 contain six antitheses: murder (vv. 21-26); adultery (vv. 27-30); divorce (vv. 31-32); swearing (vv. 33-37); retaliation (vv. 38-42); and love of enemy (vv. 43-47).

## THE TEXT

First, a translation of Mt 5:21-48.

(1) *Murder*

21 You have heard that it was said to the men of old, "You shall not kill; and whoever kills shall be liable to judgment."

22 But I say to you that every one who is angry with his brother shall be liable to judgment; whoever insults his brother shall be liable to the council, and whoever says, "You fool!" shall be liable to the hell of fire.

23 So if you are offering your gift at the altar, and there remember something that your brother has against you,

24 leave your gift there before the altar and go; first be reconciled to your brother, and then come and offer your gift.

25 Make friends quickly with your accuser, while you are going with him to court, lest your accuser hand you over to the judge, and the judge to the guard, and you be put in prison;

26 truly, I say to you, you will never get out till you have paid the last penny.

(2) *Adultery*

27 You have heard that it was said, "You shall not commit adultery."

28 But I say to you that every one who looks at a woman

lustfully has already committed adultery with her in his heart.

29 If your right eye causes you to sin, pluck it out and throw it away; it is better that you lose one of your members than that your whole body be thrown into hell.

30 And if your right hand causes you to sin, cut it off and throw it away; it is better that you lose one of your members than that your whole body go into hell.

(3) *Divorce*

31 It was also said, "Whoever divorces his wife, let him give her a certificate of divorce."

32 But I say to you that every one who divorces his wife, except on the ground of unchastity, makes her an adulteress; and whoever marries a divorced woman commits adultery.

(4) *Swearing*

33 Again  you have heard that it was said to the men of old, "You shall not swear falsely, but shall perform to the Lord what you have sworn."

34 But I say to you, Do not swear at all, either by heaven, for it is the throne of God,

35 or by the earth, for it is his footstool, or by Jerusalem, for it is the city of the great King.

36 And do not swear by your head, for you cannot make one hair white or black.

37 Let what you say be simply "Yes, yes" or "No, no"; anything more than this comes from evil.

(5) *Retaliation*

38 You have heard that it was said, "An eye for an eye and a tooth for a tooth."

39 But I say to you, Do not resist one who is evil. But if any one strikes you on the right cheek, turn to him the other also;

40 and if any one would sue you and take your coat, let him have your cloak as well;

41 and if any one forces you to go one mile, go with him two miles.

42 Give to him who begs from you, and do not refuse him who would borrow from you.

(6) *Love of enemy*

43 You have heard that it was said, "You shall love your neighbor and hate your enemy."
44 But I say to you, Love your enemies and pray for those who persecute you,
45 so that you may be sons of your Father who is in heaven; for he makes his sun rise on the evil and on the good, and sends rain on the just and on the unjust.
46 For if you love those who love you, what reward have you? Do not even the tax collectors do the same?

47 And if you salute only your brethren, what more are you doing than others? Do not even the Gentiles do the same?

*Concluding verse*

48 You, therefore, must be perfect, as your heavenly Father is perfect.


Introduction formulas mark the beginning of each antithesis. The first halves of the first and fourth antitheses, practically identical, are the longest of all: "You have heard that it was said to the men of old" (v. 21; cf. v. 33: "Again you have...."). The formulas of the second, fifth, and sixth omit "to the men of old": "You have heard that it was said" (vv. 27, 38, and 43). The third has only: "It was also said" (v. 31). The first half of the formula is always followed by: "But *I* say you." The opposition is twofold: against the men of old" (= the elders, the ancestors) stands "you" (= the disciples and the listening people); and against those who spoke in the past stands, very strongly emphasized, Jesus.

Who is the agent of the passive verb "it was said"? Some exegetes argue that it is God; others postulate Moses. In both cases (and particularly the first!), the opposition involved is hardly tolerable. In the light of vv. 17-20, where the Matthean Jesus opposes an erroneous understanding and living of the Law, it is better that we do not think immediately of Moses (and certainly not God) but rather of the expounders of the Law of the past, of the Jewish scribes with all their "traditions" that were still in force (cf. 15:1-9).

## THE SO-CALLED PRIMARY AND SECONDARY ANTITHESES

In the judgment of many exegetes, primary and secondary antitheses must be distinguished in 5:21-47. This distinction requires some explanation.

a) The "primary" antitheses are those that had the antithetical form from the beginning (stemming from Jesus): the first, second, and fourth. The form, moreover, is an essential feature of the saying. Thesis and antithesis are so related to each other that what Jesus says (= the antithesis) is only intelligible in conjunction with the thesis. And in contrast to the secondary antitheses, the Old Testament prohibition cited is not abolished but radicalized.

It used to be often argued that both the form and the radicalization were typical of Jesus. Recently, however, E. Lohse has shown that this is not the case. Antithetical ways of expression are also to be found among the rabbis, and the radicalization of commands is also encountered in the Qumran texts and in some rabbinical texts. What is unique to Jesus, it is now said, is that he does not argue with contemporary scribes but with the entire tradition, that he does not support his new explanation with Scriptural arguments, and most of all that he invokes God's will with unprecedented power and authority.

b) The remaining three antitheses, the third, fifth, and sixth, are called "secondary" because, as is widely accepted, they were not originally cast in the antithetical form. They were most probably forced into this form by the Matthean rewriting in order to fit the primary antitheses. I must stress that "primary" and "secondary" here only concern the form. The content of the so-called secondary antitheses could go back to Jesus, and thus be as authentic and original as the others.

Luke has preserved a more original version of the fifth and sixth antitheses in his Sermon on the Plain: for the retaliation antithesis, see Lk 6:29-31; for the love-of-enemy antithesis, see Lk 6:27-28, 32-36.

For the divorce antithesis, there is also a Q-parallel, but none in the Lucan Sermon on the Plain. See Lk 16:18: "Every one who divorces his wife and marries another commits adultery, and he who marries a woman divorced from her husband commits adultery." This logion also apparently followed Lk 16:17 in Q, a saying that Matthew already included in 5:18. But Matthew places parts of Mk 9:43-48 in 5:29-30, and Mt 5:32, with the addition of "except on the ground of unchastity," is very similar to 19:9 "except for unchastity," which verse is a rewriting of Mk 10:11. Therefore, with the divorce antithesis (Mt 5:31-32), we have a Matthean combination of a Q-text and a Marcan text. The introductory formula also has something special. We do not read as everywhere else: "You have heard that it was said (to the men of old)", but only "It was also said" (v. 31). Matthew sees divorce as thematically bound to adultery, and perhaps this is the reason for the short transitional phrase.

.While the Law is radicalized in the primary antitheses, it is directly opposed in the secondary, and the Old Testament commandments cited are abrogated: letter of divorce, an eye for an eye, hate for the enemy. A new attitude replaces the old.

## IS THE DIVISION TOO RIGID?

The division of the antitheses into two groups (primary and secondary) has won wide acceptance and retains its attractiveness because of the clear separation it provides. The primary antitheses are concerned with *prohibitions* (cf. Ex 20:13-14 and 16 [?]; fifth, sixth, and eighth prescriptions of the decalogue) that are radicalized; the secondary with *commands* that Jesus abrogates. Matthew took the primary

antitheses from his own source, where they had their antithetical form from Jesus; the secondary antitheses received
their antithetical introduction from Matthew, which he borrowed from the primary ones, but the content is traditional
(and from Jesus): the content of the fifth and the sixth comes
from the Q-Sermon on the Mount, that of the third can be
found in Q (not the Sermon on the Mount) and in Mk.

It can also be noted here that apparently only the primary
antitheses were given an added commentary. The murder
antithesis, the first, received a three-fold expansion: v. 22bc
(casuistic detailing, S or R?); vv. 23-24 (on the way to the
altar, S); and vv. 25-26 (accommodating one's opponent, Q;
cf. Lk 12:57-59). With the adultery antithesis, the second,
Matthew placed sayings in vv. 29-30 that dealt with scandal
(from Mk 9:43-48). And in the middle of the oath-taking
antithesis, the fourth, there is also a casuistically detailed
summary in vv. 34b-36. Now, is the fact that additions only
occur in the primary antitheses not a confirmation that
Matthew simply copied these antitheses and commented on
them, while he himself had to form the secondary antitheses
and, because of this redactional work, forgot, as it were, to
add any further comments?

Still, not everyone agrees with this rigid division. Indeed,
there a considerable number of uncertain factors remains.
First, does the distinction between commandment and prohibition apply everywhere? What, for example, is one to do
with the so-called prohibition of v. 33 and the so-called
command of v. 43? Second, the distinction between radicalization and abrogation is also sometimes contested. Thus it
is argued that it is more an abrogation than a radicalization
in the oath-taking antithesis and more a sharpening than an
abolishment in the love antithesis. Third, some exegetes
hold that Matthew found the antithetical introduction in
the Sermon on the Mound of Q. Luke would have ommitted
it as being too Jewish. Lk 6:27 with its "But I say to you that
hear," would then be the remainder of it and thus still a
witness to an antithetical form in Q. Fourth, not all exegetes
agree that Matthew simply took the three primary antitheses from S. It is not to be excluded *a priori* that the

antithetical introduction of these three is also to be attributed to Matthew. Thus, G. Dautzenberg recently demonstrated rather convincingly that Matthew himself wrote the primary oath-taking antithesis. In the Letter of James we read: "But above all, my brethren, do not swear, either by heaven or by earth or with any other oath, but let your yes be yes and your no be no, that you may not fall under condemnation" (5:12). James' parenesis seems to be more original that Matthew's. While the traditional Jewish criticism on oath-taking was directed against the multiple and frivolous use of the name of God, the Greeks devoted more attention to the moral aspect of truthfulness in this regard. James, in a sense, already sharpens the Jewish criticism, but it still is not a criticism of the Law, and his exhortation is not a saying of Jesus. But Matthew was influenced by hellenistic Jewish-Christianity. So Dautzenberg supposes that Matthew has taken an exhortation as we find in James and cast it in antithetical form and also presented it as a saying of Jesus that criticized the traditional Law.

Could Matthew not also have formed the adultery antithesis in an analogous manner from traditional information that he read in Mk 9:43-48 and placed in Mt 5:29-30? And why not then the murder antithesis as well, although it is not excluded that Matthew found this antithesis in S?

The distinctions which the first and second points above call into question must be discussed further. The hypothesis of the third point is impressive, but that of the fourth point is much more so. As an evangelist Matthew was probably more active and more personally involved than was thought in the past. Is it now possible to arrive at an acceptable hypothesis about the way Matthew proceeded in the composition of 5:21-48?

## A COMPOSITIONAL WHOLE

One thing is certain: Matthew is responsible for this remarkable composition. What were, if the question may be so framed, the various stages of his redaction?

a) The point of departure was the short Sermon on the Mount of Q, which already provided Matthew with some beatitudes (see 5:3-12). From the Q-text that Luke reproduces in 6:27-36, Matthew took the last two antitheses and the concluding verse. It is possible that something like an antithetical introduction already existed in Q (cf. Lk 6:27), and it could have inspired Matthew in the formation of his antitheses. In the concluding verse, the term "perfect" is, in all probability, a Matthean alteration (cf. 19:21); the Lucan parallel verse preserves the Q-version (Lk 6:36: "be merciful"). In Matthew's conception, perfection is the same as the greater righteousness he wrote about in 5:20. This is not optional advice for someone who is already keeping the commandments. Perfection is required in order to enter the Kingdom.

b) Matthew was prompted to form still other antitheses with traditional material that was not in the Q-Sermon on the Mount. As he added new beatitudes to the already existing ones, so, too, he expanded the two antitheses he formed from Q by the addition of four others. It is primarily Marcan material that is at the basis of the antitheses about adultery (cf. Mk 9:43-48) and divorce (cf. Mk 10:2-12, but also Q = Lk 16:18). For the oath-taking antithesis, we can refer to a tradition that is also found in Jas 5:12. For the murder antithesis, we are in the dark. Whether we may speak of vv. 22b-26, 29-30, and 34b-37 as a commentary added "later" is very doubtful. The composition of 5:21-37 probably occurred in one phase.

c) Matthew gave this unit (5:21-48) a solemn introduction, 5:17-20. The result is a compositional whole. The form and content of the separate parts were originally heterogeneous, and Matthew brought order into this diversity. The six stereotyped antithetical introduction formulas mark the parts, but there is no rigid, enslaving scheme. Matthew makes additions and thus betrays his tendency to fill out his themes. What belongs thematically to an antithesis was simply added, even though it somewhat disturbed the six-part structure. Perhaps we may consider the present Matthean antitheses as ordered in two groups: the first three (murder, adultery, and divorce) and the last three (oath-taking, retaliation, and love of enemy). The last two of each group are closely related to each other in content. With the long introductory formula of the fourth (v. 33, cf. v. 21), a new beginning is made. The theme of love of one's fellow person at the end undeniably forms the high point of the entire series. One can consider v. 48 as the conclusion of the sixth antitheses, but it is more probable that Matthew intended this verse as an inclusion with v. 20 and thus as a conclusion to the whole passage.

## III. Jesus and Matthew

If this presentation is close to being correct — and a number of exegetes such as I. Broer, M.J. Suggs, and G. Dautzenberg attach a great deal of importance to Matthew's part in the redaction — then it necessarily follows that one must distinguish more than was formerly the case between the earthly and the Matthean Jesus. As in the Matthean version of the beatitudes, here too the Matthean portrait of a Jesus who speaks in the antitheses will cause many Christians to wonder whether Matthew was justified in so presenting Jesus. Is there a continuity between the earthly and the Matthean Jesus?

## THE EARTHLY JESUS

The conclusion of this long literary-critical analysis is partially negative. We do not know with certainty whether Jesus used the antithetical form or not. It is also uncertain whether the content of, for example, the adultery and the oath-taking antitheses goes back to him. What remains undisputedly from Jesus is the saying against divorce (cf. 5:32) and his command to love one's enemies (cf. 5:44). The first saying was not in the Q-Sermon on the Mount, although it appears elsewhere in Q (cf. Lk 16:18) and in Mk 10:11-12. The love of one's enemy was stressed in the Q-sermon by means of many arguments (all from Jesus?).

Luke probably preserved the original Q-version of Jesus' saying in 16:18 better than Mk 10:11-12 and Mt 5:32 and 19:9. It is short, clear, and radical, and the matter is considered one-sidedly in the Jewish manner, i.e. from the standpoint of the man: "Every one who divorces his wife and marries another commits adultery, and he who marries a woman divorced from her husband commits adultery."

"Love your enemies" was repeated over and over again and driven home in the Q-sermon with varying expressions and examples (see Mt 5:44 and 39-42 = Lk 6:27-30). Offering no resistance and non-violence go together with the command to love. Jesus also explains that we must avoid the worldly mentality of only giving to those who give something to us. Only disinterested love assures reward in heaven (see Mt 5:46-47 = Lk 6:32-35ab). We must become children of God and follow him who is merciful and who is good to all people (see Mt 5:45 and 48 = Lk 6:35c and 36).

In both cases — divorce and love of enemy — Jesus does not actually speak intentionally, universally, or expressly *against* the Law. Nevertheless, his concept of the Law brought him more than once to critical positions and actions with respect to the Torah. When the Jews appealed to the Law to divorce and to remarry, or to hate the enemy, then Jesus presented the pure will of God. Jesus also did this in other areas such as ritual purity and keeping the sabbath.

## THE MATTHEAN JESUS

The Jesus of the antitheses is a Matthean Jesus. The information that Matthew added in 5:21-48 to his portrait of Jesus is an extension of the image that already emerged from 5:1-2, 3-12, 13-16 and 17-20. In 5:21-48, he is more than ever a self-aware Jesus. Six times he repeats his majestic, solemn "but *I* say to you." He opposes what was taught formerly and what was still respected tradition. It seems to me that Jesus according to Matthew was neither against the Law nor against Moses. No, the Matthean Jesus deepens and interiorizes, radicalizes and specifies, clarifies and concretizes the Law. Thus he "fulfills" the Law and the

Prophets; thus he explains what God's will and the greater righteousness consist in. When Jesus abrogates laws (e.g., in 5:32, 34, 39, and 44), then it is actually not the Law itself he envisages but the human traditions, i.e., the erroneous explanation and mistaken living of this Law. The Matthean Jesus speaks against the scribes and Pharisees, who were already part of the past for Matthew, but at the same time he firmly warns the Christian antinomians, who were Matthew's contemporaries.

It is difficult to maintain that the Matthean Jesus, with his six antitheses, wanted to give a new codification of laws. Even when he uses juridical language, his position breaks through every legalistic and casuistic mentality. In this regard, P. Hoffmann uses the expression "maxims that guide behavior" (*Gerechtigkeit*, p. 267). These are not laws or prescriptions that must be carried out to the last detail. How we are to perceive the Sermon on the Mount in the concrete will differ for each of us according to the time and the circumstances. But for Matthew, the Sermon on the Mount with its antitheses is certainly the will of God and is therefore realizable.

Prohibitions ("Thou shalt not kill") or casuistic prescriptions ("When..., then you must...") can often be obeyed literally and completely. But with demands that also fix an interior disposition, with a positive command for perfection or mercy, one is never finished, particularly when, as in 5:48, God is presented as the example. Did the Matthean Jesus therefore only want to indicate a disposition? Is the concrete act of less importance? I have already noted that much has been written about the impracticability of the Sermon on the Mount. Without any doubt, Jesus placed great emphasis on interior disposition, but by that he did not at all relativize the concrete action. His message contains authentic, enduring imperatives. Following G. Bornkamm, for example, the authors of *A New Catechism: The Catholic Faith for Adults* (Search Press, London, 6th ed. 1974) write perceptively: "All the changes that are here made have the effect of turning something external into something internal — without abandoning the external precept. They could be summed up in the words, 'not only ... but also.' Not only murder is forbidden, but also the thought in which hatred is cherished and the word through which hatred is expressed. Not only divorce outside due form of law is forbidden, but any divorce at all. The same idea lies behind the demand for veracity without oaths, the command never to contemplate revenge, and finally the call for a love which like God's sunshine and God's rain is bestowed impartially on all men, including enemies" (p. 129).

The analysis of Part II may well have surprised many readers. Did Matthew the Evangelist then work so independently, freely, and radically? After the exposition in Part III, however, nobody can say that Matthew's portrait of Jesus is essentially incorrect or unhistorical. Even though the earthly Jesus did not say everything that Matthew ascribes to him, even though Jesus sometimes said other things than the Evangelist presents, the picture of the Matthean Jesus is not only an actualized and adapted one but also a legitimate presentation of what the earthly Jesus was in reality. Thus, there is not a gap but rather a continuity. The requirement of inner sincerity, total commitment including thoughts, radical love of one's fellow person: all this is typical of Jesus! Therefore, one should certainly not be overly disturbed by the casuistic lists of v. 22 and vv. 34-36, which do not seem to fit Jesus' way of thinking or his way of acting.

Sometimes it is argued that the Matthean Jesus softens the radical concepts of the earthly Jesus and adapts them pastorally — an argument supported by reference to the "unchastity clause" in v. 32 and the so-called "substitute" for oaths in v. 37. Is this the case? In order to decide we must go on to the next section.

## THE FIRST FOUR ANTITHESES

It would be beyond the scope of this book to give a complete, detailed exegesis of all the verses with equal thoroughness. Thus, I will limit myself to one peculiarity in each of the first four antitheses and then give somewhat more attention to the last two from Q.

(1) It is best to see v. 22 as building to a climax. "Fool" (= godless) is worse than "raka" (= rattle-brained, blockhead), which in its turn is a worse reproach than "being angry." The three terms that indicate the consequences coincide with the gravity of the sin. "Hell" is more to be feared than the "Sanhedrin" (of Jerusalem), which in turn is more frightening than the local "court" of one or another city.

(2) Often, v. 28 is translated as "everyone who looks at a woman *in order to* desire her." Biblical Greek permits the two verbs to be considered as simultaneous: "everyone who, with *desire*, looks at a woman" (RSV: "lustfully").

(3) With good reason, eminent exegetes still defend the position that "unchastity" (in Greek: *porneia*) in v. 32 is not the same as adultery. Matthew would have meant here the marriages of pagans who, before their conversion, had married within the forbidden degree of relationship. Such marriages were abhorred by the Jews and the Jewish-Christians and were illicit; the partners had to separate (cf. the title of Wambacq's study: "obligation de rompre une union illégitime"). If this explanation is accepted — it remains a minority position — then the unchastity clause in no way softens the radical demand of Jesus' saying. According to the other explanation, Matthew saw adultery on the part of the wife as valid grounds for divorce. This exception to indissolubility would then witness to pastoral realism.

However that may be, the Christian is confronted with the difficult question of whether the Matthean (and earthly) Jesus meant that "marriage *may not* be dissolved" or that "marriage *cannot* be dissolved." Also, those who shrink from the consequences of the position that marriage may not but can be dissolved must realize that some serious moralists are seeing "indissolubility" more and more as a task, as something dynamic. In their opinion, when a marriage has radically failed and is dead as far as love is concerned, then the bond and the reality of marriage have also disappeared.

(4) With reference to the Slavonic Henoch (a Jewish apocalyptic writing) which was originally written in Greek and which dates probably from the first or second century after Christ, some exegetes explain v. 37 as a substitute for oath-taking: should one want to reinforce a contention, then one used a double yes or a double no instead of an oath. This procedure is still permitted, but a real oath is excluded! But this explanation is unworthy of Matthew. It is forced and masks the appeal for truthfulness, which is also clearly present in the letter of James.

## THE LAST TWO ANTITHESES

The reconstruction of the Q-text of the last two antitheses will have to be discussed again in the seventh chapter of this book which is devoted to the Lucan Sermon on the Plain. Generally, it is accepted that Matthew has preserved the original sequence. Along with the antithetical introductions of vv. 38-39a and v. 43, he added v. 41 (perhaps, but this is not certain); he shifted the Golden Rule (cf. Lk 6:31) to 7:12. Without discussing the minor changes, I would suggest the following reconstruction of Q.

| *Mt 5* | | *Lk 6* |
|---|---|---|
| 39b | If anyone strikes you on the right cheek, turn to him the other also; | 29 |
| 40 | and if anyone would sue you and take your coat, let him have your cloak as well; | |
| 42 | Give to him who begs from you, and do not refuse him who would borrow from you. | 30 |
| (7,12) | Whatever you wish that people would do to you, do so to them. | 31 |
| 44 | I say to you, Love your enemies, do good to those who hate you, bless those who curse you, pray for those who abuse you, | 27 28 |

| 45 | and you will be sons of your Father, for he makes his sun rise on the evil and on the good and sends rain on the just and on the unjust. | 35c |
| 46 | For if you love those who love you, what reward have you? Do not even the tax collectors do the same? | 32 |
| 47 | And if you salute only your brethren, what reward have you? Do not even the Gentiles do the same? | 33 |
| 48 | Be merciful, even as your Father is merciful. | 36 |

In the Sermon on the Mount of Q, this passage thus begins with a double appeal not to offer resistance (vv. 39b-40) and a double invitation to give (v. 42) followed by the Golden Rule (7:12). Then, introduced by "I say to you," comes the command to love one's enemy and to pray for those who abuse one (v. 44). In this way, one will become a son of the good Father (v. 45). That normal human reciprocal love is not sufficient is twice indicated in the form of rhetorical questions (vv. 46-47). One must be merciful like the merciful God, who is also here called Father (v. 48). Specialists try to show that this Q-text itself already has a "layered" appearance and was not written as one unit and that the command to love (vv. 44-45, 48) is the oldest nucleus. We need not concern ourselves further with these questions here (see the second part of the seventh chapter below).

Violence must not be answered with violence; give always, love one's enemy, and follow God in his merciful, fatherly goodness: this is the fundamental position of the source text Matthew had at hand. Three important redactional interventions show how Matthew understood this Q-pericope.

a) The evangelist Matthew made two units of this pericope: two antitheses. The antithetic formula, "You have heard that it was said ... but I say to you" is twice placed before a saying: see vv. 38-39 and 43-44. Matthew cites the Old Testament twice in this formula: "An eye for an eye and a tooth for a tooth" in v. 38 and "you shall love your neighbor and hate your enemy" in v. 43. "Hate your enemy" is not a literal citation; moreover, as I have already said, Matthew had in mind more the Jewish traditions and the spirit they disseminated than Moses and the Law directly. Jesus is the authoritative opponent of these Jewish authorities. What in Q was a rather loose set of exhortations to a radical love of people, enemies included, was structured by Matthew into two distinct parts. The first thesis postulates "retaliation," the second "hate of the enemy." Each time Jesus reacts with an antithesis. The new stands in opposition to the old. Thus Jesus is presented as someone with authority, someone completely different from the scribes (cf. 7:29).

b) It is certainly not by chance that these two antitheses are the last of the series. Matthew split the Q-source to make them so: between the beatitudes and the command to love, he inserted four antitheses. In this way, he intentionally placed the last two at the end as the high point. They are both concerned with the second great commandment, which is like the first "You shall love your neighbor as yourself. On these two commandments depend all the Law and the Prophets" (cf. 22:34-40). All of the antitheses are included in this second commandment.

c) Matthew changed the concluding verse. "Be merciful as your Father is merciful" becomes "You, therefore, must be perfect, as your heavenly Father is perfect." Matthew alone among the evangelists uses the term "perfect." He uses it one other time in the pericope of the rich young man: "If you would be perfect" (19:21; different in Mk 10:21). In the Sermon on the Mount, the perfect God becomes the example to be followed. Perfection is a task for each Christian. It is the more abundant righteousness (5:20) that is absolutely necessary to enter the Kingdom of heaven. One becomes perfect, the Matthean Jesus teaches, by observing the radical demands expressed in the antitheses.

## IV. The Contemporary Christian

We have seen that Mt 5:20 stands like a title verse at the beginning of the antitheses: "For I tell you, unless your righteousness exceeds that of the scribes and Pharisees, you will never enter the kingdom of heaven." More abundant, better righteousness: this is the greater righteousness. But what is this righteousness? Is righteousness here a synonym for justice or rectitude? Does righteousness consist of being just, of granting rights, or of having justice done? Why is God's righteousness, which is bound closely to his Kingdom, called greater? Is this greater righteousness really imposed on the disciples of Jesus as a radical requirement, a *conditio sine qua non*, lest they be excluded from the Kingdom?

Justice is a much used, often emotionally charged term today. The word sounds like a call, a challenge, an urgent, world-encompassing duty. Justice and peace in the world, *justitia et pax*! Every right-thinking person feels that this concerns human dignity, a basic datum of the human community, a protest against inhuman exploitation and oppression. But does the biblical "greater righteousness" coincide with what we mean today by "more justice"? This question will be considered in three stages: the concept will be defined, its dimensions described, and finally a comparison will be made. What is righteousness according to the New Testament? What are its dimensions, its height and depth? Is the biblical notion of righteousness very different from the contemporary feeling for justice?

## RIGHTEOUSNESS

When speaking of God's righteousness we almost automatically understand this term as the righteousness that God requires of us and that we must thus provide. Righteousness is a human task.

a) *God's Saving Righteousness in Paul.* One can say of God himself that he is righteous, that he is just. We then think of God primarily as a judge delivering a verdict at the end of our lives or at the end of the world. For all of us will appear before his judgment seat. Then "God's righteous judgment will be revealed. For he will render to every man according to his works: to those who by patience in well-doing seek for glory and honor and immortality, he will give eternal life; but for those who are factious and do not obey the truth, but obey wickedness, there will be wrath and fury.... For God shows no partiality" (Rom 2:5-8, 11).

I have intentionally cited the Epistle to the Romans here because Paul also speaks in another way about God's righteousness. He does this with great emphasis particularly in two important epistles, Galatians and Romans. According to Paul we must not only and not even primarily see God's righteousness as the justice of a judge who, without respect for persons, condemns the sinner and frees the sinless. Even less may we set God's righteousness in opposition to his grace and mercy. God's righteousness is, according to Paul, salvific: forgiving sin, creating life. His justice creates just people. God is righteous by being unconditionally faithful to his election, his promises, his covenant. Anselm said that God is just in a divine way precisely by taking pity on sinners ("*Dum parcis peccatoribus, iustus es; decet enim Te!*").

According to Paul, a person becomes justified. The individual does not achieve his or her own righteousness: it is a gift received from God in Christ, a free gift that is not earned. Rom 3:21-24 says this clearly: "But now the righteousness of God has been manifested apart from law ... the righteousness of God through faith in Jesus Christ for all who believe. For there is no distinction; since all have sinned and fall short of the glory of God, they are justified by his grace *as a gift*, through the redemption which is in Christ Jesus."

Naturally, Paul also knows that the individual will have to answer for this gift and live morally, live a life in the Spirit by serving the other in love, by doing good to everyone (cf. Gal 5:13-6:10). But Paul particularly stresses God's initiative, his gift to humankind. And so we come to that astonishing, breathtaking, and simultaneously space-creating insight that God, unlike us, displays his justice in salvation history by being merciful, by not insisting on his rights, by saving and healing, by making people just. Thus, righteousness is here synonymous with goodness, salvation, and mercy.

Elsewhere in the New Testament, God's new initiative in Jesus Christ is almost as central. But to express this idea, the term "righteousness" is normally not used. Nevertheless, it is good that we began first with Paul: before we can do anything, God is there with his grace. This biblical definition of the concept is thus at first surprising. The term "righteousness" is indeed sometimes used in the Bible in a way other than we, with our modern mentality, would expect.

b) *Righteousness in Matthew: To Do What God Wills.* But there is still another surprise. In Matthew's Gospel, righteousness always means what the person must do, what he or she must accomplish. Thus, not the gift but the task is envisaged. Still, this righteousness in Mt has a much broader field of application than our "justice," which is concerned with the distribution of goods or possessions.

The verse cited above from the Sermon on the Mount, "unless your righteousness exceeds..." (5:20), is followed by a series of six antitheses, six examples that are intended to show in what this better righteousness consists. They concern murder, adultery, divorce, oaths, retaliation, and hatred of one's enemy. These are only examples: the list is in no way complete. But, for us, this summary is already amply sufficient to determine that this righteousness embraces more, much more than the classic concept of justice. Who is the person who practices such righteousness? When is someone truly "righteous"? Matthew the evangelist would certainly answer with the further explanation that to live righteously means to do the will of God and that God's will extends to all areas of human existence, to the relationships of people with each other and with God. Righteousness thus comprises all the virtues. All that God desires of people is a demand of righteousness. Jesus said that whoever does the will of his Father in heaven is his brother, sister, and mother (cf. Mt 12:50). He could just as well have said that such a person is righteous or just.

This is our second surprise. The first concerned *God's* righteousness, which, according to Paul, is actually goodness and mercy as long as the world endures. The second concerns that of *human beings*: the New Testament teaches us that this righteousness must be seen as being very broad and all-encompassing — everything that God wills, all human obligations! From this fuller biblical definition of the concept there arises automatically the question of whether the modern idea of striving for justice is sufficiently present in the biblical concept or whether we would not do better to stop supporting this legitimate striving with particular biblical texts. But this is something for our third stage; now for the second. For by saying that the biblical concept of righteousness is all-embracing and possesses a very wide field of application, I have yet to describe it fully. What are the actual dimensions of the greater righteousness of Christians?

## GREATER RIGHTEOUSNESS

Three considerations will help us gain a better understanding of these dimensions.

a) *Radicalization.* Jesus showed in what the righteousness of God consists. Both when he criticizes the too humanly interpreted, narrow, and rigid Law and when he radicalizes and internalizes it, it is clear that this righteousness is greater, better, more sincere than what the scribes and the Pharisees propounded and also what an individual is likely to present for himself or herself: a divine Law in human proportions, often obscured and rigid. Again, Jesus discloses the first intention of God. God calls the whole person: the person who makes plans and carries them out, who thinks and acts, not only sometimes or occasionally, but always. In this way a righteous person serves God.

b) *Love as the Foundation.* But there is still more. Matthew cites Hosea 6:6 twice in his gospel: "I desire mercy, and not sacrifice" (9:13; 12:7). It is noteworthy that the first occurs when Jesus is criticized because he eats with tax collectors and sinners. Jesus says to his accusers, the Pharisees: "Those who are well have no need of a physician, but those who are sick. Go and learn what this means, 'I desire mercy, and not sacrifice.' For I came not to call the righteous, but sinners" (9:12-13). The "just" or the righteous stand here in opposition to the sinners. The righteousness that Jesus practices and demands of others is one that consists in mercy, not for the righteous, because they do not need it, but for sinners. By Jesus' example and teaching we are, somewhat unexpectedly, reminded of the salvific righteousness that Paul so clearly described.

Law and justice can be applied wrongly in our society. The greatest justice sometimes threatens to turn into the greatest injustice. Often one hears the ideal of justice being presented as "to each his due." But many people, many Christians, wonder with good reason what justice is without love and what remains of justice without mercy.

Let us consider the father in the Parable of the Prodigal Son. The elder son had stayed outside; when he returned from the fields and approached the house, he heard music and dancing, and he asked one of the servants what was happening. The servant told him that his brother had returned and that his father had killed the fatted calf because he had returned safe and sound. The elder son became angry. When the father came out and urged him to enter, he told his father: "Lo, these many years I have served you, and I have never disobeyed your command; yet you never gave me a kid, that I might make merry with my friends. But when this son of yours . . . ", and he continues by comparing the unrighteousness of his brother with his own righteousness. His father was dismayed. He searched for words: "Son, you are always with me, and all that is mine is yours. It was fitting to make merry and be glad, for . . . "(Lk 15:25-32). For the father of the parable and for Jesus the better righteousness is manifestly different, i.e., more merciful and more loving than the strict, cold justice of the elder son. "To each his due" is here, almost without one realizing it, shattered by "all that is mine is yours."

Thus, in this second consideration, we are automatically brought back to the most important commandment of this better righteousness. A lawyer asked: "Which is the greatest commandment of the Law?" Jesus answered: "You shall love the Lord your God with all your heart, and with all your soul, and with all your mind. This is the great and first commandment. And a second is like it, You shall love your neighbor as yourself. On these two commandments depend all the law and the prophets" (Mt 22:34-40). Without love of neighbor, there is no love of God possible in a Christian perspective nor any fulfillment of his will, and thus also no greater or better righteousness.

c) *God's Perfection as a Criterion.* Looking for the dimensions of the abundant righteousness that Jesus demands of his disciples, I made use of two considerations and, indeed, discovered the height and the depth of that righteousness. Jesus radicalizes God's will, he interiorizes and deepens his commandments. And Jesus teaches that righteousness actually cannot come to perfection without love. Love is the central, primary, greatest commandment. God and people are inextricably united in love. It is a divine-human enterprise.

I complete this stage with the third consideration. In the sixth antithesis we find the command to "love your enemies and pray for those who persecute you." Jesus adds: "so that you may be sons of your Father who is in heaven; for he makes his sun rise on the evil and on the good, and sends rain on the just and the unjust" (Mt 5:44-45). Here we see not only the objective ("so that you . . ."), but also the motivation ("for he makes . . ."). This motivation prompts us to follow God's example, to act the way God acts. And a few verses further, the six antitheses are concluded with "You, therefore, must be perfect, as your heavenly Father is perfect" (5:48). For the evangelist, it is obvious that the greater righteousness of v. 20 is nothing other than perfection. Indeed, the beginning (v. 20) and end (v. 48) of the antitheses pericope correspond to each other. And what is more, even though mere human perfection is difficult to achieve, the Sermon on the Mount still presents the perfection of God as the ultimate criterion.

It ought not surprise us, therefore, that many commentators have considered that this greater righteousness is not intended for everyone — not even for all Christians — and that they admit that it is impracticable. Some contend that Jesus did not impose these antitheses as a strict Law but only as a model, an unattainable ideal to be striven for. Thus, they would have been proposed as a disposition rather than as actual acts to be performed. But such explanatory efforts are opposed to the clear sense of Jesus' words. The greater righteousness is meant as a rule to be observed, as an imperative that is universally valid and absolutely obligatory, a *conditio sine qua non*, as it is expressed in 5:20. Jesus desires a specific attitude that permits no conflict between faith and life. Righteousness is not added to faith optionally; authentic faith is lived out in righteousness. In the Epistle to the Galatians, Paul gives the essence of it when he says that nothing is of any avail except "faith working through love" (5:6).

Perhaps this greater righteousness leaves many of us with a feeling of powerlessness. Who is perfect as God is perfect, who is righteous so abundantly? But with these questions it is necessary again to call to mind what Paul understands by God's righteousness: God's salvation, God's gift, God's forgiveness and justification. It is precisely the freely given grace that transforms the weak person, the faith received that is active in us and that works through love.

The greater righteousness meant by Jesus engages the entire person; it has its center of gravity in love; God's perfection is its model. This is the three-fold dimension of this righteousness. Do Christians know, do we understand sufficiently what this involves? Is all this not a reason to be justly proud of this incomparably noble, eminent way of life? Thus it becomes clear in this second stage that biblical righteousness not only involves much more than what is generally meant by justice today (first stage), but also that it is rightly called greater and better, more abundant (second stage).

## RIGHTEOUSNESS AND JUSTICE

The third stage compares the biblical concept with the contemporary concept and poses the question of whether they are similar enough to discuss in the same context. Does the biblical call for righteousness lead, in fact, to more justice as we now conceive it? Or, in other words, is a Christian experience of righteousness at issue in the struggle for a more just society?

a) *Justice in the Prophets of the Old Testament.* The theologies of secularization and liberation both like to cite the prophetic message of the Old Testament. For in this message, secular injustice is sharply criticized. Widows and orphans are oppressed; the poor are exploited; people murder each other; even the authorities who must maintain the laws are thieves and corrupt judges; they have become hardened egoists! At the end of the Song of the Vineyard in Isaiah 5, it is stated: "He [God] looked for justice, but behold, bloodshed; for righteousness, but behold, a cry!" (v. 7).

Archbishop Oscar Romero, confessor and martyr, in his speech entitled "The Political Dimension of Faith from the Side of the Poor" given on the occasion of his receiving an honorary doctorate at the University of Leuven on 2 February 1980, less than two months before his assassination, also cited the Old Testament prophets: "The economic and political structures of our country dominate and daily oppress the impoverished majority. The hard words of the prophets of Israel are contemporary for us. Indeed, there are, in our country, people who sell the righteous for money and the poor for a pair of sandals; people who amass their loot taken with violence in palatial houses; people who crush the poor, who convene a kingdom of violence and still sleep in beds of ivory; they buy houses and more houses, and land and more land until they have everything, but they are still isolated. What I cite here freely from Amos and Isaiah is not merely respectful liturgical reading. This is reality and its intense cruelty we experience every day. We experience it when the mothers and wives of prisoners and 'the disappeared' visit us, when mutilated corpses are found in secret cemeteries, when people who speak out of justice and peace are murdered."

Let us pause to consider this indictment. I repeat the question: Is that against which Archbishop Romero protested the absence of righteousness, and, if so, is this the righteousness that is meant in the New Testament? Are Romero and those like him the righteous as Jesus meant it? The answer is, obviously, yes.

b) *Justice in Modern Society.* Perhaps we remember the clear but bleak definitions of moral theology. Justice would give "each his due." There is commutative justice when people deal with each other honestly in commerce; there is distributive justice, which administrators must provide primarily to protect the weak; and there is finally the obligatory just contribution of the individual to the general welfare in the form of taxes. This morality was also taught in capitalistic, individualistic societies with clearly distinguished classes, and it was respected to a certain extent. But we all feel that it would be a caricature to limit the modern Christian conscience to these definitions. For social justice destroyed, at least theoretically, the monopoly held on the rule of "to each his due" by the propertied class.

Moralists know that striving for justice may no longer be concerned only with the individual person but must also be concerned with the establishment of just structures and laws. And people today like to speak — and rightly so — of making the world livable for everybody, a better place. They understand that justice involves prosperity, peace, mutual respect, esteem, and happiness in addition to welfare.

We know well that we must not be naive in this area. Much of the striving for justice today is not for evangelical righteousness. It is often purely secularly oriented and ignores the eternal destiny of humankind; it often excludes God, sometimes as a matter of principle; it ignores or neglects the deepest roots of evil, human sinfulness. All this is too often true. Still, something striking has happened in the course of our argument. We were concerned with two extensions. First, it appeared that biblical righteousness is more than economic justice; it is oriented to God's will and embraces all of life. Then, too, the modern experience of justice is also concerned with the true well-being of the individual and society: it envisions more than "to each his due." Is it not so that, due to these extensions, biblical righteousness and contemporary justice have come very close to each other in their concrete application?

A Christian knows that God cannot be loved without the love of neighbor. He or she will, therefore, resolutely take as his or her own the application of the modern striving for social justice. Naturally, the evangelical dimensions of God's righteousness remain in force for the Christian. It must be greater, better, that is to say, more profound and more internalized, oriented to the will of God. It will consequently, be based on love and mercy, and this means concretely, an option for the poor, the association with the disenfranchised, and the non-abandonment of sinners. Finally, it must strive for a perfection that is modeled on God himself.

c) *Powerless Christians and Encouragement.* Let us conclude with a word of encouragement for ourselves. In the Gospel of Matthew, in addition to the religious revolutionary John the Baptist, the silent Joseph of Nazareth is also called just, even before he accepts Mary (1:19). Are not, therefore, many ordinary people — diligent, honest and loyal, silent Christians — righteous and just? The famous French political philosopher, Roger Garaudy once wrote: "To change yourself, you *must* militantly participate in the changing of the world structures" (*De Tijd*, 5, 1978, no. 224, p. 63). In and out of season, many are preached at and talked to in this way, causing the ordinary citizen to be assailed by feelings of powerlessness. Most Christians look on with bewilderment and perplexity. What should they actually *do*? They tend to repeat the question of the lawyer in the Parable of the Good Samaritan, though without his devious intention: "Who is my neighbor?" (Lk 10:29). What structures and which people can I, in fact, reach? Does it make sense to be burdened by what is called collective guilt? Is not everything more complex than the extreme right and the extreme left would have it? Are we then all unjust, unrighteous people? Probably an answer of "no" to this question (or at least "no, not completely") is more correct than an unqualified "yes." After all, this answer is also a better stimulus for a serious practice of the righteousness according to the program that Jesus presented to the lawyer: stop asking the theoretical question of "who is my neighbor?", and begin to become a neighbor to the one who is the nearest to you, the one whom you can most realistically reach (Lk 10:30-37).

Elsewhere in the Gospel, Jesus says: "Whoever receives one such child in my name receives me; and whoever receives me, receives not me but him who sent me" (Mk 9:37). This statement applies to all times and to all peoples. And many Christians have lived it and are now living it. Whoever makes it the guideline for his or her life practices righteousness and also contributes to the authentic improvement of the world, and, in fact, demonstrates solidarity with the weak and the oppressed wherever they may be on this earth. This person works for justice in the world and, indeed, for biblical righteousness.

## Bibliography

See also the general works cited on pp. 41-44 above.

Banks, R., *Jesus and the Law in the Synoptic Tradition* (Soc. New Test. Stud. Mon. Ser. 28), Cambridge, 1975.

Banks, R., "Matthew's Understanding of the Law: Authenticity and Interpretation in Matthew 5,17-20," *Journ. Bibl. Lit.* 93 (1974) 226-242.

Barth, G., "Matthew's Understanding of the Law," in: G. Bornkamm, G. Barth, and H.J. Held, *Tradition and Interpretation in Matthew* (The N.T. Library), ET by P. Scott, London, 1963, pp. 58-164.

Betz, O., "Die hermeneutischen Prinzipien in der Bergpredigt (Mt 5,17-20)," in: E. Jüngel, J. Wallmann, and W. Verbeck (eds.), *Verifikationen. Fs. G. Ebeling*, Tübingen, 1982, pp. 27-41.

Broer, I., *Freiheit vom Gesetz und Radikalisierung des Gesetzes. Ein Beitrag zur Theologie des Evangelisten Matthäus* (Stuttg. Bib. Stud. 97), Stuttgart, 1980.

Broer, I., "Plädierte Jesus für Gewaltlosigkeit? Eine historische Frage und ihre Bedeutung für die Gegenwart," *Bib. Kirche* 37 (1982) 61-69.

Crossan, J.D., "Jesus and Pacifism," in: J. Flanagan and A. W. Robinson (eds.), *No Famine in the Land. Fs. J.L. McKenzie*, Missoula, 1975, pp. 195-208.

Dautzenberg, G., "Ist das Schwurgebot Mt 5,33-37; Jak 5,12 ein Beispiel fur die Torakritik Jesu?" *Bibl. Zeitschr.* 25 (1981) 47-66.

Descamps, A., "Essai d'interprétation de Mt 5,17-48. 'Formgeschichte' ou 'Redaktionsgeschichte'," *Stud. Ev. I* (Texte u. Unters. 73), Berlin, 1959, pp. 156-173.

Descamps, A., "Les textes évangéliques sur le mariage," *Rev. Théol. Louv.* 9 (1978) 259-286; 11 (1980) 5-50.

De Vriese, J., *De uitleg van Mt. 5,18 in de recente exegese* (unpublished licentiate thesis, Religious Sciences, K.U. Leuven), Leuven, 1981.

Dietzfelbinger, C., *Die Antithesen der Bergpredigt* (Theol. Ex. H. 186), Munich, 1975.

Dietzfelbinger, C., "Die Antithesen der Bergpredigt im Verständnis des Mätthaus," *Zeitschr. Neutest. Wiss.* 70 (1979) 1-15.

Dumbrell, "Logic" (see p. 78 above).

Dupont, J., "L'appel à imiter Dieu en Matthieu 5,48 et Luc 6,36," *Rivista Biblica* 14 (1966) 137-158.

Fitzmyer, J. A., "The Matthean Divorce Texts and Some New Palestinian Evidence," *Theol. Stud.* 37 (1976) 197-226.

Guelich, R. A., "The Antitheses of Matthew V. 21-48: Traditional and/or Redactional," *New Test. Stud.* 22 (1975-76) 444-457.

Geulich, R. A., "Mt 5, 22: Its Meaning and Integrity," *Zeitschr. Neutest. Wiss.* 64 (1973) 39-52.

Hahn, F., "Mt 5,17 — Anmerkungen zum Erfullungsgedanken bei Mätthaus," in: U. Luz and H. Weber (eds.), *Die Mitte des Neuen Testaments. Einheit und Vielfalt neutestamentlicher Theologie. Fs. E. Schweizer*, Göttingen, 1983, pp. 42-54.

Hamerton-Kelly, R. G., "Attitudes to the Law in Matthew's Gospel," *Bibl. Res.* 17 (1972) 19-32.

Hanssen, "Verständnis" (see p. 43 above).

Hoffmann, P., "Die bessere Gerechtigkeit. Auslegung der Bergpredigt III (Mt 5, 17-37)," *Bib. Leb.* 10 (1969) 175-189; "IV (Mt 5, 38-48)," *ibid.* pp. 264-275.

Hoffmann, *Jesus* (see p. 78 above), pp. 73-94.

Honeyman, A. M., "Matthew V. 18 and the Validity of the Law," *New Test. Stud.* 1 (1954-55) 141-142.

Jensen, J., "Does 'Porneia' Mean Fornication? A Critique of Bruce Malina," *Nov. Test.* 20 (1978) 161-184.

Kilgallen, J. J., "To What Are the Matthean Exception-Texts (5, 32 and 19, 9) an Exception?" *Bibl.* 61 (1980) 102-105.

Linskens, J., "A Pacifist Interpretation of Peace in the Sermon on the Mount?" *Concilium* (1983), no. 164, pp. 16-25.

Lohse, E., "Ich aber sage euch," in: Lohse, *Die Einheit des Neuen Testaments. Exegetische Studien zur Theologie des Neuen Testaments,* Göttingen, 1973, pp. 73-87.

Mahoney, A., "A New Look at the Divorce Clauses in Mt 5, 32 and 19, 9," *Cath. Bibl. Quart.* 30 (1968) 29-38.

Malina, B., "Does 'Porneia' Mean Fornication?" *Nov. Test.* 14 (1972) 10-17.

Martin, B. L., "Matthew on Christ and the Law," *Theol. Stud.* 44 (1983) 53-70.

Meier, J. P., *Law and History in Matthew's Gospel. A Redactional Study of Mt. 5, 17-48* (An. Bibl. 71), Rome, 1976.

Meier, J. P., *The Vision of Matthew: Christ, Church and Morality in the First Gospel* (Theological Inquiries), New York, 1979.

Merklein, *Gottesherrschaft* (see p. 79 above), pp. 72-80, 222-237.

Minear, P. S., "Yes or No: The Demand for Honesty in the Early Church," *Nov. Test.* 13 (1971) 1-13.

Piper, J., *"Love your Enemies." Jesus' Love Command in the Synoptic Gospels and in the Early Christian Paraenesis. A History of the Tradition and Interpretation of Its Uses* (Soc. New Test. Stud. Mon. Ser. 38), Cambridge, 1979.

Przybylski, B., *Righteousness in Matthew and His World of Thought* (Soc. New Test. Stud. Mon. Ser. 41), Cambridge, 1980.

Rausch, J., "The Principle of Nonresistance and Love of Enemy in Mt 5, 38-48," *Cath. Bibl. Quart.* 28 (1966) 31-41.

Sabourin, L., "Why is God Called 'Perfect' in Mt 5, 48?" *Bibl. Zeitschr.* 24 (1980) 266-268.

Sand, A., *Das Gesetz und die Propheten. Untersuchungen zur Theologie des Evangeliums nach Matthäus* (Biblische Untersuchungen 11), Regensburg, 1974.

Schmahl, G., "Die Antithesen der Bergpredigt. Inhalt und Eigenart ihrer Forderungen," *Trier. Theol. Zeitschr.* 83 (1974) 284-297.

Schnackenburg, R., "Christian Perfection According to Matthew," in: Schnackenburg, *Christian Existence in the New Testament I,* Notre Dame, 1968, pp. 158-189.

Stock, A., "The Matthean Divorce Texts," *Bibl. Theol. Bull.* 8 (1978) 24-33.

Strecker, G., "Die Antithesen der Bergpredigt (Mt 5, 21-48 par)," *Zeitschr. Neutest. Wiss.* 69 (1978) 36-72.

Suggs, M. J., "The Antitheses as Redactional Products," in: G. Strecker (ed.), *Jesus Christus in Historie und Theologie. Fs. H. Conzelmann*, Tübingen, 1975, pp. 433-444.

Tannehill, R. C., "The 'Focal Instance' as a Form of New Testament Speech: A Study of Matthew 5, 39b-42," *Journ. Rel.* 50 (1970) 372-385.

Trilling, W., *Das wahre Israel. Studien zur Theologie des Matthäus-Evangeliums* (Stud. A.N.T. 10), Munich, ³1964, pp. 167-186, 207-211.

Vawter, B., "Divorce and the New Testament," *Cath. Bibl. Quart.* 39 (1977) 528-542.

Vögtle, A., *Was ist Frieden? Orientierungshilfen aus dem Neuen Testament*, Freiburg-Basel-Vienna, 1983.

Wambacq, B. N., "Matthieu 5, 31-32. Possibilité de divorce ou obligation de rompre une union illégitime," *Nouv. Rev. Théol.*, 114 (1982) 34-39.

Yarnold, E., "*Teleios* in St. Matthew's Gospel," *Stud. Ev. IV* (Texte u. Unters., 102), Berlin, 1968, pp. 269-273.

Zeller, D., *Die weisheitlichen Mahnsprüche bei den Synoptikern* (Forsch. Bib. 17), Würzburg, 1977.

# Chapter Four

# EXTERIOR DISPLAY AND PRAYER (Mt 6:1-18)

Mt 6:1-18 can be considered a well-rounded unit within the Sermon on the Mount. In this passage, Matthew is concerned with the practice of righteousness "before men" (v. 1). Giving alms (vv. 2-4), praying (vv. 5-6), and fasting (vv. 16-18) are dealt with in turn. These counsels are striking for the uniformity of their structure: first the negative triptych and then a matching positive triptych. In the following presentation of the text, along with the verse numbering, are indicated the triptychs (A and B) and their three parts (a: introductory phrase; b: prohibition or commandment; c: motivation).

> 1 Beware of practicing your righteousness [RSV: piety] before men in order to be seen by them; for then you will have no reward from your Father who is in heaven.
>
> A a 2 Thus when you give alms,
>  b sound no trumpet before you, as the hypocrites do in the synagogues and in the streets that they may be praised by men.
>  c Truly, I say to you, they have their reward.
> B a 3 But when you give alms,
>  b do not let your left hand know what your right hand is doing,
>  4 so that your alms may be in secret;
>  c and your Father who sees in secret will reward you.
> A a 5 And when you pray,

b you must not be like the hypocrites, for they love to stand and pray in the synagogues and at the street corners, that they may be seen by men.

c Truly, I say to you, they have their reward.

B a 6 But when you pray,

b go into your room and shut the door and pray to your Father who sees in secret;

c and your Father who sees in secret will reward you.

A a 16 And when you fast,

b do not look dismal, like the hypocrites, for they disfigure their faces that their fasting may be seen by men.

c Truly, I say to you, they have their reward.

B a 17 But when you fast,

b anoint your head and wash your face,

18 that your fasting may not be seen by men but by your Father who is in secret;

c and your Father who sees in secret will reward you.

In the first chapter (pp 38-39), I referred to these three counsels and concluded that Matthew had found them already grouped together in his *Sondergut*. The evangelist must have judged not only that the antitheses (5:21-48) but also that the three "good works" (6:1-18) could illustrate his abundant righteousness.

How has Matthew altered this three-strophe exhortation from S? First, the introductory sentence, the title verse, is completely Matthew's work. Here Matthew gives the central idea in his own words before he gives the three examples. One may not, he says, perform pious practices in the sight of people in order to be noticed by them, for then one will not receive a reward from God. The vocabulary of this verse is typically Matthean: "beware", "righteousness," "to be seen by," "Father in heaven." Second, Matthew has also made a considerable insertion. Between the second and the third strophes, he places a passage on prayer, which is the theme of the second good work: vv. 7-15. Third, in the English translation, it cannot be seen that Matthew has replaced the original second person singular twice by the plural, i.e., in the introductory verses of vv. 5 and 16.

Fourth, perhaps the three-time "truly, I say to you" (plural! vv. 2, 5, 16) is also from the evangelist.

In 5:17-48, the Matthean Jesus rejects the Jewish interpretation of the Law, which was still in force; he opposes the faulty righteousness of the scribes and Pharisees. In 6:1-18, he censures the attitude of the hypocrites and protests against their pious practices. These two passages are sometimes sharply separated. In the first, Jesus cites the Law; the second is concerned with "good works" not prescribed in the Law. But did Matthew actually consider the two passages dissimilar? Do they differ in essential points? I do not think so. In the woes (23:13 and 15) Matthew expressly calls the scribes and Pharisees "hypocrites," so one may presume that he has the same people in mind in 6:1 as in 5:20. Indeed, both verses concern the same righteousness. The two textual units, 5:17-48 and 6:1-18, stand next to each other. For Matthew, the commands on pious practices as well as the antithetical directives in 5:21-48 have the same binding force. In 6:1-18, the Matthean Jesus continues his explanation of how the better Christian righteousness must be practiced.

In the choice of David by Samuel, we read: "for the Lord sees not as man sees; man looks on the outward appearance, but the Lord looks on the heart" (1 Sam 16:7). And Paul writes: "For he is not a real Jew who is one outwardly .... He is a Jew who is one inwardly .... His praise is not from men but from God" (Rom 2:28-29). Thus Matthew tells us in 6:1-18 that one can give a false orientation to one's pious acts. He is not so much concerned here with vanity. The hypocrisy that is censured here is much worse; it is the degeneration of religion. By his acts, the hypocrite contends that he is serving God, but his ostentatious charity, public praying, and visible fasting are only means by which he seeks his own honor and pursues approval among other people. This is not the way to practice the true righteousness! The Matthean Jesus will not have any exterior display. Is there perhaps a contradiction in 6:1-18 with what is said in 5:14-16 about good works not being able to remain hidden? Matthew himself would be astonished at this question, and his answer would certainly be a denial.

The concern here is primarily with prayer. In the middle of Mt 6:1-18 we find the Lord's Prayer, the Our Father. Luke also has a version in his gospel, but not in the Sermon on the Plain. After the discussion of the contexts in Mt and Lk, the two texts of the Lord's Prayer will be compared. Next comes an explanation of the Lord's Prayer as it may have been taught by Jesus, and then that of the evangelist Matthew. At the end we offer an actualizing consideration about Jesus and our prayer.

How Matthew understood the arrival of the Kingdom and the prayer for bread for today and how we still can pray certain portions of the Lord's Prayer will be dealt with in the fifth chapter. There I will examine Mt 6:19-34, a pericope that ends with the exhortations to seek first God's Kingdom and God's righteousness and not to be anxious about tomorrow (cf. vv. 33-34).

## I. *The Context of the Lord's Prayer*

The Lord's Prayer has come to us in two versions, the longer one of Matthew, which is used in the liturgy and elsewhere (cf. Mt 6:9-13) and the shorter one of Luke, which has escaped the attention of most Christians (cf. Lk 11:2-4). Each version has its own context.

### PRAYER IN Mt 5

In four places in Mt 5 something is said that is directly or indirectly related to prayer. In 5:44c-45 in the sixth antithesis, a second command is given after "You shall love your neighbour and hate your enemy. But I say to you, love your enemies": "and pray for those who persecute you, so that you may be sons of your Father who is in heaven; for he makes his sun rise on the evil and on the good, and sends rain on the just and on the unjust." Praying is here expressly mentioned. One must pray for one's persecutors.

Two other antitheses may also be mentioned. The first of the series is based on the Old Testament commandment "Thou shalt not kill." Jesus radicalizes it. Being angry at one's brother and insulting him are already guilty acts. Vv. 23-24 comment further: "So if you are offering your gift at the altar, and there remember that your brother has something against you, leave your gift there before the altar and go; first be reconciled to your brother, and then come and offer your gift." Offering gifts is normally accompanied by prayer and is in essence already a prayer. Jesus points to an essential condition for good contact with God: the good relations with one's neighbor. The fourth antithesis, which is about swearing and truth (vv. 33-37), is also concerned with God and prayer as well as with human relationships, though in a somewhat broader sense.

Up to this point, the concern is with the prayer of those whom Jesus addresses in the Sermon on the Mount, and first of all the disciples. The exhortations of vv. 13-16 are also intended for them. They, by their behavior, must be the salt of the earth and the light of the world. Jesus concludes: "Let your light so shine before men, that they may see your good works and give glory to your Father who is in heaven." Here, curiously enough, Jesus mentions the prayer of non-disciples.

## Mt 6:5-15

5 And when you pray, you must not be like the hypocrites; for they love to stand and pray in the synagogues and at the street corners, that they may be seen by men. Truly, I say to you, they have their reward.

6 But when you pray, go into your room and shut the door and pray to your Father who is in secret; and your Father who sees in secret will reward you.

7 And in praying do not heap up empty phrases as the Gentiles do; for they think that they will be heard for their many words.

8 Do not be like them, for your Father knows what you need before you ask him.

9 Pray then like this: Our Father who art in heaven, hallowed be thy name,

10 thy Kingdom come, thy will be done, on earth as it is in heaven.

11 Give us this day our daily bread;

12 and forgive us our debts as we also have forgiven our debtors;

13 and lead us not into temptation, but deliver us from evil.

14 For if you forgive men their trespasses, your heavenly Father also will forgive you;

15 but if you do not forgive men their trespasses, neither will your Father forgive your trespasses.

Mt 6:5-15 is a kind of lesson on prayer. Matthew repeats in v. 7 the ideas of the introductory sentences in vv. 5 and 6. In these verses one phrase specifies time ("when you pray"). In v. 7, Matthew uses a participle ("in praying" = in your prayer). Then the negative directive: "do not heap up empty phrases as the Gentiles do; for they think that they will be heard for their many words. Do not be like them, for your Father knows what you need before you ask him" (vv. 7-8). Notwithstanding the parallelism in the beginning and the comparison with "Gentiles," which corresponds to the comparison with "hypocrites," the structure of vv. 7-8 is not the same as that of vv. 5-6 (and vv. 2-4 and vv. 16-18). Vv. 7-8 are only a very partial imitation of vv. 5-6. The idea of display is absent, and the positive directive is also lacking, unless the Lord's Prayer (vv. 9-13) itself functions as a positive directive for Matthew: "Pray then like this" (v. 9a).

Still, there is a certain tension between vv. 7-8 and vv. 9-13. If God already knows in advance what is necessary (cf. v. 8), why add a prayer like the Lord's Prayer? Further, it is also somewhat strange that, after the warning about the use of many words, another prayer formula — however brief it may be — is taught.

The separation of vv. 2-4, 5-6 and vv. 16-18, the lack of symmetry between vv. 5-6 and vv. 7-8, the difference in content, the tension between vv. 7-8 and vv. 9-13: all this indicates that Matthew makes use of vv. 5-6 (on praying) in order to put together a lengthy pericope of instruction on prayer (6:5-15). With vv. 14-15, finally, Matthew wishes to stress the condition for obtaining God's forgiveness, which is already mentioned in v. 12. For v. 14, he depends on Mk 11:25. Moreover, in Mt 21:20-22 (this passage parallels Mk 11:20-25) he does not take up Mk 11:25. (Does not this last verse suggest that Mark also knew the Lord's Prayer?)

We now have enough information to illustrate the very different origins of Mt 6:5-15:

Mt 6:5-6:  pre-Matthean material (S)
      7-8:  probably of Matthean origin (R)
    9-13:  Q-material (cf. Lk 11:2-4)
      14:  Marcan material (see Mk 11:25)
      15:  probably of Matthean origin (R).

## Lk 11:1-13

As in Mt, we can also speak of an entire pericope devoted to an instruction on prayer in Lk (11:1-13). This pericope is situated close to the beginning of Luke's long travel narrative (9:51-19:46). In Mt, the Lord's Prayer stands in the middle of various counsels. Luke begins his eleventh chapter — chapter 10 ends with the pericope on Jesus' visit to Martha and Mary — with his typical "and it happened" without an actual transition: "He was praying in a certain place, and when he ceased, one of his disciples said to him, 'Lord, teach us to pray, as John taught his disciples'" (11:1). Jesus responds to this request and teaches them the Lord's Prayer (11:2-4).

Thus the occasion for the teaching of the Lord's Prayer was, according to Luke, very concrete. The disciples see Jesus praying and also know that John taught his disciples to pray. After the Lord's Prayer, Luke stresses constant prayer: "Ask, and it will be given you; seek, and you will find; knock and it will be opened to you. For every one who asks receives, and he who seeks finds, and to him who knocks it will be opened" (vv. 9-10). This threefold call is preceded by the parable of the friend who comes at an inconvenient time (vv. 5-8) and is followed by a comparison of the heavenly Father with an earthly father (vv. 11-13). If the latter knows how to give good things to his son — a fish and not a serpent, an egg and not a scorpion — how much more will God then give the Holy Spirit to those who ask! With all these verses (parable, call, comparison), Luke stresses the bread petition of v. 3 in a way that is comparable with the way in which Matthew emphasizes, with the help of 6:14-15, the petition for forgiveness.

As in Mt, the multiple origins of Lk 11:1-13 clearly show that Luke also wanted to compose an instruction on prayer:

Lk 11:1: probably of Lucan origin (R)
    2-4: Q-material (cf. Mt 6:9-13)
    5-8: Lucan *Sondergut*
    9-13: Q-material (cf. Mt 7:7-11; see chapter five below)

For example, one can see in the introductory phrase of v. 9, "And I tell you," that Luke considers the call that follows as the application of the preceding parable. With this phrase (lacking in Mt 7:7 and probably also in Q), he unifies his prayer instruction.

Hence, Matthew and Luke both have a prayer pericope. But it is clear that Luke has given the Lord's Prayer a context very different from Matthew's: it is not in a sermon, but after an event. Luke urges perseverance in prayer; Matthew is concerned rather with the manner of praying (not many words, not ostentatious). With J. Jeremias, may we conclude from this that Matthew addresses himself to people who were apt to fall into externalism and formalism because of their Jewish past, while Luke has in mind Christians who, as converted Gentiles, still had everything to learn about prayer and thus had to be encouraged simply to pray? Jeremias obviously goes too far. Many Gentiles were also very religious and many Jews no doubt sincere.

## II. The Two Versions of the Lord's Prayer

In this part, the two versions of the Lord's Prayer, Mt 6:9-13 and Lk 11:2-4, will be compared. First, the two versions will be given in very literal translation; then the differences will be discussed, and a Q-reconstruction attempted.

## THE TEXT

| | *Mt 6* | | *Lk 11* |
|---|---|---|---|
| 9b | Our Father in the heavens, | 2c | Father, |
| 9c | hallowed be thy name, | 2d | hallowed be thy name, |
| 10a | come thy Kingdom, | 2e | come thy Kingdom. |
| 10b | be done thy will as in heaven so also on earth. | | |
| 11 | Our bread, the *epiousion*, give us today; | 3 | Our bread, the *epiousion*, give us every day; |
| 12a | and forgive us our debts, | 4a | and forgive us our sins, |
| 12b | as we also have forgiven our debtors; | 4b | for we ourselves also forgive everyone who is indebted to us; |
| 13a | and lead us not into temptation, | 4c | and lead us not into temptation. |
| 13b | but deliver us from the Evil One. | | |

It is generally accepted that Luke has preserved more of the original form and length, and that Matthew, in the common parts, has preserved more of the original wording. As regards the length, the reasoning runs as follows: it is not very likely that the Lord's Prayer would have been shortened by Luke (or by the pre-Lucan tradition), while it would be expected that this prayer, like many liturgical texts, would have been expanded during its transmission and frequent use. The Matthean version is, therefore, probably an expanded text. Instead of five prayers, Matthew gives seven. In Mt 6:10b, we read at the end of the first part of the Lord's Prayer: "Be done thy will as in heaven so also on earth"; and in 6:13b at the end of the second part: "but deliver us from the Evil One."

A good many manuscripts of Matthew's gospel, but not the oldest ones or the early patristic commentaries, add another sentence glorifying God after the last petition: "For thine is the Kingdom and the power and the glory, forever, Amen." This secondary acclamation or doxology was probably formed in imitation of 1 Chron 29:11-12: "Thine, O Lord, is the greatness, and the power, and the glory, and the victory, and the majesty; for all that is in the heavens and in the earth is thine; thine is the Kingdom, O Lord, and thou art exalted as head above all. Both riches and honor come from thee, and thou rulest over all. In thy hand are power and might; and in thy hand is to make great and to give strength to all." Not all the witnesses have precisely the same text. The *Didache*, an early Christian text from the end of the first or the beginning of the second century after Christ, gives essentially the Matthean Lord's Prayer (see Did 8:2). In 8:3 (cf. 10:5), there is a two-part doxology: "For thine is the power and the glory forever."

## COMPARISON

It seems to me that the following alterations can probably be attributed to Luke for the following reasons.

First, as in Mt 6:9, a typically Jewish phrase with heaven / heavens is also present in Mk 11:25 ("your Father in the heavens"; cf. Mt 6:14: "your heavenly Father") and Lk 11:13 ("the Father from heaven"). Further, elsewhere in his gospel Luke apparently likes to use "Father" by itself (see 15:12, 21; 22:42; 23:34, 46; the vocative without a pronoun is better Greek). It is therefore probably advisable to consider the Matthean "Our Father in the heavens" more original than the Lucan "Father." Many exegetes, however, are of the opinion that Luke has preserved the original "Father" — *Abba*, and that Matthew (or his church community) expanded the text. These exegetes point to the typical Matthean expression "in the heavens;" except for Mk 11:25, only Matthew uses this phrase (13 times).

Second, the imperative "give" in Lk 11:3 is in the present tense; Matthew uses an aorist. The Greek present tense stresses continuous, enduring giving or the continuity of the giving. One may assume that Luke had to choose this tense when he replaced the "today" (cf. Mt 6:11) by "each day." These two changes (to the present tense, each day) are related to each other. Luke sees further than one single day; he de-eschatologizes the text.

Third, in 11:4a, Luke writes "sins," i.e., the matter that is intended by the metaphorical term "debts" (so Mt 6:12a). The use in Lk 11:4b of the verb "to be indebted to" is an indication that most probably this metaphor was also original in the first half of the verse.

There remain the differences between Mt 6:12b and Lk 11:4b. Matthew writes: "as we also have forgiven our debtors;" Luke: "for we ourselves also forgive every one who is indebted to us." There is again the difference in the tense of the verb (Matthew: aorist; Luke: present); Matthew compares ("as we"); Luke motivates ("for we ourselves" which adds emphasis); Matthew is talking about debtors; Luke uses a general phrase with a Greek participle: literally: "everyone owing." Although absolute certainty in such details can hardly be expected, it seems to me that here, too, Luke is less original. The Lucan generalization "everyone" and the emphasis created by the addition of "ourselves" betray, it seems to me, a more reflexive character than the Matthean parallel and witnesses to a later stage. Lucan redaction also seems the more probable for "we forgive" than the position that both verb forms, the aorist in Mt 6:12b and the present in Lk 11:4b, would ultimately go back to the same Aramaic basic form (a "perfectum coincidentiae": the act "coincides" with the present). The specific character of Lk 11:4b, moreover, must also be seen in the light of the Lucan change in 11:4a ("sins") and in 11:3. It seems more likely that Luke, who had already introduced changes earlier in the Lord's Prayer, does the same here in 11:4b. Whether Matthew also changed something in 6:12b cannot be excluded *a priori*, but it is difficult to demonstrate.

## RECONSTRUCTION OF Q

The text that emerges from this discussion is both pre-Matthean and pre-Lucan and may presumably be considered the source text for both Matthew and Luke. Some authors, however, point out that one must take into account a long liturgical tradition with a text such as the Lord's Prayer, and that the two versions in Mt and Lk would be the written offshoots of that tradition. This is why, they say, it is risky to consider both the expansions of Matthew and the wording changes of Luke as interventions to be ascribed to the evangelists themselves. Nevertheless, I think that these scholars too easily underestimate the redactional work that has taken place, and particularly how much was done by Luke.

The oldest Q-text then would look roughly like this:

> Our Father in the heavens,
> hallowed be thy name,
> come thy Kingdom.
> our bread, the *epiousion*, give us today;
> and forgive us our debts,
>    as we also have forgiven our debtors;
> and lead us not into temptation.

## III. The Lord's Prayer of Jesus

J. Carmignac ardently defends the position that Jesus prayed and taught the Lord's Prayer in Hebrew. The majority of exegetes, however, is of the opinion that the Greek Q-text goes back to an Aramaic original that was used by the first Palestinian Christians and ultimately comes from Jesus himself. This position seems to be the most likely.

The reconstructed Greek source text (Q) common to Mt and Lk is not necessarily the text that Jesus taught to his disciples. Before giving a short explanation of the Lord's

Prayer of Jesus, something must be said about this question. In two recent articles, A. Vögtle argues for the possibility (and even the probability) that the second part of the petition for forgiveness (Mt 6:12b; cf. Lk 11:4b) does not belong to the original Lord's Prayer, but was added very early, already before Q was established. This opinion rests on two facts. Without this second clause, the sentence is shorter and has a simpler structure; the petition for forgiveness would then be about as long as the bread petition and also the temptation petition. Like the others, it would have only one clause. Further, it is striking that in this second part (and only here) attention is focused on what the human person does. Everywhere else in the Lord's Prayer the subject is God and his activities. Was there a saying of Jesus, such as that in Mk 11:25, that led the early church to add the concluding clause to the prayer on forgiveness? This is not impossible, but such hypothetical questions are very difficult to answer.

One can also ask whether the argumentation concerning the structure and the God-man distinction is not based too much on the assumption that Jesus had intended to construct a totally pure prayer-form and a strictly logical whole. Moreover, the word-play on "debt, debtors" seems to be evidence for the originality of the second part of the verse.

The structure of this prayer is clear. After the address or title come two short, very symmetrically composed invocations (*vota*) without a conjunction, followed by a verb in the third person imperative: your name, your Kingdom. Then we have three petitions (*petitiones*) concerning bread, debt for sin, and the danger of temptation: these somewhat longer prayers are in the second person singular imperative and are connected by the conjunction "and."

Is the Lord's Prayer a specifically Christian prayer? Almost everything that is desired and asked for in it can be found in one or another Jewish prayer. Still the Lord's Prayer is not like the Jewish prayers, first, because of its soberness, brevity, and simplicity of form (Jewish prayers generally have a longer introduction and a more extended conclusion); second, because of the universality of its contents (Jewish prayers often ask for a future salvation that will also bring a national and political recovery for the people of Israel); and third, because of the particular order: God's name and Kingdom are considered first, and then human needs are mentioned. Except for the form, all of this applies to the ancient "Eighteen Benedictions" that the Jews prayed and still pray three times a day. Around 100 AD, this prayer received its definitive form (eighteen, actually nineteen, petitions, prayers, blessings), but parts of it presumably pre-date Christ. The agreements with the Lord's Prayer are striking: short petitions, end rhymes, as probably the Aramaic original of the Lord's Prayer also had; *the* prayer of the Jew, as the Lord's Prayer is *the* prayer of the Christian; recited three times a day (for the Lord's Prayer, cf. the same prescription in the *Didache*, 8:3).

The discussion here will be restricted to questions that have arisen in recent studies.

## THE ADDRESS

If it is true that Luke has shortened a more original "Our Father in the heavens" to "Father," then Jesus desired that attention be given to the three elements of this address. First, "Our" shows that Jesus intended a church-establishing prayer. "Our" refers to the disciples, not simply to all people. Still, this word does not limit the disciples numerically as a group. Every person who joins them will be allowed to use this prayer. Second, the expression "in the heavens" distinguishes God from earthly fathers (but also from the Jewish expression "our father Abraham"; cf., e.g., Mt 3:9 = Lk 3:8; Jn 8:39; Rom 4:12). Third, anyone who sets out to explain the title of address "Father" will first have to investigate how God is called father among many non-Jewish peoples and then study how the Old Testament and late-Jewish usage of this title is unique (i.e. by reflection on its own past and by a vision of the future).

More important here is that Jesus in his own prayer addressed God as "Abba" = Father; cf. Mk 14:36: "Abba, Father, all things are possible to thee; remove this cup from me." The first Christians, in imitation of Jesus, also prayed in this way; cf. Gal 4:6 and Rom 8:15: "For you did not receive the spirit of slavery to fall back into fear, but you have received the spirit of sonship. And by him we cry, 'Abba! Father'." J. Jeremias, and many others after him, are convinced that we have here the *ipsissima vox Jesu*, a word literally spoken by Jesus. We know of no prayers in which Jews address God in this way. The Jewish author D. Flusser attributes the absence of Abba as an address of God in the Targum to the fact that the Targum has only preserved prayers that are not very charismatic. But his explanation has not been generally accepted. The Aramaic word is a term from the language of children that can be rendered as "daddy" or "dear father"; it also sometimes occurs in the familiar language of adults. The use of this term by Jesus indicates the very particular, intimate relationship that existed between the Father and the Son. When Jesus taught his disciples the "Our Father in the heavens," he was aware that also among them, his disciples, something of this relationship with God was already present.

## GOD'S NAME AND KINGDOM

a) The name refers to the bearer of the name, points to him and manifests his person. For a Jew, more than for us, the name was connected, indeed identical with the person and his deepest essence, and just as inviolable. "Hallowed be" is a passive. In Judaism after the exile, the pronunciation of the name of God was avoided. One of the means to do this was the so-called "theological passive," in which the non-expressed acting person is God: that your name be hallowed by you, God!

People can profane God's name. Even the chosen people of Israel did it: "You who boast in the law, do you dishonor God by breaking the law? For, as it is written, 'The name of God is blasphemed among the Gentiles because of you'" (Rom 2:23-24). But God, who called Israel, does not remain idle. He acts, he punishes his people, saves them from the hand of the enemy, promises restoration. Through the prophet Ezekiel God proclaims his way of acting: "Therefore say to the house of Israel, Thus says the Lord God: It is not for your sake, O house of Israel, that I am about to act, but for the sake of my holy name, which you have profaned among the nations to which you came. And I will vindicate the holiness of my great name, which has been profaned among the nations, and which you have profaned among them; and the nations will know that I am the Lord, says the Lord God, when through you I vindicate my holiness before their eyes" (36:22-23; see also vv. 24-28). At the end of time God will hallow his name definitively and openly in the presence of all nations.

With "hallowed be thy name," Jesus' disciples must pray for this eschatological hallowing expected from God. A Christian knows, however, that, with Jesus' first coming, with his preaching and works, his suffering and resurrection, this event of the end-time has already received its first accomplishment, and that the believer himself, precisely like Israel of the Old Testament, has a responsible and active role in this hallowing among the peoples.

This exposition, and also what follows in the next section, is a brief summary of what J. Dupont has worked out in detail in his monograph on the Lord's Prayer.

b) The English word "kingdom" is indefinite enough to cover two nuances: kingdom as an area, i.e. the royal domain, and kingdom as kingship, the royal power, i.e., the exercise of sovereignty, dominion. From late Jewish texts, it appears that the more abstract expression "the Kingdom of God shall be revealed" was often chosen in preference to the direct "God rules." Like the passive phrase "hallowed be," this can be explained on the basis of respect for God rather than by a conceptual shift. It is God himself who must come and rule.

Like the first, the second invocation is a prayer for the definitive breakthrough and coming of the Kingdom and not — or not so much — for a progressive confirmation of it. In the meantime, the Kingdom has come nearer in Jesus' earthly actions: "The time is fulfilled, and the Kingdom of

God is at hand; repent, and believe in the gospel"(Mk 1:15). By the saving grace of Jesus and by our faith and repentance, we know ourselves to be already "sons of the Kingdom" (Mt 13:38).

The two invocations regarding the name and the Kingdom are parallel both in sentence structure and in concept. Nevertheless, the second invocation expresses something more than the first, and therefore is correctly placed in the second place. As we have seen, "name" refers to the person and his inner essence; "Kingdom" is concerned more with exterior activity. The essence of the person is expressed in his acts. God hallows his name by the exercise of his sovereignty.

## THE NEEDS OF THE CHRISTIANS

The first part of the Lord's Prayer is thus rightly called an eschatological prayer, however strange this eschatological character may appear to us. The disciples of Jesus have to pray to God their Father for the hallowing of his name and the coming of the Kingdom. Human beings cannot accomplish this. God himself, God alone, can cause his name to be openly and universally called holy and his Kingdom to appear definitively and to be universally recognized. This is the eschaton, the eschatological completion. "Father," so Jesus taught his disciples to pray, "let this happen soon; hasten the coming of the Kingdom!"

But is the second part of the Lord's Prayer eschatological in the same sense? Did Jesus teach us to pray for the heavenly bread, for forgiveness on the last day, for safety during times of trial — messianic woes — that will immediately precede the coming of the Kingdom in the end time? Probably not. The disciples must pray that they now already, today and tomorrow, do not enter into a situation of evil that is too dangerous and do not yield to the temptation to sin. They must pray for forgiveness of sins for now and not only for the future. And also the necessary bread that is prayed for today is ordinary bread, food for the body.

a) With this, a position is taken in the ongoing controversy about the rare adjective *epiousios*, which was left untranslated above. As yet, there is no consensus on this question. What is the difficulty with the bread in the Lord's Prayer? Next to the word bread is an adjective that must be the translation of an Aramaic word. Up until recently, it has usually been translated by "daily." The Lord's Prayer is the only place that *epiousios* appears in the entire Bible, and, as far as we know, it is not used in non-biblical Greek. We can only guess at its derivation. Does it come from "*epi*" (preposition meaning "with") and "*einai*" (the verb "to be") or from "*epi*" and "*ienai*" (the verb "to go," "to come")? If we knew the meaning of this adjective, then we would probably also know with certainty what kind of bread is meant in the Lord's Prayer. Very many proposals have been made in the course of the history of exegesis regarding both the philological explanation and the meaning in the context.

As regards the origin of this adjective, there are two possibilities. First, *epiousios* is derived from the verb *epi-ienai* (= to come) and contains a time indication: (bread) for the future or for the coming day (tomorrow) or for the day now starting (today). Second, the adjective is related to the verb *epi-einai* (= to be; cf. the noun *epi-ousia* = substance) and then probably means: (bread) necessary for being or life, (the bread) we need. A spiritual and even eschatological sense is sometimes readily assigned: bread as the word of God, as eucharist, as symbol of the salvific grace or of the heavenly feast. But does the petition with "give us today" allow this?

For a good review of the recent discussion, see A. Vögtle, *Der "eschatologische" Bezug*, pp. 348-353, which, among other things, discusses and refutes the positions of Carmignac (simultaneously material and spiritual meaning) and Jeremias (eschatological meaning of "bread for tomorrow"). Against the eschatological interpretation, he writes: "It can be pointed out that 'bread' in Israel does not apply as the representation of the feast at the end of time and that 'us' is disturbing if one understands 'bread' as a share of the glory of the end time" (p. 350). I have reviewed a number of the more recent proposals in *Broodbede en menselijke inzet* (pp. 145-147).

The discussion, however, continues, and the opinions and positions diverge considerably. There is no consensus in any area of the question. Indeed, there is no agreement as yet even on the question of the root the adjective *epiousios* is derived from. There is division about the question of whether the bread petition contains an allusion to the story of the manna and must thus be understood against this Old Testament background. Controversy continues about the alternative of "ordinary, material bread" and "spiritual bread," and some defend the presence of both meanings simultaneously. Finally, because of all of this, translation remains guesswork: daily bread, the bread for today, the bread for tomorrow, the essential, actual bread, the true bread of life, and so on.

Perhaps we can ease our discouragement at this state of affairs with the following considerations. In general, the proposals can be reduced to two categories. In the one category the concept of "time" predominates: daily, today, tomorrow; in the other, the idea of necessity, need. The two kinds of meanings are not so very far from each other, however, because in both there is the additional idea of quantity: the quantity for the day (first category), the quantity that one needs (second category). The nuance of quantity, quantum, ration or measure needed and sufficient for a particular time, seems to be present at least implicitly in most translations.

In these last considerations, I have assumed that the meaning of "bread" is that of ordinary bread, the food for the body. Indeed, it is difficult to imagine that the sense of the prayer that Jesus taught, "give us today our bread," would be purely spiritual — or exclusively eschatological. Of course, "bread" is here a collective term for everything one may need. And, obviously, this is more than material bread alone. One does not live by bread alone. This line of thought leads one to reject the choice between material and spiritual and to accept layers of meaning simultaneously

present in the term "bread." However attractive this sugges-
tion may be, I am still hesitant. It seems to me that the one
who prays is praying for food for his earthly body at least
primarily if not exclusively .

Still, the bread petition apparently is not simply or solely
a prayer to be preserved from hunger. Jesus calls for freedom from anxiety: see Mt 6:25-34 = Lk 12:22-31. With the
bread petition, most probably, Jesus therefore meant this:
Father, give us the necessary bread so that we are not so
preoccupied with material cares that we lose sight of the
only truly important thing. "Martha, Martha, you are anxious and troubled about many things; one thing is needful."
(Lk 10:41-42).

b) In a revolutionary way in the Lord's Prayer, Jesus has
broken open our this-worldly closedness. Our horizon has
been immeasurably widened by his speaking about God.
Three hindrances can still cause us problems: absorption in
material existence, actual sin, and the danger of sin. With
the three petitions of the second part, we ask that we, in our
concrete daily lives, may not forget or forfeit eschatological
salvation at the end of time.

With regard to this last petition "and lead us not into
temptation," there is first the question of whether "temptation" is the correct translation of the Greek word *peirasmos*.
Some have said that the reference here is to the events in the
desert where Yahweh tested his people (cf. Deut 8:2 "and
you shall remember all the way which the Lord your God
has led you these forty years in the wilderness, that he might
humble you, testing you to know what was in your heart,
whether you would keep his commandments, or not"). Consideration has also been given to the great trials that will
announce the coming of the Kingdom at the end of time, the
oppression and the tribulations caused by the powers that
are enemies of God. Jesus would have taught his disciples to
pray to be spared all this. Without completely excluding
these opinions, I would ask whether Jesus did not have in
mind the danger of sin and apostasy, i.e., human failure in
the test of faith about which Jesus' encouragement of Peter
in Gethsemane is concerned in Mk 14:38: "Watch and pray

that you may not enter into temptation; the spirit is willing, but the flesh is weak." In the Lord's Prayer, the definite article, which could characterize the temptation as *the* eschatological danger, is lacking. The Jews, too, prayed in the time of Jesus to be freed from the temptation to sin. And of the 21 places where *peirasmos* occurs in the New Testament, it refers only once to the dangers of the end times (Rev 3:10).

James wrote in his letter: "Let no one say when he is tempted, 'I am tempted by God'" (1:13). In order not to be forced to accept that, according to the Lord's Prayer, God himself brings man into temptation, it has been suggested that we have here an Aramaic verb in the causative "aphel" form (or Hebrew "hiphil"): "to make that." When this form is used with a denial, the negation (depending on the context) can refer either to the auxiliary verb "to make" or to the main verb. Applied to the last petition, there are, considered abstractly, two possible translations: do not cause us to enter into temptation (God is the cause); or see to it that we do not enter into temptation (we are the actual cause). Jesus would then have intended the second meaning in this petition. Naturally, up to a certain point, this all remains very hypothetical. To contend that the evangelists (and even Q) would have understood this petition in this way goes one more step too far and accepts much too easily, in my opinion, that Matthew and Luke knew Aramaic well and also that they wanted to have their Greek understood with reference to the Aramaic. Furthermore, we should not be too ready to assume that both Jesus and the early church were concerned with a theological objection that is somewhat forced.

## IV. The Lord's Prayer of Matthew

The Matthean version must now be discussed further, particularly because it is the version used in the liturgy and in the prayer of Christians. The differences in regard to Lk have already been briefly indicated and discussed. In this section, I will discuss the Matthean additions in 6:10b and 13b, the translation of the verb in 6:12b, and, more generally, the way in which Matthew understood the Lord's Prayer as a whole.

## GOD'S WILL

The third invocation "thy will be done" may not be understood as an expression of resignation. This would conflict with the context and particularly with the spirit of the first two invocations. Here, too, the request is primarily for God himself to accomplish his will. In Mt 26:42b, Jesus prays: "My Father, if this cannot pass unless I drink it, thy will be done." Matthew has expanded his source text, Mk 14:39, with this entire clause. In Gethsemane, too, it is the Father who must assert his will. But the praying Jesus expresses his surrender and gives witness to his obedience.

Perhaps we may also perceive such obedience in the Lord's Prayer. This nuance of human involvement and readiness is new with respect to the first two invocations. Further, "your will" means desire and command (moral aspect) as well as decision for salvation history. And the specification "as in heaven so also on earth" is not specifically eschatological, which again differentiates it from the first two. Thus, the question arises whether, like Jesus, Matthew had fulfillment and realization of God's dominion at the end of time in mind with this added invocation as he did with the first two. To the extent that the eschatological stress is softened and that concern for human obedience also echoes in "thy will be done," Matthew presumably also understood the first two invocations less eschatologically and less theologically!

We should note here in passing the position, which is again being defended by Carmignac, that the phrase "as in heaven so also on earth" applies not only to the third invocation but also to the invocations as a whole.

## OUR ACT OF FORGIVING

"As we have forgiven" in 6:12b is a literal translation of the Greek verb in the aorist, *aphēkamen*. Philologists sometimes call this form the "dramatic" aorist, a tense used for acts that have just been performed and of which the result still endures into the present (e.g., he has just slandered = he slanders).

Because this past tense thus presents the human act not only as a condition but also, as it were, as an example and model for God's act ("as we have done!"), it is postulated, on the basis of the Lucan present tense, that the Matthean version renders the Aramaic "perfectum coincidentiae" less accurately (cf. p. 132 above). But again this is all quite hypothetical. It would certainly be hazardous to presume that Matthew was aware of this possible Semitic background. In the Matthean Lord's Prayer, the forgiveness of the other in advance can indeed be considered a condition for the receiving of God's forgiveness. The same idea is present in 6:14-15, Matthew's commentary on this prayer. Twice the forgiveness of the other occurs in the conditional clause, which chronologically precedes the future of the concluding clause. This succession (first human forgiveness and then that of God) is the same as in the petition of the Lord's Prayer.

The parable of the unforgiving servant (18:23-35), however, warns us against hardening this position into an absolute dogma. In this parable, it is the forgiveness already received from God that obliges the individual to be merciful and forgiving toward his fellow person. However, this task, which follows from the gift, is also seen in the parable as a necessary condition for keeping the gift.

## THE EVIL ONE

It is clear that, with his last petition in 6:13b "but deliver us from the Evil One," Matthew intended to make a positive addition to the negative "and lead us not into temptation." One may thus understand it as "lead us not into temptation but, *on the contrary*, deliver us from the Evil One." The two clauses form one conceptual whole. It is therefore better not to consider the Matthean Lord's Prayer as consisting of seven elements, with 13a and b expressing separate ideas, but to see v. 13 as one petition having two rather symmetrical parts. After the address, there is the first part with three invocations (name, Kingdom, will) and then the second part also with three petitions (bread, forgiveness, temptation).

Grammatically, a choice is possible between the neuter and the masculine case for the Greek *tou ponērou*: evil or the Evil One. Complete certainty cannot be gained from the Matthean context, and interpreters have been at odds since antiquity. Nevertheless, it is very probable that Matthew had in mind here the devil and, more specifically, the Evil One. With a neuter word, one would expect the preposition *ek* (= out) after "deliver" and a further specification (out of all evil). In 13:19 (the parable of the sower), *ho ponēros* is (for Matthew) the devil (cf. 13:39: "the enemy who sowed them is the devil"). We probably have to understand the "sons of the Evil One" also in 13:38, and this notwithstanding the parallel phrase in the same verse: "the sons of the Kingdom" (impersonal). If Matthew indeed intends the Evil One in 6:13b, it follows that for him the temptation of 6:13a is the work of Satan.

## V. Jesus and Our Prayer

According to Lk 11:1 the disciples formulate their request "Lord, teach us to pray" after they had seen Jesus in prayer. The praying Jesus is our exemplar. But that same Jesus, as we have seen, also taught us to pray; he gave instructions about prayer: Mt 6:5-15 and Lk 11:1-13. However, he is above all the Lord to whom we go (cf. John 6:68). What does this last sentence mean for Christian prayer today?

## PRAYING THROUGH CHRIST AND TO CHRIST

At Jacob's well in Sichem with her gaze directed to Mt. Gerizim, the Samaritan woman said to Jesus: "Our Fathers worshiped on this mountain; and you say that in Jerusalem is the place where men ought to worship" (John 4:20). Jesus answers her: "Woman, believe me, the hour is coming when neither on this mountain nor in Jerusalem will you worship the Father. You worship what you do not know; we worship what we know, for salvation is from the Jews. But the hour is coming, and now is, when the true worshippers will worship the Father in spirit and truth" (4:21-23). That hour of which Jesus speaks is our own time. Through Jesus Christ Jews and Gentiles have access to the Father in one Spirit (cf. Eph 2:18). Thanks to Jesus the Son we have become children of God. We have received the spirit of sonship which makes us cry out: Abba, Father (Rom 8:15; Gal 4:6). With this term Jesus prayed to God, and so we pray ever since, sharing in the glorious freedom of the children of God. The Spirit comes to help our weakness. We do not know how we ought to pray. But the Spirit himself — the Spirit of Christ and the Spirit of him who raised Jesus from the dead — intercedes for us with unutterable sighs (cf. Rom 8). Christian prayer then is prayer in spirit and truth, "through Christ our Lord," the formula with which, in fact, so many liturgical prayers conclude.

In one radical respect Christian prayer, though, does differ from Jesus' prayer. Since the time not long after Easter — the time in which people experienced that the Crucified lived again and that God had exalted him (cf. Phil 2:6-11) — since that time, people have not only begun to proclaim what that figure of the past, Jesus of Nazareth, did and said, how he lived and died and rose on the third day, but Christians have also come to recognize him as the living, present and commanding Lord. People not only pray through Christ; they also pray to him. For Christians the actual Lord is at the same time the Son of Man who will come again: *Marana tha*, Lord, come! (1 Cor 16:22; cf. Apoc 22:20). Jesus Christ, alpha and omega: as confessed Christ, adored Lord and expected Son of Man-Judge he brings together past, present and future.

Since that time many people — women and men, old and young, saints and sinners — have in fact prayed to their brother and Lord. He has become the mystical bridegroom of the soul, the companion on apostolic journeys, the true friend of many abandoned people, the comforter, the intimate guest. For many he is someone who understands, and not the one who condemns. He it is who lifts us up and inspires us and, with his appropriate demands, grasps people, compels them and raises them up above their small human measure.

## JESUS PRAYS IN OUR PLACE

In the Letter to the Hebrews it is said of Christ that "he is able for all time to save those who draw near to God through him, since he always lives to make intercession for them" (cf. 7:25). Jesus prays for us; he intercedes for us; he is our intercessor for all time. He prays in our place. This is a very important truth, especially in connection with the problem of so-called unanswered prayer: it is good to reflect that in and through everything that we so willfully and sometimes so narrow-mindedly wish to receive from God through our prayer, Christ is there who better knows and advocates our own cause.

However comforting this truth may be, it is not, nevertheless, completely satisfactory. In this understanding Christ is too far away. His advocacy remains unexpressed and its content unknown. Therefore, Christians tell their teacher in their turn, so to speak, how he ought to pray. They place their own prayers on his lips, prayers which are full of their present experiences and needs. Why shouldn't this be so? It already happens to some extent in the Gospel.

Thus, Luke — on the basis of his knowledge of the flight of the disciples and the denial and repentance of Peter and his role after Easter — presents Jesus as saying (after the institution of the Eucharist): "Simon, Simon, behold, Satan demanded to have you, that he might sift you like wheat, but I have prayed for you that your faith may not fail; and when you have turned again, strengthen your brethren" (22:31-32). Luke ascribes Peter's repentance and his comforting, strengthening activity to the salvific power of Jesus' provident prayer. Further, are the thoughts and intentions of Jesus' high priestly prayer in John 17 not for the most part Johannine formulations, conceived in the time after Easter?

The same freedom with which Luke and John present the earthly Jesus' prayer is also used by later Christians — theologians, spiritual writers and poets — to represent the advocacy of the exalted Christ with respect to the here and now. To repeat: nothing must keep us from praying through Christ to God in such a committed, intense and human way, making Christ pray in our place.

For all of us who periodically and sometimes for prolonged stretches of time experience the difficulty of prayer, often through our own superficiality, lack of application, or sin, the image of Jesus, the man of prayer, and the directives of the teacher *par excellence* as well as the mysterious presence of the risen Lord can become a source of abiding inspiration and effective help.

## Bibliography

See also the general works on pp 41-44

Ashton, J., "Our Father," *Way* 18 (1978) 83-91.

Betz, H. D., "Eine judenchristliche Kult-Didache in Matthäus 6, 1-18. Überlegungen und Fragen im Blick auf das Problem des historischen Jesus," in: G. Strecker (ed.), *Jesus Christus in Historie und Theologie. Fs. H. Conzelmann*, Tübingen, 1975, pp. 445-457.

Boff, L., *The Lord's Prayer. The Prayer of Integral Liberation*, Melbourne-New York, 1983.

Bonnard, P., J. Dupont, and F. Refoulé, *Notre Père qui es aux cieux. La Prière oecuménique* (Cah. Trad. Oec. Bible 3), Paris, 1971.

Bornkamm, "Aufbau" (see p. 42 above), pp. 419-432.

Brown, R. E., "The Pater Noster as an Eschatological Prayer," in: Brown, *New Testament Essays*, New York, [2]1968, pp. 275-320.

Carmignac, J., *Recherches sur le 'Notre Père'*, Paris, 1969.

De Fraine, J., *Praying* (see p. 78 above), pp. 1-64.

Dorneich, M. (ed.), *Vaterunser Bibliographie*, Freiburg i. Br., 1982.

Dupont, J. (see under Bonnard).

Edmonds, P., "The Lucan Our Father: A Summary of Luke's Teaching on Prayer?" *Exp. Times* 91 (1979-80) 140-143.

Finkel, A., "The Prayer of Jesus in Matthew," in: A Finkel, L. Frizzell, *Standing Before God. Fs. J. M. Oesterreicher*, New York, 1981, pp. 131-170.

Goulder, M.D., "The Composition of the Lord's Prayer," *Journ. Theol. Stud.* 14 (1963) 32-45.

Grelot, P., "L'arrière-plan araméen du 'Pater,'" *Revue biblique* 91 (1984) 531-556.

Harner, P. B., *Understanding the Lord's Prayer*, Philadelphia, 1975.

Hartman, L., "'Your will Be Done on Earth as It Is in Heaven,'" *Afr. Theol. Journ.* 11 (1982) 209-218.

Hill, D., "'Our Daily Bread' (Matt 6.11) in the History of Exegesis," *Ir. Bibl. Stud.* 5 (1983) 2-10.

Hoffmann, P., "Der ungeteilte Dienst. Die Auslegung der Bergpredigt V (Mt 6, 1-7, 27)," *Bib. Leb.* 11 (1970) 89-104.

Jeremias, J., *The Lord's Prayer* (Facet Books, Bibl. Ser.), ET by J. Reumann, Philadelphia, 1964.

Lambrecht, J., "Broodbede en menselijke inzet," in: *Thuis in Gods ruimte. Over gebed en gebedsopvoeding in onze tijd* (Nikè-reeks 1), Leuven, 1981, pp. 139-157.

Lambrecht, J., "Jesus and Prayer," *Louv. Stud.* 6 (1976-77) 128-143.

LaVerdière, E., *When We Pray ... Meditation on the Lord's Prayer*, Notre Dame, 1983.

Moule, C. F. D., "'... As we forgive...' — A Note on the Distinction between Deserts and Capacity in the Understanding of Forgiveness,' in: E. Bammel, C. K. Barrett, and W. D. Davies (eds.), *Donum gentilicium. Fs. D. Daube*, Oxford, 1978, pp. 68-77.

Orchard, B., "The Meaning of 'ton epiousion,'" *Bibl. Theol. Bull.* 3 (1973) 274-282.

Schürmann, H., *Praying with Jesus. The "Our Father" for Today*, ET by W. M. Ducey and A. Simon, New York, 1964.

Stendahl, K., "Your Kingdom Come," *Cross Currents* 32 (1982) 257-266.

Swetnam, J., "Hallowed Be Thy Name," *Bibl.* 52 (1971) 556-563.

Van Tilborg, S., "A Form-Criticism of the Lord's Prayer," *Nov. Test.* 14 (1972) 94-105.

Vögtle, A., "Der 'eschatologische' Bezug der Wir-Bitten des Vaterunser," in: E. E. Ellis and E. Grässer (eds.), *Jesus und Paulus. Fs. W. G. Kümmel,* Göttingen, 1975, pp. 344-362.

Vögtle, A., "Das Vaterunser — ein Gebet fur Juden und Christen?" in: M. Brocke, J. J. Petuchowski, and W. Strolz (eds.) *Das Vaterunser. Gemeinsames im Beten von Juden und Christen*, Freiburg, 1974, pp. 165-193.

Walker, W. O., "The Lord's Prayer in Matthew and John," *New Test. Stud.* 28 (1982) 237-256.

# Chapter Five

# CONCERN AND UNCONCERN (Mt 6:19-7:12)

Up to 6:18, the Matthean Sermon on the Mount gives the unmistakable impression of a certain order and structure: nine beatitudes, six antitheses, and a three-strophe warning against exterior display. This impression vanishes with 6:19-7:12. One is confronted with a plethora of commands, arguments, exhortations, and questions of all kinds. Of course, there are focal points and main themes: Jesus' warning against exaggerated earthly concern (6:19-34), Jesus' prohibition against judging (7:1-5), and his call for perseverance in prayer (7:7-11). But, in this context, what is the function of the sayings about the eye (6:22-23) and holy things and the pearls (7:6), and what is the Golden Rule (7:12), as it has been called for more than two centuries, doing here?

In 6:25-34, Matthew denounces misplaced, excessive concern, restless and irreligious anxiety, an anxiety that engrosses a person and cuts him off from God. This is an apt exhortation for most readers of this text, including moderr ones. But still, in a certain sense, Jesus' words bother us. The concern with daily, concrete existence occupies a great deal of time for most people. For many, it is an exhausting and monotonous task that flows from the responsibility for their standard of living and the future of their families. Jesus' call too easily appears as an invitation to indifference. The analogy of the birds and the lilies of the field limps, to put it

151

mildly . Inactivity is certainly not a manifestation of confidence! And a confidence in God that would ignore making elementary provision for tomorrow is dangerous and cannot be the will of God. In addition, Jesus — here in the Sermon on the Mount and elsewhere in the same chapter —teaches us to pray for the bread we need in order to live. To be occupied with one's daily bread is, therefore, not wrong.

Mt 7:12 ends with "for this is the Law and the Prophets." Almost all exegetes see this clause as a bracket, an inclusion with 5:17 ("The Law or the Prophets"). In the third chapter above, we saw that Matthew moved the Golden Rule from its original Q-context (cf. Lk 6:31) to 7:12. What follows in the Sermon on the Mount (7:13-27) is obviously a conclusion. Matthew probably wanted to round off and summarize a unit of exhortational instruction (5:17-7:11): "So whatever you wish that men would do to you, do so to them, for this is the Law and the Prophets."

There is still another fact that argues for treating the pericopes of 6:19-7:12 together. What Matthew writes in 7:7-11 about perseverance in prayer is also found in Lk 11:9-13, which is close to the Lucan Lord's Prayer (11:2-4). Why did Matthew not place this pericope in his exhortation to prayer (6:5-15)? Does the answer to this question lie in the possibility that Matthew is still dealing with the theme of the Lord's Prayer not only in 7:7-11 but also elsewhere in 6:19-7:12 and particularly in 6:25-34? For in this last passage he treats the search for the Kingdom of God and unconcern for food and clothing, which reminds the reader of "thy Kingdom come" and the bread petition. We thus have to see the extent to which the Lord's Prayer makes itself felt in 6:19-7:12, and this investigation will make it possible to take up again the double question posed at the beginning of Chapter Four: Did *Matthew* understand the coming of the Kingdom and the prayer for bread in precisely the same way as did the earthly Jesus, and how should the *contemporary Christian* best pray the Lord's Prayer?

This chapter will begin with the problem of the extent to which the Lord's Prayer and the prayer theme in general determine the structure of Mt 6:19-7:12. Then two sections will be devoted to the problem of the actual relationship (according to Matthew) between evangelical unconcern and human effort, with particular attention being given to 6:25-34 in this regard. In the last section, the focus returns to 6:19-7:12 as a whole and an attempt is made to discern Matthew's train of thought. As in the last two chapters, the concern is almost exclusively with Matthew's Sermon on the Mount. Along with the Golden Rule (7:12 = Lk 6:31), 7:1-5 also occurs in the Lucan Sermon on the Plain (= Lk 6:37-42), but the Lucan parallel texts will be discussed in Chapter Seven below.

## I. The Sermon on the Mount and Prayer

For the content of Mt 5 and 6:1-18 regarding prayer, the reader is referred to Chapter Four (pp. 125-128).

### MORE DATA

Prayer is not specifically discussed in 6:19-34. Nevertheless, the advice given in vv. 25, 28, and 31-32 reminds us of prayer and more particularly of the content of the bread petition: "Therefore I tell you, do not be anxious about your life, what you shall eat or what you shall drink, nor about your body, what you shall put on... And why are you anxious about clothing? ... Therefore do not be anxious, saying, 'What shall we eat?' or 'What shall we drink?' or 'What shall we wear?' For the Gentiles seek all these things; and your heavenly Father knows that you need them all." "Gentiles" here reminds us of 6:7-8 (Gentiles and their many words). The text continues: "But seek first his Kingdom and his righteousness and all these things shall be yours as well. Therefore do not be anxious about tomorrow, for tomorrow will be anxious for itself. Let the day's own trouble be sufficient for the day" (6:33-34). The reader may well wonder how this explicit instruction can be reconciled with the positive petition of the Lord's Prayer: "Our bread give us today."

In 7:7-11, Jesus exhorts perseverance in prayer: "Ask and it will be given you; seek, and you will find; knock, and it will be opened to you. For every one who asks receives, and he who seeks finds, and to him who knocks it will be opened. Or what man of you, if his son asks him for bread, will give him a stone? Or if he asks for a fish, will give him a serpent? If you then, who are bad, know how to give good gifts to your children, how much more will your Father who is in heaven give good things to those who ask him!" In Matthew's conception, v. 12 also belongs to this unit: "So whatever you wish that men would do to you, do so to them; for this is the Law and the Prophets." Prayer to God and effective openness to one's fellow-persons are connected to each other according to Matthew.

In 7:21-23, Jesus cites the sterile prayer of some Christians at the judgment: "Not every one who says to me 'Lord, Lord,' shall enter the Kingdom of heaven, but he who does the will of my Father who is in heaven. On that day many will say to me 'Lord, Lord, did we not prophesy in your name, and cast out demons in your name, and do many mighty works in your name. And then will I declare to them, I never knew you; depart from me, you evildoers.'" "Not every one who says to me 'Lord, Lord,' . . . ": for Matthew this praying is only "saying," an appeal in panic to Christ the judge and the citing of what one has done in his name. Such a prayer, without the doing of the will of God —which for Matthew is equivalent to the hearing and doing of Jesus' words in the Sermon on the Mount (cf. v. 24) — such a prayer is worthless. This will be made manifest on the day of judgment, the day on which this "prayer" is said.

The large number of times that the prayer theme occurs in the Sermon on the Mount is striking: eight times in all, four times in the fifth chapter (5:16; 5:23-24; 5:33-37; and 5:44c-45; see pp. 125-126), twice in the sixth chapter (6:5-15 and 6:25-28, 31-32), and twice in the seventh chapter (7:7-12 and 7:21-23). Matthew often speaks about God using the term Father: 45 times in all. He does this seventeen times in the Sermon on the Mount and twelve of these seventeen times it is in a prayer context.

Many aspects of prayer are mentioned: how one must pray and for what, and examples of good and bad prayers are given. Generally, the concern is with prayers of petition, but there is also glorification of God and the prayer that we may presume when offering sacrifice and in the striving for truthfulness. Generally, Jesus deals with the praying of his disciples, but at the beginning of the Sermon he mentions —almost incidentally — the glorification of God by other people (cf. 5:16). At the end of the Sermon, Jesus also discusses the "prayer" of disciples who have misled other disciples and have committed unrighteousness.

## THE STUDY OF G. BORNKAMM

Is prayer in the Sermon on the Mount more than just one theme among many? Several exegetes have contended that the Lord's Prayer is central to the Sermon on the Mount, not only as concerns its place, about mid-way through, but also as a structural element. According to some, the entire Sermon on the Mount is a commentary on the Lord's Prayer. Most of the proposals seem to be forced and are not convincing. Is this also the case with the most recent proposal, which was put forward by G. Bornkamm?

At the annual meeting in 1977 of the International "Studiorum Novi Testamenti Societas" held in Tübingen, Bornkamm, who was the president of the Society that year, devoted his inaugural address to the "Structure of the Sermon on the Mount." His address was published a year later in the journal of the Society, *New Testament Studies.* Bornkamm argues that Matthew's manner of composition in this programmatic sermon is not uniform: "Ungleichartigkeit der Komposition." The "redactional methods" do "not appear everywhere with the same clarity"(p. 421). He shows briefly that Mt 5 and 6:1-18 and also 7:13-27 have a clear structure, which was intended by the evangelist. But at first sight there is not much order or structure in 6:19-7:11. However, since Matthew very obviously imposes an order elsewhere — consider, for example, the Matthean introductions of 5:20 and 6:1 and the concluding verse 12 of chapter 7 corresponding to 5:17 — it would be very strange, in Born-kamm's opinion, if Matthew's compositional creativity were totally absent in 6:1-7:12. In his study, therefore, Born-kamm's attention is focused primarily on 6:1-7:12, the large middle part of the Sermon on the Mount. How does he proceed?. I will summarize his argument. But first something should be said about the components of this long textual unit.

Matthew compiled material from various places. The following table will clarify this point.

| Mt | | Lk | Lk | Lk | Lk |
|----|----|----|----|----|----|
| 6:1 | introduction | R | | | |
| 6:2-4 | alms | S | | | |
| 6:5-6 | Jewish praying | S | | | |
| 6:7-8 | Gentile praying | R/S? | | | |
| 6:9-13 | Lord's Prayer | Q | 11:2-4 | | |
| 6:14-15 | forgiveness (Mk 11:25-26) | | | | |
| 6:16-18 | fasting | S | | | |
| 6:19-21 | treasures | Q | | 12:33-34 | |
| 6:22-23 | eye | Q | 11:34-36 | | |
| 6:24 | two masters | Q | | | 16:13 |
| 6:25-33 | anxiousness | Q | | 12:22-32 | |
| 6:34 | tomorrow | R/S? | | | |
| 7:1-2 | judging | Q | 6:37-38 | | |
| 7:3-5 | speck/log | Q | 6;41-42 | | |
| 7:6 | holy things | S | | | |
| 7:7-11 | asking | Q | | 11:9-13 | |
| 7:12 | Golden Rule | Q | 6:31 | | |

Matthew used material from various Q-contexts to compose this middle part.

Bornkamm first raises an important question. Luke placed his own exhortation on prayer in another place than in the Sermon on the Plain, namely in 11:1-13. Nowhere in his gospel does Matthew give the parable of the friend's inconvenient arrival at night (Lk 11:5-8) but he does place the Lord's Prayer (6:9-13 = Lk 11:2-4) and the passage on perseverance in prayer (7:7-11 = Lk 11:9-13) in his Sermon on the Mount. Why, asks Bornkamm, did not the systematic Matthew place this last pericope next to his parenesis on prayer (6:5-15) rather than at the end of this middle part, in 7:7-11? There must be a reason for this, Bornkamm thinks, and all the more so because in Matthew's source the Lord's Prayer and the pericope on perseverance in prayer presumably stood close together (cf. Lk). There must have been a reason to place them so far apart!

After the question, an observation. Mt 6:1-18 obviously has three parts. The exhortation written by Matthew himself, "Beware of practicing your piety before men in order to be seen by them" (cf. v. 1) is clarified by three examples: giving alms, praying, and fasting. Bornkamm, like many others, uses here the Greek term *didachē* (instruction, teaching intended for people who are already Christians) to distinguish from *kerygma* (message announced to non-Christians). Mt 6:1-6, 16-18 is an instruction on cult or *Kultdidache*. This threefold warning was a unit in Matthew's source. Matthew disrupted this unity, and expanded considerably the "prayer" example: he inserted an instruction on prayer or *Gebetsdidache* (6:7-15) that, in the context of the *Kultdidache* (= 6:2-6, 16-18), clearly possesses its own importance (p. 426). It is, therefore, not completely subordinate to the theme that is so strongly emphasized in the introduction of 6:1: no ostentatious display! Does this *Gebetsdidache* perhaps have a structural function for the content of the Sermon on the Mount in 6:19-7:12?

## ANALYSIS OF Mt 6:19-7:12

a) *Mt 6:19-34*

19 Do not lay up for yourselves treasures on earth, where moth and rust consume and where thieves break in and steal,

20 but lay up for yourselves treasures in heaven, where neither moth nor rust consumes and where thieves do not break in and steal.

21 For where your treasure is, there will your heart be also.

22 The eye is the lamp of the body. So, if your eye is sound, your whole body will be full of light;

23 but if your eye is not sound, your whole body will be full of darkness. If then the light in you is darkness, how great is the darkness!

24 No one can serve two masters; for either he will hate the one and love the other, or he will be devoted to the one and despise the other. You cannot serve God and mammon.

25 Therefore I tell you, do not be anxious about your life, what you shall eat or what you shall drink, nor about your body, what you shall put on. Is not life more than food, and the body more than clothing?

26 Look at the birds of the air; they neither sow nor reap nor gather into barns, and yet your heavenly Father feeds them. Are you not of more value than they?

27 And which of you by being anxious can add one cubit to his span of life?

28 And why are you anxious about clothing? Consider the lilies of the field, how they grow; they neither toil nor spin;

29 yet I tell you, even Solomon in all his glory was not arrayed like one of these.

30 But if God so clothes the grass of the field, which today is alive and tomorrow is thrown into the oven, will he not much more clothe you, O men of little faith?

31 Therefore do not be anxious, saying, "What shall we eat?" or "What shall we wear?"

32 For the Gentiles seek all these things; and your heavenly Father knows that you need them all.

33 But seek first his Kingdom and his righteousness, and all these things shall be yours as well.

34 Therefore do not be anxious about tomorrow, for tomorrow will be anxious for itself. Let the day's own trouble be sufficient for the day.

What is the origin of the material of vv. 19-34? The table above tells us. Except for vv. 22-24, everything comes from the same Q-context; Luke places this material in the twelfth chapter of his gospel. In Lk, and probably also in Q, warning is given against being anxious about food and clothing. Jesus said: the Gentiles also strive for these things; your Father knows that you need them. Seek the Kingdom, and all of these things will be given to you in addition (cf. Lk 12:22-31). At the end of the pericope then we find an exhortation: acquire a treasure in heaven "where no thief approaches and where no moth destroys. For where your treasure is, there will your heart be also" (Lk 12:33-34).

What did Matthew do with this text? Three differences can be noted: First, the sequence is different: treasure comes first (vv. 19-21) and then anxiety (vv. 25-34). Second, the text on treasure is expanded: vv. 22-23 develop the idea of v. 21 ("for where your treasure is, there will your heart be also") with the image of the clear eye that is like a lamp that illuminates the whole body. V. 24 is concerned with two masters, God and mammon, and fits well with the heaven-earth opposition of vv. 19-21. Third, at the end of the second part ("do not be anxious," vv. 25-34), Matthew has made several redactional changes. He repeats as a conclusion (cf. v. 25) the warning "do not be anxious about tomorrow" and justifies it with "for tomorrow will be anxious for itself. Let the day's own trouble be sufficient for the day." This is the added v. 34. Moreover, he rewrote v. 33. "Seek God's Kingdom" becomes in Matthew: "seek *first* his (= of the Father, v. 32) Kingdom and *his righteousness*."

What does Bornkamm conclude from this thoroughgoing Matthean redaction? One must keep in mind, Bornkamm states, that the "prayer-anxiety" contrast is a common, often varied motif, used already in the psalms and also in early Christian preaching. One example is the First Letter of Peter, which cites Ps 55:23: "Cast all your anxieties on him, for he cares about you" (5:7). To entrust one's anxieties to God is a form of prayer! According to Bornkamm, Matthew included vv. 19-34 in his Sermon on the Mount precisely because of the prayer theme. The sentence, "seek *first* his Kingdom," moreover, shows us why Matthew altered the sequence of his source text. The first part of the Lord's Prayer is also devoted to God's Kingdom; the first three invocations (name, Kingdom and will) develop the same fundamental concept. The opposition between the two masters and between treasures on earth and treasures in heaven is clearly alluded to at the end of the third petition: "Thy will be done as in heaven so also on earth." The entire first part, 6:19-24, is thus a commentary on the first half of the Lord's Prayer. The second part, "do not be anxious" (6:25-34), then works out the implications of the bread petition. One must not be excessively concerned with food, drink, and clothing, "for the Gentiles seek all these things; and your heavenly Father knows that you need them all" (v. 32). This verse clearly recalls in its turn 6:7-8, the introduction of Matthew's *Gebetsdidache* with the description of the prayer practices of the Gentiles in v. 7 and with the prohibition and the motivation in v. 8: "Do not be like them, *for your father knows what you need* before you ask him." Further, it is difficult to avoid the impression that "tomorrow" in v. 34 was written as a kind of pendant of "today" in the bread petition (6:11; cf. also "today-tomorrow" in 6:30 = Lk 12:28).

Bornkamm concludes that both the inclusion in the Sermon on the Mount as well as the inversion, expansion, and rewriting of the text that Matthew gives in 6:19-34 were guided by Matthew's *Gebetsdidache* in 6:7-15, and more particularly by the Lord's Prayer. Verses 19-24 and 25-34 are commentaries on the three invocations and the first petition of this prayer, respectively.

b) *Mt 7:1-6*

> 1 Judge not, that you be not judged.
> 2 For with the judgment you pronounce you will be judged, and the measure you give will be the measure you get.
> 3 Why do you see the speck that is in your brother's eye, but do not notice the log that is in your own eye?
> 4 Or how can you say to your brother, "Let me take the speck out of your eye," when there is the log in your own eye?

> 5 You hypocrite, first take the log out of your own eye,
> and then you will see clearly to take the speck out of your
> brother's eye.
> 6 Do not give dogs what is holy ; and do not throw pearls
> before swine, lest they trample them under foot and turn
> to attack you.

The warning "judge not, that you be not judged" is illustrated by means of a comparison between a speck and a log.
Matthew had found vv. 1-5 in his source, the Q-version of
Jesus' Sermon on the Mount (cf. Lk 6:37-38, 41-42). In the
large middle part, Mt 6:1-7:12, this is the only long passage
that comes from this source.

After the bread petition in the Lord's Prayer comes the
petition for forgiveness. The condition is that one must first
forgive one's neighbor. Matthew stresses this in particular in
the added verses 14-15 of chapter 6: "If you do not forgive
men their trespasses, neither will your Father forgive your
trespasses." Although 7:1-5 has no vocabulary in common
with the forgiveness petition of the Lord's Prayer and the
added explanation, the similarity in content is so striking in
Bornkamm's opinion that this unit can be considered a
commentary on this petition. In both places, the one who
judges his brother or refuses him forgiveness will be shown,
on the day of God's judgment, his own guilt and the consequences of his attitude (cf., pp. 427-428). Bornkamm sees
"not judging," therefore, as a further explanation of the
disposition of forgiveness.

Only one more verse separates us from 7:7-11, the pericope on perseverance in prayer with which we began this
analysis. Mt 7:6 reads: "Do not give dogs what is holy; and
do not throw pearls before swine, lest they trample them
under foot and turn to attack you." Could the place of this
mysterious, difficult saying (S) also be related to the
sequence of petitions in the Lord's Prayer? If the conclusions above are correct, then, in Bornkamm's opinion, this
is to be expected. He thus suggests that 7:6 be considered a
commentary on the last petition (6:13 as a whole). He
understands very well, however, that this proposal can only

be an attempt to explain both the location and the meaning of this verse. He had not yet stated his proposal in Tübingen. But later, supported by the eminent Church historian, H. von Campenhausen, he worked out this theory in the published version of his address. What are the arguments?

This verse contains a strict prohibition against wasting holy things on unworthy people. In the context of the Sermon on the Mount, "what is holy " must be a comprehensive concept of everything entrusted to the disciples in this sermon and particularly in the Lord's Prayer. "Dogs" and "swine" are metaphors for unworthy Gentiles. In what then is the attitude recommended for the disciples? What does the not throwing away, the preservation of the holy consist? Precisely in that, Bornkamm argues, to which they are called in the beginning of the sermon: "You are the salt of the earth; but if salt has lost its taste, how shall its saltness be restored? It is no longer good for anything except to be thrown out and trodden under foot by men" (5:13). Twice, in 5:13 and 7:6, the disciples are told what horrible consequences their defection would have and what is at stake in their mission. The verbs "throw" and "trod" occur in both places. Christians abandon the holy things to the Gentiles and throw their pearls to be scrambled for when their light darkens and their salt becomes tasteless, when their life does not engender good actions by which the Gentiles glorify God.

Bornkamm now relates this warning to the last petition of the Lord's Prayer: lead us not into temptation, but deliver us from the Evil One. For Christians, he says, their own failure is the great temptation.

c) *Mt 7:7-12*

> 7 Ask, and it will be given you; seek, and you will find; knock, and it will be opened to you.
> 8 For every one who asks receives, and he who seeks finds, and to him who knocks it will be opened.
> 9 Or what man of you, if his son asks him for bread, will give him a stone?

10 Or if he asks for a fish, will give him a serpent?
11 If you then, who are bad, know how to give good gifts
to your children, how much more will your Father who is
in heaven give good things to those who ask him!
12 So whatever you wish that men would do to you, do
so to them; for this is the Law and the Prophets.

The study began with the question of why Matthew, systematic as he is, did not place the pericope of 7:7-11 in the parenesis on prayer of 6:7-15. This question must certainly be asked when one considers that this passage probably stood close to the Lord's Prayer in Matthew's source text (cf. Lk 11:1-13). According to Bornkamm, we now have an answer to this question. Everything that precedes this passage is commentary on the Lord's Prayer: 6:19-24 on the three invocations (6:9-10); 6:25-34 on the first petition (6:11); 7:1-5 on the second (6:12), and 7:6 on the last (6:13). Mt 7:7-11 no longer explains one particular petition but emphasizes the need for perseverance and the certainty that prayers will be heard. Everything from 6:5 to 7:11 is concerned with prayer. Mt 7:7-11 thus is not "in an apparently odd place." At the beginning of this middle part, in 6:8, we read: "for your Father knows what you need before you ask him." At the end, in 7:7-11, Matthew writes: "Ask, and it will be given you ... how much more will your Father who is in heaven give good things to those who ask him!" The agreement between these framing verses is striking.

Before proceeding to a brief evaluation of this remarkable proposal, I would note that Bornkamm says nothing about the connection of 7:12 (the Golden Rule) with 7:7-11. I myself am of the opinion that Matthew wanted to stress again the accompanying condition of authenticity for all prayer to God, namely, the attitude toward one's fellows.

## SHORT EVALUATION

G. Bornkamm concludes his argument as follows. The middle part of the Sermon on the Mount is "in no way a loose conglomeration of disparate sayings, but rather a meaningfully organized whole following the structure of the Lord's Prayer" (p. 430). Can we accept this conclusion? Is Bornkamm's analysis completely convincing?

One ticklish point is his explanation of 7:6. To argue that this verse is truly a comment on "lead us not into temptation. . . " seems somewhat farfetched. In addition, it is not so obvious that Matthew, in 7:1-5, intended to explain the forgiveness petition of the Lord's Prayer. One may justifiably doubt that "judge not, that you be not judged" is a development of "forgiving others to receive God's forgiveness oneself." These two critical observations lead me to hesitate to consider the Lord's Prayer as the structuring principle of Mt 6:19-7:12, and thus I am not inclined to support Bornkamm's conclusions in their entirety.

But this negative evaluation ought not to cause us to lose sight of the many positive qualities of Bornkamm's research. His analysis confirms the finding that the Sermon on the Mount is controlled by the prayer theme. Moreover, Bornkamm has brought out very well the unity of Matthew's conceptual scheme in the Lord's Prayer and in 6:19-34: the Kingdom of God and earthly concerns; bread for today and no anxiety for tomorrow. And it is precisely this problem of prayer for bread and the anxiety-free Christian life that will be treated in the next two sections.

## II. Seeking Righteousness

Matthew introduces 6:1-18 with a warning: "Beware of practicing your righteousness before men in order to be seen by them: for then you will have no reward from your Father who is in heaven." However important this warning is for Matthew, he seems to devote still more attention to three other aspects of Christian prayer: human forgiveness as a condition for God's forgiveness, human faithfulness to God's will (for otherwise all prayer is false display) and human confidence and surrender.

The first aspect, that of forgiveness as a condition, is clearly expressed in the forgiveness petition of the Lord's

Prayer, but Matthew stresses this idea again by means of the double saying in 6:14-15, which he places immediately after the Lord's Prayer. Moreover, he had already spoken about it in 5:23-24, i.e., in the first antithesis. And the call not to judge others in 7:1-5 is also related to forgiveness.

The second aspect, that of doing God's will, is already in the foreground in 5:13-16. Christians must be the salt of the earth and the light of the world. They must be this to such a degree that the Gentiles will glorify God in heaven because of it. I am convinced that Matthew, by placing the Golden Rule (7:12) directly after the exhortation to persevere in prayer (7:7-11) has in mind the same relationship between praying to God and doing good for one's fellow person. Finally, this is very emphatically stressed once again at the end of the Sermon on the Mount. At the judgment, the pathetic prayers of unfaithful Christians — those who mislead, false prophets, workers of unrighteousness — will be fruitless. It will gain them nothing to call: "Lord, Lord, did we not prophesy in your name, and cast out demons in your name, and do many mighty works in your name?" (7:22). This aspect is thus related to the better righteousness of the Christian without which there is no entry into the Kingdom of heaven and all praying becomes meaningless.

The second aspect, albeit in a more veiled manner, is also present in the third, which I have called here human confidence and surrender. However, we may not understand these terms in a passive sense. For Matthew, they imply a conscious and active Christian attitude toward life. This last aspect is the subject with which this section is concerned. More particularly, the question is how Jesus' exhortation to pray for bread is related to his warning about being anxious about food and clothing.

## KINGDOM AND RIGHTEOUSNESS

At the end of his study on the structure of the Sermon on the Mount, G. Bornkamm, like others, states that Matthew indicated the double central theme of Jesus' preaching with two of his favorite terms: the Kingdom of heaven (*basileia tōn ouranōn*) and righteousness (*dikaiosynē*). The first concept expresses God's saving initiative, his free gift to man, and the second God's will, his commands and demands, i.e., the task that each person must carry out in thankfulness. Those who pray the Lord's Prayer ask for the coming of the Kingdom and not to be excluded from it by their sins. Matthew, as pastor, often presumes the gift of the Kingdom and also mentions it now and then, but he still emphasizes the necessity of the human response. This he does clearly in 6:33: seek first God's Kingdom and God's righteousness!

Mt 6:33 is part of a well-defined pericope in the middle of the Sermon on the Mount that warns against earthly concerns: 6:25-34. V. 33 is at the end of the pericope and is no longer a warning but rather a call. There is a double opposition in this pericope. In opposition to anxiety about life, about food and clothing, Jesus sets the search for righteousness. The second opposition is meant for those he is addressing. Jesus does not want his disciples to remain people of little faith, and he also wants them to live differently than the Gentiles, who are only concerned with earthly things.

By "searching," Jesus means an active effort. In the pericope on anxiety two verbs stand in opposition to each other, in Greek, *merimnaō* and *zēteō*. Both indicate "being occupied with," but the first, *merimnao*, is used here in the negative sense in the sense of anxious, excessive concern, of worrying without confidence in God. The second verb, *zēteō* (to seek), has positive overtones in v. 33. In Jesus' command "seek first . . . ", therefore, it is a matter of praiseworthy effort. Through the entire pericope, Jesus warns against a troubled, irreligious anxiety with respect to food and clothing. He states that this anxiety is a Gentile attitude. He justifies his warning with the reference to God's concern for birds and plants, and asks reproachfully if the disciples with such little faith are not of more value than these creatures. Finally, he tells them that their heavenly Father knows that they need all these things. This is Jesus' admonishment. One may not act and live in this way. But how then? Jesus replies: seek first God's Kingdom and his righteousness! Thus, Jesus calls for diligence, for human activity.

In the Sermon on the Mount, the term "righteousness" occurs five times: twice in the beatitudes (5:6 and 10); in 5:20 at the beginning of the antitheses: the greater righteousness; and in 6:1 at the beginning of the warning against ostentation: "Beware of practicing your righteousness before men in order to be seen by them." Finally it occurs once again in 6:33 at the end of the passage on earthly anxiety: "But seek first his Kingdom and his righteousness." Righteousness is a typically Matthean concept. With the verbs "to do" and "to seek" he encourages his readers to practice this better righteousness. Perhaps the Christian suffers, being hungry and thirsty in its absence; perhaps its practice brings persecution. But Jesus paradoxically calls the Christian blessed in such situations. What the study here has made clear is the consciously intended stress that Matthew places on the necessity of Christian commitment as the only appropriate answer to God's salvific initiative. For the pastorally-minded Matthew, this is a matter of ultimate importance, for there will be no salvation at the judgment for those who are negligent and who commit injustice (cf., e.g., 7:21-23; 13:41-42 and 48-50).

## THE PRIORITY TASK

Let us examine the Matthean redaction in 6:32-34 once again (cf. 158-160). In his source text, Matthew probably read: "But seek the Kingdom of God and these things [i.e. food and clothing] will be yours as well" (cf. Lk 12:31).

Several changes are important. First, Matthew writes "seek *first*." I have the impression that he somewhat weakens his source with this "first." The other may also be sought, but one is obliged to pay attention to the priorities. Is not Matthew here harmonizing the radicality of the Q-saying with the bread petition? For in the Lord's Prayer, Jesus teaches us to pray for bread, and such praying already presumes a seeking, thus an active effort. Matthew appar-

ently takes this fact into account in his rewriting of 6:33-34.
Second, Matthew expands the text: not only God's Kingdom, but also *God's righteousness*. He tells us in this way
that the seeking of God's Kingdom includes the seeking of
God's righteousness by means of concrete acts. According
to Matthew, that person who accomplishes the will of God
and obeys his commandments is righteous. God's Kingdom
is primarily eschatological, something that is yet to come.
Nevertheless, God's will can be known and done already on
earth. We are reminded of another addition in the Matthean
Lord's Prayer (literally): "Be done thy will as in heaven so
also on earth." Like righteousness in v. 33, "will" also follows "Kingdom" in the Lord's Prayer. Indeed, righteousness and will are linked to each other. Third, Matthew
added the word "all" to "these things": "and *all* these things
shall be yours as well." He also added a generalizing "all" to
v. 32: "your heavenly Father knows that you need them *all*."
Fourth and finally, Matthew added v. 34: "Therefore do not
be anxious about tomorrow, for tomorrow will be anxious
for itself. Let the day's own trouble be sufficient for the
day." In the Lord's Prayer, the corresponding petition is
"Our bread give us today"; thus, the bread we need for
today. Matthew in his added v. 34 agrees with this, but there
should be no excessive concern about tomorrow!

This explanation of vv. 32-34 clearly indicates what Matthew wants to emphasize. He demands that the effort for
God's Kingdom be given a priority which is experienced in
the concrete by searching for God's righteousness, by thirsting for it, by practicing it, by doing God's will. Not all
exegetes subscribe to this presentation of Matthew's harmonizing and mitigating intention. Some argue that "first"
in v. 33 does not indicate a priority or an order in a sequence
but means "first and foremost, before everything," almost
the same as "exclusively" (cf. Riesenfeld, pp. 49-50). They
find in Matthew no concern for "seeking" for bread, not in
the bread petition (to beg for something from God is not
human seeking) nor in 6:32-34 (the earthly things are simply

given with it; v. 33b). And they consider the stress I would place on the distinction between "today" (the bread petition) and "tomorrow" (6:34) to be forced and not intended by Matthew. The evangelist is concerned in 6:19-34, they argue, only with God's Kingdom and righteousness, and there is no allusion to a permissible and justified concern for today. Although I would not reject this alternative explanation out of hand, I still prefer the other.

## THE LAYING UP OF HEAVENLY TREASURES

Verses 32-34 conclude the passage 6:25-34. The analysis of Matthew's rewriting gives us a better insight into what Matthew has in mind in 6:19-24. At the beginning of the Lord's Prayer stands God's name, God's Kingdom, and God's will in heaven and also on earth. This means, Matthew explains in 6:19-24, that the attachment of the heart and the clarity of the eye must be directed to the wholehearted service of God, not to that of mammon, and that we must lay up treasures in heaven and not on earth. Matthew seems to be wanting to explain to the Christians of little faith that praying is not enough. Praying well implies transcending material worries and earthly anxieties. Praying well includes and active accomplishment of what God desires of us.

## *III. Human Effort*

An entire set of problems is generated by the so-called eschatological character of the Lord's Prayer. Can we still pray for the speedy final arrival of the Kingdom, which would also mean the end of history? Is such a prayer still appropriate for contemporary Christians? And how does the bread prayer function in the life of a Christian who seeks God's Kingdom and God's righteousness? How is the prayer for bread and for the coming of the Kingdom understood by Jesus, by Matthew, and by the modern Christian?

## THE PRAYER FOR BREAD

a) According to the interpretation given in the fourth chapter above, the "our bread" of Mt 6:11, in the sense that *Jesus* intended, is certainly ordinary, material bread, but still the follower of Jesus should not worry about it in view of the coming Kingdom and his or her apostolic task. This is the way Jesus taught his disciples to pray.

b) In addition to the unavoidably hypothetical character of such an interpretation, there is also the question of whether *Matthew*, fifty years later, still understood the bread prayer so eschatologically. The analysis given above leads me to doubt it. Matthew took Jesus' saying about laying up treasures and about not being anxious (6:19-34) into the Sermon on the Mount and placed it very near the Lord's Prayer as his commentary on it. That was my conclusion. To "seek God's Kingdom" he added not only "his righteousness" but also "first." According to Matthew, there is a priority, a gradation: a first and a then. The seeking of the Kingdom of God and the doing of God's righteousness certainly take precedence and must be given priority by the Christian. But apparently, according to Matthew, one may then seek for and be concerned about material bread, but naturally without unchristian anxiety and excessive worry. For Matthew, the prayer for bread is no longer a total shift of this concern onto God. By the adding of "first," therefore, Matthew tempers the eschatological radicality. In a certain sense, he de-eschatologizes the bread prayer.

V. 34, the concluding verse that Matthew adds, also leads in this same direction: "Therefore do not be anxious about tomorrow, for tomorrow will be anxious for itself. Let the day's own trouble be sufficient for the day." Praying for bread for today is recommended in the Lord's Prayer; here anxiety for tomorrow is rejected. Matthew sees no contradiction between them. On the contrary, they complement each other.

c) The application today must go still further with the de-eschatologization process that is already visible in Matthew's gospel. For Matthew, the terms "today" and "tomorrow," although they are probably not to be taken strictly literally as 24-hour periods, are still real time indications. Consequently, they leave little or no room for long-term planning. The *contemporary Christian* has a different and more adequate vision of history, its duration and evolution, and of the secular human vocation. For him, therefore, the prayer for bread for today and Jesus' warning against excessive concern certainly remain applicable, but still they must neither inhibit being occupied with the future of the world nor prevent planned effort for its improvement. This has not made this prayer any easier for the modern Christian. He or she will have to succeed in combining unflagging confidence in God's providence with serious and loyal work for a better society. But, in the earthly task, the Christian may never lose sight of the priority of the search for the Kingdom of God.

## THE COMING OF THE KINGDOM

a) The original Lord's Prayer contained two invocations at the beginning: "hallowed be thy name; come thy Kingdom." The verb-noun structure and the thought are parallel. In the opinion of most exegetes, *Jesus* taught his disciples to pray for the coming of the Kingdom and the definitive, public hallowing of God's name at the end of time. They must ask God for it. Only he can bring it about. Moreover, they must ask God to hasten the eschatological breakthrough, for they are convinced that the time is fulfilled and the Kingdom of God is near. Jesus of Nazareth began his public life with this announcement.

The Christians of today no longer live in the tense atmosphere of expectation of an imminent end (*Naherwartung*) and eschatological hope. How should they then pray "come thy Kingdom"? Has not the better exegesis that made possible the discovery of the echatological dimension of Jesus' message become a hindrance to the actual praying of the Lord's Prayer? Does Matthew provide us with any help here?

b) In 6:33, Matthew writes: "Seek first his Kingdom and his righteousness." Seeking, thirsting for righteousness is, according to *Matthew*, as we have seen, the doing of God's will, the keeping of what God has commanded. The righteousness of the Christian must exceed that of the scribes and the Pharisees (5:20); it may not be practiced in order to win human approval (6:1).

It strikes me as something special that this same Matthew, who added "righteousness" in 6:33, also formulated a third invocation to follow the first two in his version of the Lord's Prayer: "Be done thy will as in heaven so also on earth." It is not necessary to argue that it was certainly Matthew who created this third invocation, for it is possible that it already existed in Matthew's church community. We do not know for certain, but it seems to me that the parallelism between the succession of Kingdom and will in the Lord's Prayer and that of Kingdom and righteousness in 6:33 is not a matter of chance. I think that Matthew has the Christian express submission and readiness to obey by means of this added invocation (cf. Jesus in 26:42). The first two invocations thereby become less eschatological (the fulfillment is shifted from the end-time) and less theological (it is not only God who acts).

This perception is confirmed by the conclusions arrived at above regarding 6:33. With the expression "seek his Kingdom and his righteousness," Matthew intends the complete human effort, moral and religious, to do God's will on earth. This is the characteristic pastoral encouragement with which Matthew interlaces his gospel.

c) The *contemporary Christian* does well to continue with actualization in Matthew's manner. When we pray "come thy Kingdom," then our prayer asks not so much the hastening of the end of the world, the great day of parousia and judgment. We rightly ask that God's dominion on earth become, now already, more and more a reality. And like Matthew, we do not exclude the eschaton from this invocation. Although we do not know the time of that end, we know all too well that God's judgment awaits us, not only at some undetermined point in the far-distant future, but already at the end of our mortal life. Like Matthew and in fact like Jesus himself, we realize that there is a link between this future of salvation or failure and the quality of our life on earth. The entry into the Kingdom of God — God's supreme gift — is also a task for the individual person. Matthew, moved by his pastoral concern, has strongly emphasized this second aspect. And this Matthean call appeals to modern man.

When people maintain the double command of love of God and love of neighbor, when they do to others as they would have others do to them, when Christians strive for a greater righteousness by doing such things as renouncing retaliation and revenge and even by loving enemies and praying for their persecutors, then they are the children of God, then they will certainly enter the Kingdom of heaven, and then the Kingdom of God has already come. The Christians of today in no way exclude the future coming of the Kingdom, but when they pray, "come thy Kingdom," they may rightly ask for God's grace and help so that they themselves, their relatives and friends, and the entire human family will find the courage to hasten, with their moral and religious effort, the coming of God's dominion to this world.

## ORDINARY LIFE

If we, following Jesus, must pray again each day for bread ("give to us today!"), then we must pray each day also for the coming of the Kingdom. The Talmud tells how the disciples of Rabbi Simeon ben Johai (ca. 150 A.D.) asked him why the manna did not fall from heaven all at once instead of every day. Like many rabbis, Simeon answered with a parable. An earthly king had a son, and he gave him the food he needed once a year. This son only came once a year to greet his father in gratitude. The father decided to give him what he needed every day, and the son then greeted his father every day. We pray for bread, we pray for the coming of the Kingdom. We devote ourselves to our earthly tasks, we work for the establishment of God's Kingdom now already on earth, tangible and visible. Maybe Jesus taught his disciples to pray the Lord's Prayer every day so that they would remain conscious of their creatureliness and realize that all their worrying and toiling cannot force God's grace and can never replace God's blessing.

We come now to the conclusion of this section. The reconciliation that Matthew accomplished between concern, worry, toil, the labor of every day "for bread," often "by the sweat of one's brow" *and* the seeking for God's Kingdom and God's righteousness is, for us, very welcome. He condemns neither of the two concerns; rather he orders them with a "first" and a "then." He clearly assigns priority to the seeking of God's Kingdom and righteousness, but he seems to leave room for many other cares. Two conclusions are now in order.

The first is one of reassurance. Most Christians should be convinced that they need not give up their profane efforts. The Kingdom of God and God's righteousness do not demand that everyone literally abandon his fish nets, sell all his property, and follow Jesus. The collaboration in the task of creation, both for what concerns one's own person, family, and community as well as for technology and progress, leisure and culture, production and consumption, is and remains a noble task, meaningful and worthy, very much from the point of view of a Christian. But this reassurance may not lull the Christian to sleep. The second conclusion emphasizes the priority call: seek *first*. . . God has priority. It would be naive to want to suppress this call. Property and luxury, and certainly the materialism of our consumer society so easily suffocate our deeper questions. Therefore, God's righteousness must be preached in season and out of season: God's name, God's Kingdom, God's will — these take first place in the thoughts and the striving of the Christian.

In Mt 6:25-34, there is certainly a distinction between earthly concerns and the righteousness of God. Matthew brings these two opposing poles together in a "seek first. . . " but they still remain apart. These are my two conclusions: Matthew issues a reassurance and a warning. But many are presumably still uncomfortable. One can theoretically separate the poles and oppose them, but in the real life of the Christian the question arises how, in the concrete, this righteousness must be sought first.

At the end of the eschatological sermon is the pericope on the last judgment (Mt 25:31-46). The king concludes his judgment with the pronouncement: "And they [those without love] will go away into eternal punishment, but the righteous into eternal life" (v. 46). Why are the latter "righteous"? The parable provides the explanation: everything they did for one of the least of the brothers of the King, they did to the King himself! Feeding the hungry, giving drink to the thirsty, welcoming strangers, clothing the naked, visiting the sick, and going to those in prison: this is being righteous. Our love or lack of love is not a matter of indifference to God. God himself is affected by it!

When we hear such texts, we are moved to think further. Do the two areas distinguished above not largely overlap, at least materially, as far as the work itself is concerned? Do they not continuously and of themselves flow into each other? Everywhere, in one's work and contact, one encounters one's neighbor; everywhere the Christian is called to the greater righteousness in his concrete existence and not in a vacuum. It is thus possible in ordinary life, not only on Sundays but also during the week, at work and in the community, in the family and in one's social intercourse, to be righteous and just. It is not only possible, it is also a Christian duty, for it will happen nowhere except in the concrete. The greater righteousness is present in "profane" existence. The seeking first of the Kingdom does not lead away from life. Instead, it orders it, transforms that life and gives it a specific Christian style, motivates and inspires it, makes it truly worth living, fruitful, and worthy.

## IV. Righteousness and Love of Neighbor

In the first three sections of this chapter, our attention was focused primarily on the close relationship between the Lord's Prayer and 6:19-7:12. More specifically, I asked how

Jesus' call to freedom from anxiety must be understood. The Matthean rewriting of a few Q-sentences that resulted in 6:32-34 was discussed in detail. But 6:19-7:12 is a long passage, and its unity is not immediately obvious. Indeed, it is uncertain whether Matthew really did intend this text to be one well-structured whole. Even Bornkamm's attempt to show this on the basis of the Lord's Prayer is not, I think, wholly successful. Let us now re-read the passage one last time, and I will explain some details, giving particular attention to Matthew's train of thought.

## SERVING GOD ALONE (6:19-24)

In 6:19-24, Matthew expands on information from 6:1-18: acting for God; reward in heaven. Still there is a shift. Matthew is no longer thinking here about display and the practice of righteousness to be seen by others. The danger discussed in this pericope is money, possessions, earthly treasures.

Matthew has assembled his material from various Q-contexts. The content of the last saying on the impossibility of serving two masters at the same time (v. 24: "hate" and "love" are here typical Semitic exaggerations, compare 10:37, "love more," with Lk 14:26, "not hate") fits quite well with vv. 19-21, which are concerned with gathering two kinds of treasure. In vv. 19-21, Matthew seems to have preserved the Q-source better than Luke. Moth and rust are images that make clear that earthly treasures are transitory. V. 20 repeats v. 19 in the same detailed descriptive style; only v. 20 is a positive command, while v. 19 was a prohibition. "For where your treasure is, there will your heart be also" (v. 21) provides at the end a motivation of prohibition and command. It would probably not be an exaggeration to state that in v. 21 Jesus is not only arguing that the heavenly treasure is the only one that is important — for there our hearts must be — but is also suggesting that being busy with something and toiling for it creates "heart" and love for it. The "treasures in heaven" are, according to the Matthean Jesus, certainly the fruit of good works (chapter 6) and acts of righteousness (chapter 5) that he has been continually referring to up to this point in the Sermon on the Mount.

The metaphorical sayings about the lamp, eye and light (vv. 22-23) are somewhat surprising. Most probably, v. 21 ("heart") led Matthew to place these verses about the "eye" here. By "eye", presumably, is meant here not so much a lamp inside the body that shines out, but a lamp and light *for* that body. In Mt, these sayings explain v. 21 further. Originally, Jesus had startled his Jewish listeners with such words: "But you are blind; you do not see what is happening; you do not understand the signs of the times." In the Matthean Sermon on the Mount, the meaning is changed. To determine this meaning, it is better not to proceed from "unsound eye" (v. 23), by which the Jews meant jealousy and envy. For in this sermon, vv. 22-23 are framed by sayings about possessions and money, and this middle part also contains a warning against greed. The eye of man must be clear, lighted, and illuminating, completely focused on God. Then will the heart also be able to abide by the true treasure.

In v. 22, what is translated by "sound" is the Greek *haplous* (simple), a term that may probably be related to "clear, perfect, undivided." One would expect *diplous* (two-fold) in v. 23 instead of *poneros* (= bad, not sound). In the following v. 24 (two masters!), Matthew presumably has this term in mind.

## FIRST THE KINGDOM AND RIGHTEOUSNESS (6:25-34)

G. Schneider, not inaptly, calls the Kingdom of God the remote goal and God's righteousness the proximate goal: *Fernziel-Nahziel.* But is not the Kingdom rather simply the final objective with righteousness being the way that leads to it (cf. Giesen, p. 176)? Matthew has added his favorite concept of righteousness at the end of 6:25-34; he states that one seeks the Kingdom of God in the concrete by practicing righteousness. I have had occasion to discuss this point at length in this chapter.

In Q, the pericope on the gathering of treasures (Mt 6:19-21; cf. Lk 12:33-34) most probably stood not before but after the passage on anxiety. Matthew altered the sequence and adds v. 25 with *dia touto legō hymin* ("therefore I tell you) as a consequence of 6:24: because Christians may serve the Lord God, *therefore Jesus says to them* "do not be anxious about your life." There is a shift in meaning: from the gathering of treasures to not being anxious about what is necessary for the body. In this first verse of the new pericope the dual theme of this anxiety already occurs: food and clothing. By means of comparisons cast in an *a fortiori* argument, this is worked out: first food and the birds (vv. 26-27), then clothing and the lilies of the field (vv. 28-30). Twice reference is made to the higher value of life itself and to the Christians as people. V. 31 forms a clear inclusion with v. 25; v. 32 adds a double reason for not being anxious: the behavior of the Gentiles, which is not to be imitated, and God's providential omniscience.

Vv. 25-32 are negative: do not be anxious; v. 33 is their positive counterpart: seek first God's Kingdom and God's righteousness. With v. 34, Matthew (not Q!) repeats the exhortation of vv. 25 and 31, but in place of food and clothing there now stands: "for tomorrow," a time indication that is somewhat surprising.

In 6:19-24 as in 6:25-34, Jesus, with his prohibitions and commands, intends that Christians do not become closed and imprisoned in themselves. To serve God alone, to seek first his Kingdom and his righteousness: what does this imply? Is this not all rather vague? But although helping one's neighbor is not explicitly mentioned in these two pericopes, the reader knows from Mt 5 and 6 that Matthew has it clearly in mind.

## THE NEIGHBOR (7:1-12)

"Judge not" in 7:1 forms a new beginning in the Sermon. Here Matthew is expressly concerned with the neighbor. When we compare 7:1-2 with the presumed Q-source (see Lk 6:37-38), we may well be surprised at Matthew's abridgment. V. 2a is now modeled after v. 2b (= Lk 6:38c): "For with the judgment you pronounce you will be judged, and the measure you give will be the measure you get back." The hyperbolic saying of vv. 3-5 has been taken over almost literally from Q (cf. Lk 6:41-42).

Did Matthew intend 7:1-12 to be a unit? If we can state that all of the parts are concerned with the neighbor, then this impression of unity would be reinforced. There are no difficulties with 7:1-5. Most exegetes are of the opinion that the Matthean Jesus in 7:6 is warning against imprudent haste in the conversion of Gentiles. And in the Golden Rule of 7:12, the love of neighbor is obviously central. But what about 7:7-11? Some would say that here one must pray with perseverance for the "good gifts" (v. 11) of the conversion of the Gentiles. But, unfortunately, this must remain uncertain, even though 7:7-11 is framed by texts concerned with the neighbor. The term "brother" in 7:1-5 makes it doubtful that Matthew has non-Christians in mind, as he probably does in v. 6 and also perhaps in v. 12. As regards v. 6, need we, according to Matthew, take "dogs" as a specific reference to the Gentiles, and does "swine" refer to the Romans, or did the evangelist intend them to be vaguer metaphors for all recalcitrant and unworthy unbelievers? The latter seems more probable.

The construction of the small unit 7:7-11 must be considered carefully. "Seeking" and "knocking" in vv. 7-8 means intensified asking or praying. In vv. 9-11 we meet, as we do so often in 6:19-7:12, the interrogatory form and an exclamation. The manner of reasoning is again *a fortiori*: human father — heavenly Father. The conclusion of v. 11 is unexpected. After vv. 9-10, the reader must conclude that God, too, will not give anything bad to his children: if the earthly father does not do this, how much less would God do it? But in v. 11 stands "how much more." Besides, v. 11 uses the second person and stresses the bad-good opposition in an almost emotional way: "If you then, who are bad, know how to give good gifts to your children, how much more will your Father who is in heaven give good things to those who ask him!" The "good things" are, of course, the bread of the bread petition, but also much more: everything that is asked for in the Lord's Prayer and, still more broadly, all that which the Sermon on the Mount is concerned with.

"So whatever you wish that men would do to you, do so to them" (v. 12ab) was known in non-Christian wisdom circles, generally in a negative formulation. However, we must clearly understand that 7:12 is not at all concerned with reciprocity: doing good or evil just as others do it to us. What we wish that men do to us is certainly good, not evil, and it need not yet have happened! Matthew allows no limitations: cf. "*whatever*" and "do *so* to them." He certainly has love of neighbor in mind. For in Q, his source, this call stood before the command to love one's enemy (cf. the reconstruction on pp. 104-105), and Matthew's addition of "for this is the Law and the Prophets" (v. 12c) anticipates the same expression that he also inserted in the pericope on the greatest commandment (22:34-40): the entire Law and the Prophets depend on these two commandments, love of God and love of neighbor.

With 7:12 Matthew concludes a large part — sometimes this part is considered to be 5:17-7:11! — of the Sermon on the Mount as indicated by the adverb *oun* (consequently, so). Matthew must have seen 7:1-11 as relevant to the love of neighbor, notwithstanding the vagueness of some of its parts.

Do the three parts of Mt 6:19-7:12 form a conceptual whole? A closed, strictly logical line of reasoning can hardly be identified here. Still, Matthew, with his emphasis on the Kingdom and righteousness, with his linking of submission without anxiety and serious effort to confidence in God and love of neighbor, has certainly created a thematic unit. A reading of 6:19-7:12 cannot leave the contemporary Christian unperturbed.

## Bibliography

See also the general literature cited on pp. 41-44 above.

Betz, H. D., "Matthew VI. 22f. and Ancient Greek Theories of Vision," in: E. Best and R. McL. Wilson (eds.), *Text and Interpretation. Fs. M. Black*, Cambridge, 1979, pp. 43-56.

Bornkamm, "Aufbau" (see p. 42 above).

Catchpole, D., "The Ravens, the Lilies and the Q Hypothesis. A Form-Critical Perspective on the Source-Critical Problem," in: A. Fuchs (ed.), *Stud. N. T. Umwelt* A 6-7, Linz, 1981-82, pp. 77-87.

Fensham, F. C., "The Good and Evil Eye in the Sermon on the Mount," *Neotest.* 1 (1967) 51-58.

Groenewald, E. P., "God and Mammon," *Neotest.* 1 (1967) 59-66.

Hendry, G. S., "Judge Not: A Critical Test of Faith," *Theology Today* 40 (1983) 113-129.

Hickling, "Motives" (see p. 43 above).

Hoffmann, "Dienst" (see p. 150 above).

Olsthoorn, M. F., *The Jewish Background and the Synoptic Setting of Mt 6,25-33 and Lk 12,22-31* (Studium Biblicum Franciscanum. Analecta 10), Jerusalem, 1975.

Riesenfeld, H., "Vom Schätzesammeln und Sorgen — ein Thema urchristlicher Paränese. Zu Mt vi 19-24," in: *Neotestamentica et Patristica. Fs. O. Cullmann* (Suppl. Nov. Test. 6), Leiden, 1962, pp. 47-58.

Strecker, G., "Compliance — Love of One's Enemy — The Golden Rule," *Austr. Bibl. Rev.* 29 (1981) 38-46.

Zeller, *Mahnsprüche* (see p. 127 above).

# Chapter Six

# THE WAY TO LIFE
# (Mt 7:13-27)

"Humanly speaking, we could understand and interpret the Sermon on the Mount in a thousand different ways. Jesus knows only one possibility: simple surrender and obedience, not interpreting it or applying it, but doing and obeying it. That is the only way to hear his word. But again he does not mean that it is to be discussed as an ideal, he really means us to get on with it" (D. Bonhoeffer, *The Cost of Discipleship*, p. 175).

Whoever accepts, as I do, that Mt 7:12 (the Golden Rule) is part of an inclusion and thus rounds off a textual unit (5:17-7:12), must also see 7:13 as a new beginning, although the evangelist has hardly made this structurally obvious. I will argue in this chapter that 7:13-27 forms a unit and is the concluding part of the Matthean Sermon on the Mount. Elsewhere in this sermon, Matthew introduced many redactional and compositional changes. Likewise in this epilogue, he inserts a number of ethical exhortations and pieces of advice. He writes christologically in 7:21-23 ("Lord, Lord..."; Jesus is the judge), and he ends his sermon eschatologically, like many other addresses in his gospel; the prospect is the inevitable judgment. He also accuses certain Christians, so a polemical tone is not absent. In the New Testament there are few other passages in which the need for orthopraxis, for acting justly, comes so explicitly to the fore.

Matthew the pastor is aware of a danger within the Church: the actions of some Christians no longer correspond to Christian doctrine, confession, and status. This danger is present at all times and confronts every Christian. Matthew's exhortation remains very relevant to us! The epilogue of the Sermon on the Mount leaves the honest Christian no room for complacency.

The Q-sermon also ended with this warning, as Luke gives witness (see 6:43-49). But Matthew has considerably expanded and rewritten it. As in the three previous chapters, the discussion of the Lucan parallels will be postponed. Thus, our attention will again be primarily focused on the Matthean Jesus. I will begin with the study of the structure and the train of thought. In the following sections, the separate units, first 7:15-20, 21-23 and then 7:13-14, 24-27, will be examined. The last section, a review of the entire Sermon on the Mount, will be devoted to more general questions regarding Matthew's concept of the Law and the pertinence of the message contained in his Sermon on the Mount.

## I. Structure and Train of Thought

For this first part, I will be gratefully using the recent study of A. Denaux, *Der Spruch von den zwei Wegen im Rahmen des Epilogs der Bergpredigt*. The text of Mt 7:13-27 is given first. Matthew uses four adjectives in 7:16-19 (and 12:33-35): good (*agathos*) and bad (*ponēros*), beautiful (*kalos*) and "sick" (*sapros* = decayed, moldy, spoiled, rotten). These four terms will be used in this literal translation:

> 13 Enter by the narrow gate; for the gate is wide and the way is easy, that leads to destruction, and those who enter by it are many.
> 14 How (RSV: For) narrow is the gate and hard the way that leads to life, and those who find it are few!
>
> 15 Beware of false prophets, who come to you in sheep's clothing but inwardly are ravenous wolves.

16 You will know them by their fruits. Are grapes gathered from thorns, or figs from thistles?

17 So, every good tree bears beautiful fruits, but the sick tree bears bad fruits (RSV: evil fruit).

18 A good tree cannot bear bad fruits, nor can a sick tree bear beautiful fruits.

19 Every tree that does not bear beautiful fruits is cut down and thrown into the fire.

20 Thus you will know them by their fruits.

21 Not every one who says to me "Lord, Lord," shall enter the Kingdom of heaven, but he who does the will of my Father in heaven.

22 On that day, many will say to me, "Lord, Lord, did we not prophesy in your name, and cast out demons in your name, and do many mighty works in your name?"

23 And then will I declare to them, "I never knew you; depart from me, you evildoers."

24 Every one then who hears these words of mine and does them will be like a wise man who built his house upon the rock;

25 and the rain fell, and the floods came, and the winds blew and beat upon that house, but it did not fall, because it had been founded on the rock.

26 And every one who hears these words of mine and does not do them will be like a foolish man who built his house upon the sand;

27 and the rain fell, and the floods came, and the winds blew and beat against that house, and it fell; and great was the fall of it.

## THE FOUR UNITS

On the basis of content and structure, four parts can be distinguished in the passage Mt 7:13-27: vv. 13-14, vv. 15-20, vv. 21-23, and vv. 24-27. In vv. 13-14 are the images of the gate and the way. In vv. 15-20, there are the false prophets, who are compared to the sick tree that bears bad fruits. Vv. 21-23 deal with the many who, at the judgment, will call upon the Lord but who during their lives have committed evil. Finally, in vv. 24-27 we bring, the double parable of the house on the rock and the house on the sand. In each of the four units, therefore, there is a very specific subject.

The repetitions within the units, often antithetical-symmetrical, confirm their relative independence each from the other. The inclusion of vv. 16a and 20 performs this role for the second pericope; twice we encounter the framing sentence: "You will know them by their fruits." Every part has its own striking beginning: an imperative in v. 13 ("enter") and v. 15 ("beware") and a generalizing introduction in v. 21 ("Not every one who says to me") and in v. 24 ("Every one then who hears these words of mine").

The source texts Matthew used confirm this division:

vv. 13-14; cf. Lk 13:23-24;
vv. 15-20; cf. Lk 6:43-44;
vv. 21-23; cf. Lk 6:46 and 13:25-27;
vv. 24-27; cf. Lk 6:47-49

Matthew proceeds to another source for each new unit. The third unit is an exception. At the end of the second, Matthew has omitted a verse from Q (cf. Lk 6:45). At the beginning of his third unit, he uses the following verse, which in Q probably functioned as the introduction to the parable of the house (cf. Lk 6:46-49), but then he jumps back to the Q-context from which he has already borrowed the first unit (cf. Lk 13:23-27). Therefore, this exception does not threaten the division proposed above.

## A CONCENTRIC STRUCTURE?

Notwithstanding the clearly distinct subjects, the four units are not unrelated to each other. There is a conceptual coherence. The first impression one receives is that the first and second pericopes are parallel to each other, as are the third and fourth. The pericopes of vv. 13-14 and vv. 15-20 both begin with an imperative ("enter" in v. 13, and "beware" in v. 15) and they are both concerned with what happens during this life: one follows the hard or the easy way; one produces, like a tree, beautiful or bad fruits. In the pericopes of vv. 21-23 and 24-27, however, the end time and the judgment are in the foreground (cf. "will be like" in vv. 24 and 26, future tense!), and these parts, too, have very similar beginnings: "not every one": v. 21 (*ou pas*) and "every one": v. 24 (*pas*).

Nevertheless, another point of view is preferable. The people discussed in vv. 21-23 are most probably the same as those of vv. 15-20: the false prophets. The "not every one" in v. 21 is taken up by "many" in v. 22, and the reference in this verse is to their previous charismatic activities. The "prophets" are also mentioned here, reminding the reader of the false prophets of vv. 15-20. Moreover, the evil that many did (v. 23) is indicated in the preceding pericope by the metaphor of "bad fruits" (vv. 17 and 18), and the words of rejection in v. 23 ("depart from me") express the same thing as the metaphor of v. 19: the tree is cut down and thrown into the fire. In the entire middle part of vv. 15-20, 21-23, the Matthean Jesus thus has one group of people in mind, the false prophets. The category of people referred to in vv. 13-14 and vv. 24-27 is broader: all Christians, or better, everybody to whom the Sermon on the Mount is addressed.

In the light of these considerations, I would prefer, with Denaux, a cyclic structure:

*a*    vv. 13-14:    everybody
*b*    vv. 15-20:    false prophets
*b'*   vv. 21-23:    false prophets
*a'*   vv. 24-27:    everybody

First, the entire public is addressed in *a*, and then the false prophets are mentioned in *b*; each time, Jesus refers to a present situation, to what is done in this life by people. What follows is joined chiastically: first the *b'* part is concerned with false prophets, and the *a'* part then with all the listeners, and each time Matthew describes what will happen at the future judgment; not the people, but Christ and God will have the final word.

However, the parallelism between *a* and *b* on the one hand and between *b'* and *a'* on the other is also apparent and contributes to the coherence of the entire passage.

Moreover, this coherence is more than formal. The idea of the judgment is already present in *a* and *b*: see "destruction" and "life" in vv. 13 and 14 and the entire v. 19. In the same way, in *b'* and *a'*, we are referred back to the present: the evil (v. 23) and the building of the house (vv. 24 and 26) took place before the end, during one's earthly life. In addition, one must not lose sight of the fact that the whole of 7:13-27 is directed to the same persons (disciples and people) to encourage and inform them. Finally, the concluding "then" (*oun*) with which the last unit begins (v. 24) indicates that the textual whole has reached its conclusion.

## THE CONTENT

I will limit myself here to a global review of the principal ideas. There is no doubt that one of the thematic terms in this passage is the verb *poieō* (= to do, to bear), for it occurs nine times: see vv. 17(2x), 18(2x), 19, 21, 24, and 26. At the end of his programmatic sermon, the Matthean Jesus stresses the doing of God's will as he has just finished explaining it.

In the first pericope, the entry through the narrow gate and the finding of the hard way is nothing other than the doing of God's will. Most people choose the wide gate and the easy way, but this leads to destruction and not to life.

Initially, particularly after the reading of v. 15, one has the impression that the theme of the second pericope is the dangerous, concealed greed of the false prophets. But the comparison with the two kinds of trees and the two kinds of fruit teaches us that here, too, the actual subject is good actions. Again, two groups are set in opposition to each other: in this pericope the true and the false prophets. The outcome, i.e., the judgment, is also mentioned: see v. 19. What is new over against the first unit is the opposition between outer and inner, which implies that, in the beginning, the true nature of the false prophets is unrecognizable: one must consider their deeds in making a judgment, for only by their fruits will they be known (cf. vv. 16a, 20).

In the third pericope, the subject is directly stated for the first time without imagery: the doing of the will of the heavenly Father. Here, too, there is an opposition between those who do the will of the Father and those who do evil, with the stress being on the condemnation of the latter. Again, there is something new here, a shift in the train of thought. Not only is there the initial unrecognizability of the false prophets ("in sheep's clothing," v. 15) as in the previous unit, but there is also the opposition between their confession and prophetic activity on the one hand and the doing of evil on the other. This dissonance between doctrine and life will be the cause of the great disappointment at the end.

The same dissonance (now between hearing and doing) is present in the fourth pericope as a threat and a warning. There is also the distinction between the two groups and the causal relationship between life now and the judgment later.

The Matthean Jesus exhorts his disciples and all his hearers in this long concluding part. He calls them to think about their end, warns them about false prophets, and gives the criterion with which to judge them. Obviously, Jesus takes his own words extremely seriously ("these words of mine," vv. 24 and 26). He wants the deed to match the word, i.e., to match the Christian confession and the charisms, to match what it means to be Christian; he wants orthopraxis. And he threatens with the judgment: the Matthean Jesus refers to the coming judgment at the end of each of the five great sermons; the eschatological emphasis in 7:13-27 also appears in 10:40-42, 13:47-50, 18:23-35, and 25:31-46.

## II. The Pseudo-Prophets Among the Christians

Now that we have determined and surveyed Matthew's structure and train of thought, we must investigate in detail the way in which Matthew has composed this passage. For he has rewritten his source texts and ordered them in a new whole. First, the middle part: 7:15-20, 21-23 (*b* and *b'*).

## A MATTHEAN DOUBLET

Matthew uses the parable of the tree and its fruit again in the Beelzebul discussion in 12:33-37. The parallel parts of the two texts are juxtaposed.

| *Mt 7* | | *Mt 12* | |
|---|---|---|---|
| 18a | A good tree cannot bear bad fruits | 33a | Either make the tree beautiful, and its fruit beautiful; |
| 18b | nor can a sick tree bear beautiful fruits. | 33b | or make the tree sick, and its fruit sick; |
| 20 | Thus you will know them by their fruits. | 33c | for the tree is known by its fruit. |

In 12:34-37, we read further:

> 34 You brood of vipers! how can you speak good when you are bad? For out of the abundance of the heart the mouth speaks.

> 35 The good man out of his good treasure brings forth good, and the bad man out of his bad treasure brings forth bad things.

> 36 I tell you, on the day of judgment men will render account for every careless word they utter;

> 37 for by your words you will be justified, and by your words you will be condemned.

By comparing Mt 7:16-20 and 12:33-37 with Lk 6:43-45, we can reconstruct the following hypothetical Q-text (the numbering of the Lucan verses is used):

> 43 For no beautiful tree bears sick fruit, nor again does a sick tree bring forth beautiful fruit;

> 44 for each tree is known by its fruit. Are figs gathered from thorns, and grapes picked from a bramble bush?

45 The good man out of the good treasure produces good,
and the bad man out of his bad treasure produces bad
things; for out of the abundance of the heart his mouth
speaks.

Luke has preserved the Q-order of these sayings. Already in
Q the parable of the tree and the fruit is applied to the heart
and the mouth, i.e., to the connection between what a
person is in his inner essence and the words that he speaks.
This appears clearly from v. 45 of Q. The great differences
between the two Matthean versions are astonishing, both
with respect to each other and with respect to the Q-version.
Is the evangelist responsible for this?

### Mt 12:33-37

By placing these verses at the end of the Beelzebul discussion (Mt 12:24-37), Matthew relates Q-verse 45 to the Pharisees' accusation of sinfulness: "It is only by Beelzebul, the
prince of demons, that this man casts out demons" (12:24).
Jesus defends himself in vv. 25-37 against the Pharisees and
directs his apologia to them, which requires a number of
modifications because of this new context. I will use here the
results of a previous study.

(1) In Q the subject is a tree that either does or does not
"make" fruit. This verb also occurs in Mt 12:33, but here
Matthew uses the imperative, second person plural: the
same people are addressed as in the preceding verses (cf. v.
31: "Therefore I tell *you*"). In addition, both the construction of the sentence and the meaning of the verb have been
modified. The first part in Q (v. 43a) reads: "For no beautiful tree 'makes' sick fruit." Matthew writes: " 'Make' the tree
beautiful [in the sense of consider it beautiful] and its fruit
good." This meaning of "make = consider" only occurs here
in Mt and appears strange. It concerns the making of a
judgment, so there must be an identity between the judgment of the tree and that of its fruit. The comparison to the

tree and its fruit illustrates in this context Jesus' reproach. The Pharisees see that the fruit of his actions (casting out of demons) is good, and still they maintain that he acts by means of evil (by Beelzebul), that he is evil (12:22-24). These modifications of the Q-text are best ascribed to Matthew.

(2) The adaptation of v. 33 to the Beelzebul context, however, generates a tension in vv. 33-35. V. 33, with its beautiful tree and beautiful fruit, must be related to Jesus. He is the one who must be judged and about whom the Pharisees have, in fact, pronounced an erroneous judgment. Now if need be, one can advocate the same application in v. 35a: "The good man out of his good treasure brings forth good." But from the inserted v. 34a, "You brood of vipers! how can you speak good, when you are bad?", it is clear that in chapter 12 Matthew specifically has in mind the words and the accusation of the Pharisees: the intentional misinterpretation by the Pharisees of the casting out of demons is a result of their inner disposition. The almost silent shift of meaning after v. 33 is best explained as a consequence of a Matthean secondary insertion and of his reinterpretation of the source text.

(3) Still more changes have been made, apparently in view of the new context. In the immediately preceding verses, 31-32, we read: "Therefore I tell you, every sin and blasphemy will be forgiven men, but the blasphemy against the Spirit will not be forgiven. And whoever speaks against the Son of Man will be forgiven; but whoever speaks against the Holy Spirit will not be forgiven, either in this age or in the age to come." The great stress on speaking in vv. 34-37 is related to these verses. Further, the "being forgiven" in vv. 31-32 will take place on the day of judgment; the eschatological tone is clearly heard in the concluding phrase of v. 32: "either in this age or in the age to come." Since the emphasis on the judgment comes to the fore precisely in the verses added by Matthew, vv. 36-37, we focus here, too, primarily on Matthew's conscious redaction.

(4) Matthew takes the address "brood of vipers" in v. 34

from the preaching of the Baptist (3:7, cf. also 23:33). The phrase "when you are bad" occurs also in 7:11 (the Sermon on the Mount!). Matthew changed the order of v. 45 in Q: v. 45c is placed at the beginning of the pericope, in 12:34b, immediately after "Brood of vipers! how can you speak good, when you are bad?" Matthew does not include vv. 43-44 of Q in chapter 12.

Detailed vocabulary and style studies have also shown that the differences with Q were most probably introduced by Matthew. In the light of all these considerations, I can only conclude that the Q-text of the Beelzebul discussion did not have vv. 33-37 of Mt 12. Matthew has inserted them, and they are from a passage from the Q-Sermon on the Mount. The redactor rewrote, omitted a part, and also expanded with a phrase from the preaching of the Baptist and with words and ideas from the context. He strongly emphasized the account that one will have to give on the day of judgment for the words one has spoken. All of this is directly applied to the accusing Pharisees as a reproach..

## Mt 7:15-20

Even where Matthew has preserved the Q-context of the Sermon on the Mount for the parable of the tree and the fruit, he changed the Q-text considerably.

(1) Matthew himself created 7:15 and with this expansion of the text showed how he wanted to have the rest of the pericope understood. The study of the vocabulary and the theological motifs could reinforce this position (see also 23:25-28 with partially the same words and ideas). Other Matthean expansions are v. 17 (an anticipation of v. 18) and v. 20 (a repetition of v. 16a, so that vv. 16b-19 are framed by this inclusion). On the basis of v. 45 (Q), Matthew applies the adjectives "good" and "bad" (in addition to "beautiful" and "sick") to the tree and the fruit, which adjectives are used in Q only for people.

(2) The major change is that Matthew, unlike Q and his own chapter 12, does not apply the parable of the tree and

the fruit to words but to deeds. The deeds of the false prophets are in the foreground (note the plural "fruits" in vv. 16-18 and 20).

The three following changes can be compared with what the evangelist did in 12:33-37. (3) As in chapter 12, Matthew here too omits a part of Q, namely v. 45 of Q. (4) And also as in chapter 12, Matthew takes an element from the preaching of the Baptist, v. 19: "Each tree that does not bear beautiful fruit is cut down and thrown into the fire" (cf. 3:10 and also 23:33). This verse contains the idea of judgment that Matthew also stresses in chapter 12. (5) Again, as in chapter 12, Matthew writes in the second person: see vv. 15, 16, and 20; Jesus is thus addressing his audience directly.

It is striking that the redaction is done so thoroughly and so similarly in both chapter 7 and chapter 12. Such a large number of agreements can, in my opinion, only be accounted for if the *same* author twice rewrote the *same* source text. The contexts (Sermon on the Mount, Beelzebul discussion) give rise to the differences that remain, notwithstanding such similar treatment.

## Mt 7:21-23

This short pericope was composed by Matthew from two Q-texts: cf. Lk 6:46 and 13:25-27. Here, too, his redactional activity is very extensive. In the Q-sermon (cf. Lk 6:46), there stood: "Why do you call me 'Lord, Lord,' and do not do what I tell you?" This question functions as an introduction to the concluding parable of the house on the rock (cf. Lk 6:47-49). In 7:21, Matthew transforms the question into a general statement: "Not every one..." He talks in his own specific way about entry into the Kingdom of heaven (cf. 5:20) to which a condition is attached; he replaces the verb "to call" (i.e. to confess and thus recognize in prayer and cult) by the weaker "to say" (which is no longer actually praying in the full sense). He also replaces "do what I tell you" by "do the will of my Father in heaven" (cf. 6:10), because, for Matthew, Jesus' words in the Sermon on the

Mount express this will (cf. 7:24). And Matthew further expands the text with vv. 22-23, which are taken from another Q-context: "On that day many will say to me 'Lord, Lord' . . . ", which indicates that this supplicatory prayer is spoken on the day of judgment. What it will come down to on the day of judgment is whether or not one has done the will of God and avoided evil. The prayer of these Christians is then no longer the Lord's Prayer. With "Lord, Lord," they do not address God, their Father, directly, but Christ, their judge, and cite in their defense all they have accomplished in his name.

It would take us too far afield to reconstruct the Q-text of Lk 13:25-27 (= Mt 7:22-23) with a close analysis of the Lucan redaction, but this much is certain: in Q there was the succession of (1) the closed door of the banquet hall or room, (2) the request for admission of those who stand outside, (3) the answer of the Lord: "I do not know you," (4) the persistence of those outside and their reference to their former stay with the Lord, and, finally, (5) the definitive condemnation and dismissal.

What did Matthew do with this scene? He keeps only (4) and (5). He adapts his verses 22-23 to v. 21 and vv. 15-20: the doubling of Lord (cf. v. 21); the "many" in v. 22 are the false prophets (v. 15) who "have prophesied" in Jesus' name (repeated three times!). Those who have committed *anomia* (v. 23, probably different in Q) are those who did not do the will of the heavenly Father (v. 21). *Anomia* means literally "lawlessness, illegality," but already in the Old Testament and later in Judaism it means "evil," the opposite of righteousness. To do the will of God is, for Matthew, nothing other than to practice the abundant righteousness: both are "conditions" for the entry into the Kingdom of heaven (cf. 7:21 and 5:20).

## WHO ARE THE FALSE PROPHETS?

In the beginning of the eschatological sermon, Matthew has added a few sentences that recall 7:15-23: "And then many will fall away, and betray one another and hate one another. And many false prophets will arise and lead many astray. And because evil is multiplied, most men's love will grow cold" (24:10-12). Here, too, we have false prophets, danger of misleading, evil ("lawlessness"). Who are the false prophets of chapter 7?

It has already been noted that the same people are discussed in the second and third units (*b* and *b'*). These are the false prophets who, on the day of the judgment, want to save themselves by appealing to their previous activities and their acquaintance with Jesus. There has been much controversy about their identity. In my opinion, it can hardly be doubted that Matthew has Christians in mind and not contemporaries of Jesus. They act in Jesus' name, present themselves as sheep (belonging to the Christian fold), but are actually wolves, (bad Christians). They come to the "ordinary" Christians and are dangerous. These would have been the Christian false prophets who tried to mislead other Christians. Apparently, they came from elsewhere and presented themselves in the local churches. It is possible that they were the predecessors of certain itinerant missionary-prophets about whom later Church history speaks and against whose abuses it warns (e.g., already in the early Christian text, the Didache).

The Matthean Jesus had nothing against their prophetic activity or mighty works as such. It could be that their doctrine was unorthodox, but this is not said. They are ravenous wolves, but this is not the actual accusation. They are dangerous because they cannot be easily recognized. One must therefore look at their deeds: this is the way to identify them. What the Matthean Jesus has against them most of all is that they do not do God's will; they commit evil, and their moral lives do not correspond to their religious beliefs and their Christian status.

## III. Each Christian and All Hearers

The analysis of the pericopes *a* and *a'*, 7:13-14 and 7:24-27, can proceed much more quickly. These two units are not concerned with a particular group of Christians, the false

prophets, but a twofold possibility is presented for everyone, Christians in the first instance and also non-Christians
who are listening to the Sermon on the Mount. One is
confronted with a choice. One may not follow the majority,
not yield to the easy solution. One must listen to the warning
and the threat of the Matthean Jesus.

## Mt 7:13-14

For a thorough examination of these verses, the reader is
referred to the study of A. Denaux cited above. His principal conclusions will be summarized here. I will accept without further discussion his hypothetical reconstruction of the
Q-version of the logion that both Luke and Matthew have
rewritten: "Strive to enter by the narrow door, for many will
seek to enter but they will not find it" (cf. Lk 13:24). The
introductory verse Lk 13:23 is probably entirely Lucan
redaction, although the "few" may have come from Q.

(1) Matthew has expanded Q a great deal and constructed
two long antithetical-symmetrical sentences after "Enter by
the narrow gate." The first is causal: "for the gate is wide and
the way is easy, that leads to destruction, and those who
enter by it are many"; the second is exclamatory: "How
narrow is the gate and hard the way, that leads to life, and
those who find it are few!" The evangelist has a predilection
for parallelism.

(2) Matthew has added the way -motif, so he changed the
"door" into the "gate." He no longer has in mind a room but
rather a city and its gate to which the way leads. It would
appear that this rewriting has caused some minor irregulari-
ties, because "to go *through* the way" and "*to find* the way"
(literal translation) are somewhat disturbing phrases in the
context.

(3) Matthew stresses not only the two kinds of ways and
gates, but also the opposition "destruction" and "life."
Moreover, he sets the "many" (the crowd) in opposition to
the "few" (cf. Lk 13:23).

In the light of what follows in 7:15-27, "narrow" and
"hard" must be interpreted as referring to the difficulty of

putting Jesus' words into practice. "Wide" and "broad" then mean the opposite: the easy, loose (immoral) and unchristian way the crowd lives.

## Mt 7:24-27

This parable, which was the conclusion of the Sermon on the Mount already in Q, was thoroughly rewritten by Luke in 6:47-49. His subject is a house with or without a foundation, and he speaks about a flood without mentioning wind and rain. In fact, the vocabulary of his version is very Lucan. The Matthean version seems to be more original, certainly when he describes the storm and the water — the autumn cloudbursts accompanied by gales in Palestine — and the house built on rock or on sand.

Nevertheless, there are also Matthean changes of the Q-source. (1) In v. 24a, Matthew added the concluding "then" and also "these" (to "words of mine," which refers to the words of the entire Sermon on the Mount). (2) It is quite possible that the tenses of vv. 24bc and 26bc ("will be like," "built" ) are from Matthew. The future refers to the judgment; the aorist tense refers to the acts performed during earthly life. (3) Matthew probably added the adjectives "wise" in v. 24b and "foolish" in v. 26b to describe the two figures of the parable. Such addition of adjectives is typical of Matthew (see, for example, 25:21 and 23; cf. Lk 19:17 and 19).

After the pericopes *b* and *b'*, which were concerned with the false prophets, he expands and generalizes in *a'* again (the concluding parable): "every one who...." The theme at the end of the Sermon on the Mount is also the separation at the judgment, as in the parables of the weeds among the wheat (13:24-30 and 36-43) and of the net (13:47-50) at the end of the parable sermon, and also as in the pericope of the last judgment (25:31-46) at the end of the eschatological sermon. In *a*, 7:13-14, we perhaps still considered the distinction to be between the many non-Christians and the few Christians. In *a'*, 7:24-27, the criterion for the selection is not being Christian but the "doing" of Jesus' words. But the one who keeps Christ's words has become a Christian in the true sense of the word.

## IV. The Ethical Message of the Sermon on the Mount

Mt. 7:13-27 is the epilogue of the Sermon on the Mount. With our attentive study of this text, we have again, as in the preceding chapters, come to the same surprising conclusion. Certainly, Matthew as a writer is dependent on sources and traditions; in 7:13-27, we saw that there were two different Q-texts (cf. Lk 6:43-49 and 13:23-27). But it is the freedom that Matthew allows himself, the creativity he reveals in his composition — omissions, expansions, rewritings, and retouchings — that is striking and that surprises us. The question that automatically arises here concerns the identity of the Matthean Jesus. So many words are changed, indeed there are entire speeches placed in the mouth of Jesus by the evangelist, that the reader may rightly wonder if Matthew still allows the authentic Jesus to speak. Is there still continuity between the earthly Jesus and the Jesus presented by Matthew?

Matthew's faithfulness to his sources and to the earthly Jesus is undoubtedly something different from what most Christians thought not so long ago. We have found him to be unexpectedly much freer and much more personal. In his composition, Matthew gives a composite vision of Jesus, a Jesus whom he himself adapted to his circumstances. He takes account of the concrete needs of the Christian fifty years after the first Easter. Nevertheless, I have repeatedly and resolutely maintained the continuity between Matthew and Jesus, thus for Matthew's fundamental faithfulness to Jesus' message and his right to present his portrait of Jesus. His gospel is an extension of the historical Jesus. One can still agree with the sentiments with which Dietrich Bonhoeffer begins the foreword for his book *The Cost of Discipleship*: "Revival of church life always brings in its train a

richer understanding of the Scriptures. Behind all the slo-
gans and catchwords of ecclesiastical controversy, necessary though they are, there arises a more determined quest
for him who is the sole object of it all, for Jesus Christ
himself. What did Jesus mean to say to us? What is his will
for us to-day? How can he help us to be good Christians in
the modern world? In the last resort, what we want to know
is not, what would this or that man, or this or that Church,
have of us, but what Jesus Christ himself wants of us. When
we go to church and listen to the sermon, what we want to
hear is his Word — and that not merely for selfish reasons,
but for the sake of the many for whom the Church and her
message are foreign" (p. 29).

At the end of this long analysis, a few of the principal
elements of my argument can be summarized by answering
three questions. Who did Matthew have in mind in his
Sermon on the Mount? What is the essence of the content of
this sermon? How can we bring the Jesus actualized by
Matthew into our lives?

## EXHORTATION AND ALSO POLEMICS?

According to Matthew, Jesus taught his disciples in the
Sermon on the Mount (see 5:1-2), but after the Sermon
Matthew also mentions that the crowds were astonished by
his teaching (see 7:28-29). Furthermore, Matthew says that
this long programmatic speech by Jesus is intended for
disciples, i.e., for people who are already disciples and for all
whom Jesus invites to become disciples. For them the Sermon on the Mount is instruction, doctrine, and necessary,
useful information. In 4:17, we read of the first public
appearance of Jesus in Galilee: "From that time Jesus began
to preach, saying, 'Repent, for the Kingdom of heaven is at
hand.'" The Sermon on the Mount explains what the life of
someone who has repented must look like.

The entry into the Kingdom of heaven is linked to a
particular condition: righteousness that exceeds that of the
scribes and the Pharisees (cf. 5:20), doing the will of the

heavenly Father (cf. 7:21). We have seen that the beatitudes clarify the manner in which the Kingdom requires Christians to become the light of the world (5:3-16); the antitheses declare further what the actual will of the Father is (5:17-48). One may not practice the greater righteousness in order to attract the notice of people (6:1-18), and our first concern must always be for God's Kingdom and his righteousness and not for food and clothing (6:19-7:12). Finally, it comes down to not only knowing the will of the Father but also doing it (7:13-27). Obviously, Jesus' teaching in the Sermon on the Mount is simultaneously a call, a warning, and an exhortation.

In the third chapter above (p. 90), the "two fronts and a double level" were discussed. With the Sermon on the Mount, Matthew informs his readers of Jesus-past, his attitude toward the Law, his judgment of the scribes and the Pharisees. But at the same time, Matthew also has in mind Jesus-present, the actual Lord of his post-Easter church. Matthew hopes that his readers, his fellow Christians, will identify with the listening disciples and the listening people. The Sermon on the Mount, consequently, does indeed have a double level. But what about the double front? Jesus rejects righteousness as it is practiced by the Jewish scribes and Pharisees of his time (5:20); this same Jesus also seems to be fighting against a number of false and lax conceptions of the Law of Matthew's time. He attacks false Christian prophets in particular because their deeds do not correspond to their Christian confession: they do not do the will of the heavenly Father, which Jesus expounded in the Sermon on the Mount (7:15-23). Jesus also preaches against hypocritical display and excessive concern, against every form of "lawless" living.

Is the Matthean Jesus perhaps preaching against the concepts of Paul? Is Matthew openly or implicitly anti-Pauline? This is sometimes contended, but I think it is not true. The Sermon on the Mount has nothing in it that would indicate such a polemic. Nevertheless, Matthew and Paul differ from each other; this is not to be doubted. On pp. 107-110 above, I have gone into detail about how their understanding on the concept of righteousness differs. Matthew stresses the fulfillment of the Law by Jesus. In Paul, Jesus is the end of the Law for all who believe (cf. Rom 10:4). The Christians, Paul says, have received the Spirit not by keeping the Law but by believing in the message of the gospel (cf. Gal 3:2). One must read Mt 5:17-20 and Gal 3:1-5 together to grasp the difference of approach and mentality! According to Matthew, the new Law, explained by Jesus, can and must be obeyed. According to Paul, Jesus has redeemed us from the fatal situation of the old Law. But Paul no less than Matthew stresses (in every epistle) the necessity of an impeccable moral life, the "living according to the Spirit" (cf. Gal 5:1-6,10). And like Matthew in 7:12 and 22:40, Paul also declares in Gal 5:14 and Rom 13:10 that the whole Law is contained in the *one* commandment to love one's neighbor.

## THE BASILEIA ETHIC

*Basileia tou Theou* means the Kingdom of God, God's royal sovereignty. G. Schneider writes: "The ethic of the Sermon on the Mount is a *basileia* ethic" (*Botschaft*, p. 113); he is expressing a well-known concept. The righteousness that the Matthean Jesus demands of his disciples is related to the Kingdom of heaven whose proximity is announced. The Kingdom and righteousness are bound inseparably (see pp. 165-167). Because that Kingdom is coming with Jesus' salvation — thus as a gift already partially but truly present — one can call Jesus' righteousness *soteriological*: without his "blood of the covenant, which is poured out for many for the forgiveness of sins" (26:28), the basileia ethic would be impossible. Because the definitive coming of the Kingdom is still awaited, this righteousness can just as well be called *eschatological*: by living the *basileia* ethic, the Christian may hope to enter this Kingdom. The righteousness of the Sermon on the Mount thus lies in the tension between the already and the not yet, a tension that typifies the entire New Testament.

It is often stated that the earthly Jesus did not directly preach about himself, so the Christology that is present in his words and acts is called implicit. The Sermon on the Mount of the Matthean Jesus does not have Jesus himself as its subject, although a high *Christology* is not lacking. The entire Sermon vibrates as it were with messianic awareness. In two places in the Sermon the christological emphasis comes to the fore, at the beginning and at the end. First, we encounter the very authoritative, conscious "I" of Jesus six times in 5:21-48. The antitheses are introduced by the "I have come" of 5:17, and already in the last beatitude we read about persecution "on my account" (5:11). The Matthean Jesus speaks on the basis of his authority on earth. Second, in 7:21-23, Jesus refers to himself as the judge of the world at the end time who is solemnly addressed by "Lord, Lord" and who will pronounce the judgment. He is the King of the entire world, of all nations, who will come in glory with all the angels and then sit on his glorious throne (cf. 25:31).

But Jesus' basileia ethic is ultimately oriented to God. It is *theological*. It is God's Kingdom and God's righteousness that Jesus preaches and teaches. God is the Creator who feeds the birds and clothes the plants. It is the will of the heavenly Father that Jesus explains, explicitates, and restores to honor. It is God our Father to whom Jesus teaches us to pray. God sees in secret, and from him comes the reward. We must become his children and strive for his perfection. And people will glorify this God when they see our good actions.

There are two centers of gravity in the Sermon on the Mount: love of neighbor (including the enemy) and prayer. Love forms an impressive climax at the end of the antitheses: the Matthean Jesus transfers the Golden Rule of the Q-sermon and concludes the large middle part of his sermon with it in 7:12. Love of neighbor *is* the Law and the Prophets. Matthean righteousness is summarized in this commandment. This above all, the Christian must do. I have stressed both the central position of the Lord's Prayer as well as the importance of the prayer theme in the Sermon on the Mount. By prayer, the Christian recognizes his dependence on God. What can he do without God's prior and accompanying gift?

# THE SERMON ON THE MOUNT TODAY

Every careful reader of the Sermon on the Mount is continually struck by its radicality. Twice, like a kind of inclusion, Matthew has written, briefly and concisely, but not to be eluded, an entry saying: "Unless your righteousness exceeds that of the scribes and Pharisees, you will never enter the Kingdom of heaven" (5:20) and "Not every one who says to me, 'Lord, Lord,' shall enter the Kingdom of heaven, but he who does the will of my Father who is in heaven" (7:21). This same radicality is present just as calmly and soberly in the concluding parable of the house. At the end of time, there will be a separation, and only one criterion will then apply, the doing of Jesus' words, i.e., the practice of righteousness. This is the only way to life. Listening without doing leads to destruction. We think automatically of the blessings and curses and the end of the covenant formulas (cf. for example, Deut 27-30).

The Matthean Jesus, we have seen, is an actualized Jesus. He speaks words that are adapted to the concrete post-Easter situation of Matthew's time and church. There is much in that society and culture that differs from what we now experience and see happening. But Matthew's actualization shows us the way and confirms our freedom to transpose and make our own applications. But who would contend that the basic elements of the Sermon on the Mount are not inspiring for all times? The stress of the Matthean Jesus on the greater righteousness remains current. And people still try to hide behind the letter of the law, to minimize and distort God's commandment. And Jesus' warning against the hypocritical seeking to be seen, his plea for a healthy unconcern, and at the same time his stress on the priority of seeking the Kingdom and righteousness, his attack on insincere Christianity, Christianity in name only — all these parenetic calls apply more than ever today. Inner disposition and external act belong together. The integrity of each person that must be directed to God, and just as much the attention of each person to his or her fellow person and to society — these two emphases also belong together.

The Matthean Jesus does not fail to hold out the prospect of judgment. Then it will be too late. The reader realizes all too well that postponing the decision for action is wrong and dangerous. The choice must be made during this earthly life, now. And it must be acted on. To be Christian means living like a Christian.

Here, at the end of this section, what Bonhoeffer has written in *The Cost of Discipleship* about cheap and costly grace fits marvelously well: "Cheap grace is the deadly enemy of our Church.... Cheap grace is not the kind of forgiveness of sin which frees us from the toils of sin... Cheap grace is the preaching of forgiveness without requiring repentance, baptism without church discipline, Communion without confession, absolution without personal confession. Cheap grace is grace without discipleship, grace without the cross, grace without Jesus Christ, living and incarnate. Costly grace is ... the call of Jesus Christ at which the disciple leaves his nets and follows him... It is costly because it costs a man his life, and it is grace because it gives a man the only true life" (pp. 35-37).

## Bibliography

See also the general literature cited on pp. 41-44 above.

Betz, H. D., "Eine Episode im Jüngsten Gericht (Mt 7,21-23)," *Zeitschr. Theol. Kirche* 78 (1981) 1-30.

Denaux, A., "Der Spruch von den zwei Wegen im Rahmen des Epilogs der Bergpredigt (Mt 7,13-14 Par. Lk 13,23-24). Tradition und Redaktion," in: J. Delobel (ed.), *Logia. Les paroles de Jésus — The Sayings of Jesus* (Bibl. Eph. Theol. Lov. 59), Leuven, 1982, pp. 305-335.

Derrett, J. D. M., "The Merits of the Narrow Gate," *Journ. Stud. N. T.* (1982) no. 15, pp. 20-29.

Hill, D., "False Prophets and Charismatics: Structure and Interpretation in Matthew 7,15-23," *Bibl.* 57 (1976) 327-348

Hoffmann, "Dienst" (see p. 150 above).

Hoffmann, P., "'Pantes ergatai adikias.' Redaktion und Tradition in Lc 13,22-30," *Zeitschr. Neutest. Wiss.* 58 (1967) 188-214.

Lambrecht, J., *Marcus interpretator. Stijl en boodschap in Mc 3,20-4,34*, Bruges-Utrecht, 1969, pp. 23-29.

Mattill, A.J., "'The Way of Tribulation'," *Journ. Bibl. Lit.* 98 (1979) 531-546.

Minear, P. S., "False Prophets and Hypocrisy in the Gospel of Matthew," in: J. Gnilka (ed.), *Neues Testament und Kirche. Fs. R. Schnackenburg*, Freiburg-Basel-Vienna, 1974, pp. 76-93.

Piper, R., "Matthew 7, 7-11 par. Luke 11,9-13: Evidence of Design and Argument in the Collection of Jesus' Sayings," in: J. Delobel (ed.), *Logia. Les paroles de Jésus — The Sayings of Jesus* (Bibl. Eph. Theol. Lov. 59), Leuven, 1982, pp. 411-418.

Zeller, *Mahnsprüche* (see p. 127 above).

# Chapter Seven

# THE LUCAN SERMON ON THE PLAIN (Lk 6:20-49)

In this chapter, the Lucan Sermon on the Plain will be considered as a whole. There has already been occasion in this book to discuss this sermon in itself: in the third part of the first chapter (pp. 32-35): the presentation of the address) and in the second chapter, part 3 (pp. 68-74: the beatitudes and woes, 6:20b-26). That study will not be repeated here. Often, in each chapter, the Lucan parallels to the Matthean text were referred to and were used for the reconstruction of the source texts. But several times, too, it was stated that the rather short Lucan Sermon on the Plain also deserved to be examined as a whole and conveniently brought together in one single chapter. This will be done here.

Presumably, Luke rather faithfully preserved the Q-Sermon on the Mount with respect to its scope and construction. But Luke also rewrote his source and expanded it with a few verses, though to a much lesser extent than did Matthew. We will have to listen attentively to Luke's own tone and accentuation. Nevertheless, in this chapter Luke's source, the Q-sermon, will be used to emphasize, once again, the essence of Jesus' message and call.

The presentation will be divided as follows. First, the origin, structure, and train of thought of Luke's text will be discussed. Then, a few important verses of the Q-sermon will be selected to clarify Jesus' command to love one's neighbor. In the third section, I will return to Luke and analyze his editorial method and investigate the specific Lucan emphasis not only out of legitimate historical interest but also in view of the modern-day reader.

## I. Composition and Train of Thought

As regards the context of the Sermon on the Plain of the Gospel of Luke, see pp. 32-33. In 6:17-20a, Luke writes: "And he [Jesus] came down with them [the disciples] and stood on a level place, with a great multitude of people from all Judea and Jerusalem and the seacoast of Tyre and Sidon, who came to hear him and to be healed of their diseases; and those who were troubled with unclean spirits were cured. And all the crowd sought to touch him, for power came forth from him and healed them all. And he lifted up his eyes on his disciples, and said [to them]." After the sermon, there is in 7:1, the statement: "After he had ended all his sayings in the hearing of the people, he entered Capernaum." On p. 33 I distinguished in the sermon itself not only the introduction (vv. 20-26: beatitudes and woes) and the conclusion (vv. 46-49: the parable of the house) but also the longer middle part with its two sections: vv. 27-36 (love of enemy) and vv. 37-45 (not judging). First, here is the translation of the complete text.

> 20b Blessed are you poor, for yours is the Kingdom of God.
> 21 Blessed are you that hunger now, for you shall be satisfied. Blessed are you that weep now, for you shall laugh.
> 22 Blessed are you when men hate you, and when they exclude you and revile you, and cast out your name as evil, on account of the Son of man!
> 23 Rejoice in that day, and leap for joy, for behold, your reward is great in heaven; for so their fathers did to the prophets.
> 24 But woe to you that are rich, for you have received your consolation.

25 Woe to you that are full now, for you shall hunger. Woe to you that laugh now, for you shall mourn and weep.

26 Woe to you, when all men speak well of you, for so their fathers did to the false prophets.

b 27 But I say to you that hear, Love your enemies, do good to those who hate you,

28 bless those who curse you, pray for those who abuse you.

29 To him who strikes you on the cheek, offer the other also; and from him who takes away your cloak do not withhold your coat as well.

30 Give to every one who begs from you; and of him who takes away your goods do not ask them again.

31 And as you wish that men would do to you, do so to them.

32 If you love those who love you, what credit is that to you? For even sinners love those who love them.

33 And if you do good to those who do good to you, what credit is that to you? For even sinners do the same.

34 And if you lend to those from whom you hope to receive, what credit is that to you? Even sinners lend to sinners, to receive as much again.

35 But love your enemies, and do good, and lend, expecting nothing in return; and your reward will be great, and you will be sons of the Most High; for he is kind to the ungrateful and the selfish.

36 Be merciful, even as your Father is merciful.

c 37 And judge not, and you will not be judged; condemn not, and you will not be condemned; forgive, and you will be forgiven;

38 give, and it will be given to you; good measure, pressed down, shaken together, running over, will be put into your lap. For the measure you give will be the measure you get back.

39 He also told them a parable: Can a blind man lead a blind man? Will they not both fall into a pit?

40 A disciple is not above his teacher, but everyone when he is fully taught will be like his teacher.

41 Why do you see the speck that is in your brother's eye, but do not notice the log that is in your own eye?

43 For no good tree bears bad fruit, nor again does a bad tree bear good fruit;

44 for each tree is known by its own fruit. For figs are not gathered from thorns, nor are grapes picked from a bramble bush.

45 The good man out of the good treasure of his heart produces good, and the bad man out of his bad treasure produces bad (RSV: evil); for out of the abundance of his heart his mouth speaks.

d 46 Why do you call me "Lord, Lord," and not do what I tell you?

47 Every one who comes to me and hears my words and does them, I will show you what he is like:

48 he is like a man building a house, who dug deep, and laid the foundation upon rock; and when a flood arose, the stream broke against that house, and could not shake it, because it had been well built.

49 But he who hears and does not do them is like a man who built a house on the ground without a foundation; against which the stream broke, and immediately it fell, and the ruin of that house was great.

## THE SOURCE TEXTS

To get a better idea of the questions that must be asked, I will begin with a survey of the Matthean parallel passages. The texts from the Sermon on the Mount are placed in one column, and the other texts from Mt are in the other column.

| *Lk 6* | *Mt 5-7* | *Mt* |
|--------|----------|------|
| 20a | 5:1-2 | |
| 20b-21 | 5:2, 6, 4 | |
| 22-23 | 5:1-12 | |
| *24-26* | | |

| | | |
|---|---|---|
| *27a* | | |
| 27bc-28 | 5:44bc | |
| 29-30 | 5:39bc-42 | |
| 31 | 7:12 | |
| 32-33 | 5:46-47 | |
| *34-35ab* | | |
| 35c | 5:45 | |
| 36 | 5:48 | |
| 37-38 | 7:1-2 | |
| *39a* | | |
| 39bc | | 15:14 |
| 40 | | 10:24-25 |
| 41-42 | 7:3-5 | |
| 43-45 | 7:16, 18 | 12:33, 35 |
| 46 | 7:21 | |
| 47-49 | 7:24-27 | |
| 7:1a | 7:28a | |

An attentive examination of this table soon raises three questions. (1) Did Luke omit parts of the original Q-sermon that can be found in Mt 5-7? (2) Did Lk 6:39bc (= Mt 15:14) and 40 (= Mt 10:24-25) belong to the Q-sermon, or did Luke take these verses from other Q-contexts and insert them into his Sermon on the Plain? The second question is not applicable to Lk 6:43-45 (= Mt 12:33, 35) since this passage certainly existed in the Q-Sermon on the Mount, as Mt 7:16-20 witnesses (see the analysis on pp. 189-193). (3) The third question is this: Are the verses without parallel texts (italicized in the list, but there are probably also parts of other verses) pure Lucan redaction or were they in the Q-sermon and omitted by Matthew? Are they R (redaction) or Q? In other words, did Luke expand the sermon?

In three places the Lucan order deviates from the Matthean: in 6:20b-21, in 6:27-36, and in 6:43-45. The place of the Golden Rule (Lk 6:31) in Mt 7:12 is also noteworthy. Which of the two evangelists preserved the Q-order? Finally, we may not lose sight of Luke's more or less radical rewriting as regards sentence construction and word choice.

## THE LUCAN COMPOSITION

It is not my intention in this section to list all the Lucan alterations. Rather, I will limit myself to the principal ones and thus try to arrive at an understanding of Luke's structuring of the text. From the analysis of the Matthean Sermon on the Mount, it became evident that material that appears in Mt and not in Lk was probably added by Matthew and not omitted by Luke. This is already the answer to the first question. To answer the others, I will discuss in turn the four parts of the Lucan text.

a) As regards *vv. 20b-26*. I would refer to pp. 68-70 above. Luke presumably preserved the Q-order of the beatitudes (even that of the first three). Again, what must be stressed is the hypothetical nature of the positions that propose that the second person of the first three beatitudes is due to Luke's hand and that Luke himself composed and added the woes. If these two hypotheses are correct, then Luke did indeed drastically edit and expand the Q-source here.

b) In *vv. 27-36* his rewriting and ordering activity is also perhaps greater than one would initially be inclined to accept. It is better not to consider v. 27a, "But I say to you that hear" as a residue of the antithetical formula that Q would have had (cf. Mt 5:38-39 for this antithesis structure). The phrase "I say to you" with which Jesus makes known his extraordinary authority presumably was in Q, but by his additions in v. 27a Luke wanted to indicate that the "you" of the woes is not the same as the "you" of those who hear (see also 6:18). The Lucan Jesus addresses himself from v. 27 on, after the intervening vv. 24-26, again to the people spoken to in vv. 20-23.

On pp. 104-105 above, the Q-reconstruction of vv. 27-36 was given without further discussion. Here is the text again:

| *Mt 5* | | *Lk 6* |
|---|---|---|
| 39b | If anyone strikes you on the right cheek, turn to him the other also; | 29 |

| | | |
|---|---|---|
| 40 | and if anyone would sue and take your coat, let him have your cloak as well. | |
| 42 | Give to every one who begs from you; and do not refuse him who would borrow from you. | 30 |
| (7:12) | Whatever you wish that people would do to you, do so to them. | 31 |
| 44 | I say to you, Love your enemies, do good to those who hate you, bless those who curse you, pray for those who abuse you, | 27<br>28 |
| 45 | and you will be sons of your Father, for he makes his sun rise on the evil and on the good and sends rain on the just and on the unjust. | 35c |
| 46 | For if you love those who love you, what reward have you? Do not even the tax collectors do the same? | 32 |
| 47 | And if you salute only your brethren, what reward have you? Do not even the Gentiles do the same? | 33 |
| 48 | Be merciful, even as your Father is merciful. | 36 |

Can the text, as we find it in vv. 27-36, be explained as the result of Lucan redaction? (1) Most exegetes accept, correctly in my opinion, that *v. 34* was created by Luke himself. He uses the loan motif that he omitted in v. 30 (cf. Mt 5:42) and forms a third long sentence that is parallel to vv. 32 and 33. (2) *V. 35ab* is, in the judgment of many interpreters also a purely Lucan creation. Luke repeats the three motifs of vv. 32-34, and he frames the unit that lies between vv. 27b and 35a with "love your enemies," which actually repeats v. 27b. (3) Probably, Luke moved *vv. 27-28* forward, i.e. placed them at the beginning of the unit. This is why vv. 29-30, which were cast in the second person singular, are surrounded in his 'version by verses that are all cast in the second person plural (see vv. 27-28 and 31-36). By this change, Luke apparently wanted to indicate that the pericope as a whole is concerned with love of enemy. Did he intensify, as is sometimes contended, the specific emphasis on love of enemy by the addition of the two phrases: "do good to those who hate you, bless those who curse you" (vv. 27c-28a; vv. 27-28 have, like v. 22, four parts)? This is very uncertain, since one may suppose that Matthew with "pray for those who persecute you" (5:44c) summarizes three of the four Q-commands (cf. Lk 6:27c-28ab), as he also did in 7:1-2 (cf. Lk 6:37-38 and see pp. 178-179 above). (4) *V. 35c* has been separated by Luke from vv. 27-28 (cf. Mt 5:45 after 5:44) and is placed at the end of the pericope, but not without the repetition of v. 27b in v. 35a.

It must also be noted that Luke preserved the Q-location of v. 31 (the Golden Rule) and that his version of v. 36 seems to be the original. We need not go into the Lucan rewriting of the other verses now (see Part 3 below). The four redactional interventions in vv. 27-36 which we have noted resulted in the retaliation theme (vv. 29-31) being completely subordinated to the theme of love of enemy. If this presentation of the Lucan activity is correct, then Luke has given this entire passage a thematic unity by reordering and rewriting Q and by adding his own material (R, vv. 34-35ab).

c) In *vv. 37-45*, Luke proceeds differently. The Q-order of vv. 37-38 (not judging), vv. 41-42 (speck and log), and vv. 43-45 (the tree and its fruit) is preserved. But Luke inserts two sayings after v. 38 (v. 39b and v. 40) each of which come from another Q-context. V. 39a is a Lucan introduction (cf. 5:36; 12:16; 13:6; 14:7; 15:3; 18:1, 9; and 21:29). Luke in vv. 37-38 and 41-42 no longer has love of the enemy (the non-Christian) in mind, but rather the loveless judgment of Christians against each other within the community. Anyone who judges or condemns is like a blind leader, and he should turn to his Master, Luke says in vv. 39-40. Luke also apparently relates vv. 43-45 to the danger that a Christian would lightly and erroneously pronounce judgment: "for out of the abundance of the heart his mouth speaks" (v. 45c).

Admittedly, the conceptual unity of vv. 37-45 is weaker than that of vv. 27-36. The major cause of this is the material from tradition. Luke expanded the passage by adding two Q-verses. Whether these verses fit perfectly in the new context is an open question. But I think that Luke placed them as best he could in service of his main idea: the exhortation not to judge. Luke also abbreviated the source text of v. 40 by omitting the second "servant-master" pair (cf. Mt 10:24-25).

d) The last pericope, *vv. 46-49* (the parable of the house) stands in the position it had in the Q-source. V. 46 is the introduction to the parable. Luke probably added "(Every one) *who comes to me and* (hears my words)" to v. 47. One is immediately reminded of v. 18: "who came to hear him." In v. 27, too, he added the verb "to hear." On p. 197 above, I presented the Lucan rewriting within the parable. Luke no longer has in mind the Palestinian method of construction (on rock, on sand); with three verbs in v. 48 he stresses the placing of the foundation (and thus also the necessary actual effort of the Christian); he probably pictured a large river that overflows its banks rather than the sudden surges of a Palestinian stream during a cloudburst. Luke has hellenized the source text.

## DIVISION AND CONTENT

As far as I can judge, Luke has omitted nothing of the Q-Sermon on the Mount. He expanded it in two ways: by composing parts himself (the woes and vv. 34-35ab) and by taking two sayings from other Q-contexts (v. 39b and v. 40). He also reordered a part of the text, namely, vv. 27-36. And, of course, Luke rewrote many of the Q-verses.

Is the four-part structure with which I tentatively began (cf. p. 33 above) reinforced by the analysis of Luke's composition? I think it is. Everyone recognizes the rounding off of the first part, i.e. the introduction (vv. 20b-26). There is discussion, however, with regard to the second break after v. 36 and the third after v. 45. Does not the second part run to v. 38 and do not vv. 42-45 belong to the fourth part, i.e. the conclusion?

It seems to me that v. 36, with the command "be merciful" and the comparison with God's mercifulness, has the smack of a conclusion: be merciful toward every one, as God is,

even toward one's enemy. Although v. 36 is unconnected
with v. 35, there is a content link between vv. 35c and 36:
God is mentioned twice. I admit that the content of vv. 37-38
is also related to the theme of love of neighbor of vv. 27-36,
but in vv. 37-45, the subject is no longer hostile outsiders.
Here the Lucan Jesus is concerned with the Christian
brother or sister who judges his or her fellow Christian. Vv.
35-36 contain positive exhortations and offer the prospect
of being a son or daughter; v. 37 forbids judging and mentions the possibility of future condemnation. In vv. 27-36,
God is the example for the Christian, already in this life; in
vv. 37-45 God is the one who at the judgment will use the
same measure that was used by the individual, and the
Christian is no longer compared with God but with Christ
(cf. v. 40). The "and" with which v. 37 begins now introduces
a new idea; to paraphrase: "and further, do not judge..."
All of this supports the opinion that the caesura does indeed
lie between v. 36 and v. 37.

Because v. 45c "for out of the abundance of his heart his
mouth speaks" applies the parable of the tree and its fruit to
speaking, Luke, in my opinion, is dealing with the theme of
"not judging" up to and including v. 45. It is the Christian
brother or sister who may not produce sick fruit like a sick
tree and may not produce bad out of a bad treasure. Furthermore, v. 46 is directed to the hearers and begins a new
theme, doing what Jesus says; v. 47, with "my words," refers
to the entire sermon; and the unit of vv. 46-49 —like the
beatitudes and the woes — describes as a whole two possibilities (doing and not doing) and thus forms with vv. 20-26
the framing of the middle part. For all these reasons, it is
better to place the third caesura after v. 45

In 6:20-49, the Lucan Jesus speaks to the disciples, but the
people are also present and listening (see pp. 33-35 above).
The people, including the evangelists's contemporaries, the
non-Christians, can learn what Christian living is. The
Christians are called to love as, ultimately, every one is. The
sermon has four parts: vv. 20b-26, vv. 27-36, vv. 37-45, and
vv. 46-49. (a) With the introduction (vv. 20b-26) the poor
and the persecuted disciples are called blessed. The woes

form the contrast. (b) In vv. 27-36, the Lucan Jesus gives the great and typical Christian commandment with numerous repetitions and developments, with parable and motivation: love your enemies. (c) Vv. 37-45 are concerned mainly with the danger from within the Church of lack of love of neighbor by rash and unjust judgments. The Christian who so speaks is like someone who takes bad things out of a bad treasure; he or she is like a sick tree that produces sick fruit. (d) At the end (vv. 46-49), Jesus stresses the necessity of the concrete act with the parable of the house with or without a foundation; one must apply Jesus' words in practice, and in this way lay a secure foundation so that the house remains standing. Who hears but does not do will see his or her house immediately collapse, and the ruin will be great.

Attention must be given to two other matters. Luke has placed vv. 29-31 in unit (b) under the theme of "love of enemy." Generally, vv. 29-30 are given the name "no retaliation" or "non-violence." The two ideas are certainly present, but their passivity — pure submission and not reacting — is interrupted by v. 30a "give [literally: keep giving] to every one who asks" and by the Golden Rule of v. 31: one must take the initiative, one must act first. The second observation is related to unit (c). Here, too, there is a shift. After the two negative commands in v. 37a and b ("judge not, condemn not") there are two positive commands in vv. 37c and 38a: "forgive, give." The authentic Christian life certainly demands, out of love, that certain negative acts are not done, but it must also be marked by spontaneous and positive giving and forgiving.

## II. Jesus and the Love of Neighbor

The well-known Dutch author G. Bomans once discussed the crusades in an interview while visiting the Holy Sepulchre. "The actual object [of the crusades] was the sepulchre. From Urban the Second to Peter the Hermit, this was the recruitment theme. If you read the speech of the Pope, which started the entire movement to the East, you

will see this. The lamps above the sepulchre, which had been extinguished by the unbelievers, must burn again. He stood on the steps in Clermont and spoke these words and *promised forgiveness of all sins* to all who went to Jerusalem. It makes you giddy when you read it, a man who coolly occupies the place of God, the pretention is so stunning that it takes your breath away. Four people wrote down this speech, and it might well have been the most powerful speech that was ever given. It knocks you off your chair.... A trail of blood was laid across Europe to the Holy City. On the way, all Jews were eliminated — you know why — and there was a blood bath in Jerusalem leaving, it seems, no survivors. It is incomprehensible that none of these people saw the contradiction of all these enormous slaughters for a sepulchre in which a man was laid who preached the opposite for three years. The same mystery is there when you see a heretic being tortured with a member of the clergy nearby holding up a cross. How is this possible? What gives people the idea to do this to each other with an appeal to a person who gave his life to stop such happenings? I can't figure it out. I sometimes think that maybe there is a line in the gospel that I have never noticed, one angry word, from which all this blind wrath has come. I cannot find it..."
(*Van dichtbij gezien*, Leiden-Tielt, [5]1971, pp. 114-115).

Both the Matthean Sermon on the Mount and the Lucan Sermon on the Plain have been studied in this book as regards their sources and origins. The two sermons were compared with each other. We can now form a picture of the older Q-sermon, Matthew's and Luke's source, even though we have no absolute certainty about the precise wording and the order of all of the sayings. Three major parts can be distinguished in Q: (a) The sermon begins with four beatitudes (cf. Lk 6:20b-23). (b) Then there follows a passage about love of neighbor probably with successive exhortations not to retaliate (cf. Lk 6:29-31), to love the enemy (cf. Lk 6:27-28, 35c, 32-33, 36), and not to judge (cf. Lk 6:37-42). (c) At the end are two parables, both of which concern the actual living of the Christian life: the tree and its fruit (cf. Lk 6:43-45) and the house on the rock or the sand (cf. Lk

6:46-49). One recognizes a three-part construction of (a) proclamation, (b) command, and (c) call to act.

The hypothetical Q-composition could be studied further in itself and in the context of the entire Q-document — but not in this book. However, having arrived at Q is not *ipso facto* to have arrived at the earthly Jesus. Between the two lay the resurrection events and the first dissemination of the faith, a period, we may presume, of approximately two decades. Was the Q-sermon partially or completely compiled after Easter? It is extremely difficult to form a judgment in this matter. But even if the sermon was created after Easter (see, however, my position on pp. 39-40 above), the material included in it would not therefore be inauthentic. And even if after Easter Christians placed one or other saying in the mouth of Jesus, so that it could not be *ipsissima vox* (Jesus' own voice), still there is in this sermon without doubt the *ipsissima intentio* of Jesus, i.e., his own intention.

Jesus' beatitudes were dealt with extensively in the second chapter above (see pp. 45-58). For this second part, three other elements of the Q-sermon will be chosen that are characteristic of the earthly Jesus: love of enemy, no retaliation, and the Golden Rule. The selection is, of course, incomplete: there are also themes from Lk 6:37-49 that could be considered. But this choice is intended to be representative and is also justified by the important and central theme of love of neighbor with which all three are related. I gratefully acknowledge my debt in this presentation to the profound study by H. Merklein, *Die Gottesherrschaft als Handlungsprinzip. Untersuchung zur Ethik Jesu.*

## LOVE YOUR ENEMIES

The reconstruction on pp. 211-212 above assumes that Matthew preserved the original Q-order in 5:44-48 (therefore, the Matthean numbering will be used here). Matthew abbreviated v. 44; he changed v. 45 into a purpose sentence; he replaced "merciful" in v. 48 by "perfect." For the rest,

Matthew is also presumably more original as regards vocabulary than is Luke.

Does this entire text go back to Jesus? Vv. 46-47 are excluded, probably correctly for the three following reasons taken together. (1) The form of these verses — they are rhetorical questions — differs from that of vv. 44-45 and 48. (2) The content of vv. 46-47 interrupts the unity. The first two reasons already justify the conclusion that these verses were probably added later — although they were already present in Q — but not that they could not have been spoken by Jesus. (3) But the derogatory reference to the tax collectors does seem to be very unlike Jesus and, moreover, does not concur with the spirit of the command just given to love the enemies. Thus, we are left with vv. 44-45, 48, which possibly do go back to Jesus. However, it is not excluded that Jesus only said, "Love your enemies," and that the three following sentences in v. 44 were added after Easter.

> 44 I say to you, Love your enemies (do good to those who hate you, bless those who curse you, pray for those who abuse you,)
> 45 so that you may be sons of your Father, for he makes his sun rise on the evil and on the good, and sends rain on the just and on the unjust.
> 48 Be merciful, even as your Father is merciful.

The current tendency among exegetes is to be very careful about statements like "only Jesus could have said this or that." As regards our text, it is now generally accepted that the motifs in vv. 44-45, 48 also were known among the Jews and thus can be considered traditionally Jewish. This applies to the motif of the imitation of God, to the idea of divine sonship (on the basis of moral action or as an eschatological promise), to the reference to the goodness of the creator toward good and bad people without distinction, and also to the command to love the enemies. But why should not Jesus borrow the best of the traditions of his people? The originality of Jesus lies rather in the way in which he conceived and formulated vv. 44-45, 48: he makes no reference to the Torah; he speaks with unprecedented personal prophetic authority ("I say to you," he commands, and he promises divine sonship); he uses a simple, non-emotional form. These content and formal characteristics indeed make this textual unit something totally original. Therefore, we may correctly say that vv. 44-45, 48 are authentic, i.e., come from Jesus.

One could consider that v. 48 is a summary and a repetition of vv. 44-45. God's mercy is shown by his continuous care of, and goodness toward, all of his creatures; therefore, we, too, must be good and show mercy. But is "even as your Father is merciful" a simple repetition of "he makes his sun rise on the evil and on the good, and sends rain on the just and on the unjust"? In my opinion, we have good reason to suppose that by God's mercy Jesus intended God's new initiative in salvation history. For Jesus, this mercy is not an abstract concept, nor is it a "given" of creation. Jesus is thinking concretely of what God is doing with the establishment of his sovereignty. He is thinking of his own mission. In him, God turns unconditionally toward people, to people who are all sinners and who very much need God's mercy. As the merciful God loves his enemies, so must we love our enemies. This is the ultimate motivation: not only God's continuous goodness toward all people whoever or whatever they might be (the others), but primarily his salvific mercy now, concretely for me! Of course, the intelligent consideration of God's universal care for his creation, keeping it in existence, helps in loving the enemy; of course, one may also love in order to become a child of God; but the experience of God's forgiving mercy toward the Christian himself or herself and his or her fellow person is the most profound motive. It is obvious: for Jesus, Christian morality is theocentric, but Jesus refers to a God who is, in himself, redemption. This ethic is therefore both theological and christological at the same time.

There is still more. God is not only the ultimate and actual motivation. God's offer of salvation also makes the human response possible. Not only *because* God is merciful to us must we ourselves be merciful, but also *through* his being merciful we can in our turn risk it. With his command to love the enemy, Jesus is doing nothing other than clearly formulating as a duty the Christian possibility that he himself created by God's mercy. Purely anthropologically, this cannot be explained. The "natural" person does not understand this and will always resist it. The Christian ethic is a *basileia* ethic. The love of the neighbor flows, authentically and necessarily, from God's love for us. Thus we become, now already, children of God. All of this leads us to understand fully how, in the New Testament, love is correctly called the central, the principal, the new commandment.

## NON-VIOLENCE

If the explanation given above is correct, then Jesus introduced something truly new with his command to love the enemy. This is not simply the radicalized development of Lev. 19:18: "you shall love your neighbour as yourself: I am the Lord." Often, the Jews see this commandment in relation to Ex 23:4-5: "If you meet your enemy's ox or his ass going astray, you shall bring it back to him. If you see the ass of one who hates you lying under its burden, you shall refrain from leaving him with it, you shall help him to lift it up." The Christian, too, stands in this tradition. But still, God began something new in Jesus, which makes the Christian capable of an unusual, unknown, and new form of behavior.

Who is the enemy? Is he the personal enemy or that of the nation? Is he the religious or political opponent? Is he also the socially other, the master or the slave? This kind of casuistic question reminds us of the question of the lawyer: "Who is my neighbor?", and what was certainly for him the disconcerting answer: one must oneself become the neighbor (cf. Lk 10:25-37). One may presume that Jesus in his command intentionally did not further specify the word "enemy" and thus had in mind every kind of enemy: everyone who acts with hostility toward me.

If one wishes to speak of a further specification and concretization of the commandment, then reference can be made to vv 39b-40, 42 from Q, the passage on retaliation:

> 39b If anyone strikes you on the right cheek, turn to him
> the other also;
> 40 and if anyone would sue you and take your coat, let
> him have your cloak as well;
> 42 Give to him who begs [something] from you, and do
> not refuse him who would borrow from you.

In vv. 39b-40, two concrete situations are given: the dishonorable blow on the right cheek (given with the back of the right hand of the enemy) and the threatening danger of a lawsuit for one's possessions. Twice, Jesus intends an individual, not a party or a state. Jesus forbids resistance and violence. One's own honor or rights are not limits for love. Jesus demands more than passive submission: "turn to him the other also, let him have your cloak as well." Is this active response intended primarily for the shaming and conversion of the enemy, the conquest of evil? Paul writes: "If your enemy is hungry, feed him; if he is thirsty, give him drink; for by so doing you will heap burning coals upon his head. Do not be overcome by evil but overcome evil with good" (Rom 12:20-21). This excellent result is certainly also included in the concept as an objective to be achieved. But first and foremost, Jesus has his disciples in mind rather than the enemy. Nevertheless, this behavior according to Jesus' directive immediately elevates the entire situation to a higher level and invites the enemy to repentance.

When listening to Jesus' words, each Christian who knows history will think about the bloody crusades, the religious wars of the past and present, the inquisition, and the many forms of Christian violence. Inevitably, the Christian will also think, now perhaps more than formerly, about self-defense, just armaments, and even war, the political power of the state, which employs repressive violence, and also the demands for unilateral disarmament or conscientious objection to military service which are growing louder by the day.

In the Garden of Olives, the Matthean Jesus turned to the disciple who had cut off the ear of the servant of the high priest and said: "Put your sword back into its place; for all who take the sword will perish by the sword" (Mt 26:52). And Jesus let himself be taken prisoner. The contemporary follower of this Jesus realizes all too well that this sword has become an arsenal of nuclear weapons. May one use such weapons or even merely threaten to use them? Must we possess them to frighten off other potential users? Or is this armament in itself so radically unevangelical, morally so thoroughly repugnant that the only Christian reaction is disarmament, if necessary unilaterally? On the other hand, however, we have contemporary examples of tyranny, murder, and genocide that could only be broken by counter-violence.

In his study, *Der ekklesiale Sitz im Leben der Aufforderung Jesu zum Gewaltverzicht*, G. Lohfink rejects, rightly in my opinion, a double dilution of Jesus' call. (1) Jesus intends more than an inner disposition. His directive is more than an ideal to be striven for but never to be reached. No, Jesus intends a concrete kind of behavior that is manifested in acts. (2) Jesus' call is also not only intended for the individual. The distinction between individual (private) and society (public) is too simplistic. Lohfink demonstrates that Jesus actually has his disciples in mind with his commands, i.e., the new Israel where God's Kingdom is present. For this group of people, the call is a directive to be realized. Where Christians live with each other as church, non-violence and preferring to suffer injustice is the strict rule. In this way, Christians will indeed be the light of the world.

But Lohfink knows that Christians live in a pluralistic society, in states that do not include the Sermon on the Mount in their constitutions, and he shows how Christians can behave in them. Some of them will present prophetic witness of non-violence, for example, by conscientious objection to military service or by refusing to practice certain professions. Other Christians will have to help maintain order, sometimes even with violence. But everyone will have to work so that the spirit of the Sermon on the Mount limits and humanizes the inevitable violence as much as possible.

An exegetical work is not the appropriate place to explain these complicated questions with the necessary nuances or to propose morally justified and viable solutions. But perhaps a general consideration can help us as we form our judgments. As always with such radical sayings in the New Testament, one must seek Jesus' actual intention in his prohibition of resistance. What Jesus intended was the unconditional love for one's fellow-persons. As soon as my non-violence itself becomes the cause of injustice for someone other than my enemy, as soon as, therefore, an innocent third party will suffer by a hostile act against me or society, then, paradoxically, it is not excluded that Jesus' intention is best accomplished by resistance and, if necessary, counter-violence. It is obvious that whoever strives to make a responsible judgment will comprehend all too well how easily he can be a victim of self-delusion.

This entire argument concerns the presence of the Christian in the "world"; it is important and has an apostolic significance. But that which is specifically Christian can only be purely experienced in a group of like-minded people, in a Christian community. Are our churches by their non-violence the salt of the earth and the light of the world?

## DO WHATEVER YOU WISH THAT PEOPLE WOULD DO TO YOU

With v. 42: "Give to him who begs [something] from you, and do not refuse him who would borrow from you," Jesus gives the generalized positive complement to vv. 39b and 40 (see also p. 216 above on Lk 6:29-30). This extension is further continued in Mt 7:12 (= Lk 6:31), the Golden Rule, as we have seen in Q (and with Jesus?) following v. 42: "Whatever you wish that people would do to you, do so to them."

Does the Golden Rule go back to Jesus? There seems to be no reason to deny the possibility. But if 7:12 is from Jesus, then Jesus again took a saying from the tradition of his people. Again, the formulation may well be characteristic of him: "Do" is positive and "whatever you wish that people would do to you" — not at all a stimulus for egoistic calculation — goes very, very far indeed (see also p. 180 above).

Nevertheless, Merklein correctly points out that the Golden Rule is not an adequate summary of Jesus' ethical program. This rule is too anthropocentric. As we had to integrate the motivations of vv. 44-45 into that of v. 48b, the mercy of God in salvation history, so we must also see the Golden Rule as subordinate to the *basileia*-gift of God. God's way of acting with people as it became historically visible in Christ is not only an example and ideal but also the basis and achievement of our love of our fellow person.

## III. The Lucan Emphases

After this long discourse on Luke's source, Q, and particularly on Jesus, I will return in this third section to the evangelist and pose the question of the particular emphases of the Lucan Sermon on the Plain. First, we must briefly recall Luke's compositional method..

### STYLE

In the first part of this chapter, we saw that Luke faithfully preserved the Q-order, vv. 27-36 (unit b) excepted. He expanded his source text here and there: vv. 24-26 (R; woes), vv. 34-35ab (R; end of unit b), and vv. 39-40 (Q-parable of the blind leader and the Q-saying of the disciple and master). Besides this expansion, vv. 20-49 are charactrized by the new structure that Luke gave to this sermon. Like the original Q-sermon, the Sermon on the Plain has an introduction and a conclusion. With the woes, the introduction in Luke (a: vv.20-26) has become longer; the conclusion (d: vv. 46-49) is shorter, since vv. 43-45 in Luke's composition still belongs to the large middle part. Q also has a middle part, consisting of three units (see pp. 217-218 above); Luke divided it in two: b (vv. 27-36: love of enemy) and c (vv. 37-45: not judging). This structure is the result of his view of the content.

Of course, there is also the rewriting. As regards the beatitudes and woes and the parable of the house on rock or on sand, I refer again to pp. 68-74 and p. 197 above. Here attention must be called to 6:32-35. The symmetrical sentence construction is striking:

> 32 If you love those who love you,
>         what credit is that to you?
>     For even sinners love those who love them.
> 33 And if you do good to those who do good to you,
>         what credit is that to you?
>     For even sinners do the same.
> 34 And if you lend to those from whom you hope to receive,
>         what credit is that to you?
>     Even sinners lend to sinners, to receive as much again.
> 35 But love your enemies,
>     and do good,
>     and lend, expecting nothing in return;
>         and your reward will be great, and you will be sons of the
>         Most High; for he is kind to the ungrateful and the selfish.

In vv. 32-34, Luke repeats the same sentence construction three times, like a refrain. More than one finds in Matthew, who prizes symmetry highly, Luke breaks through the monotony of a too slavish repetition by means of small variations. Since v. 34 is Lucan redaction and v. 35a takes up again the three verbs of the preceding verses (see p. 212 above), we must presume that Luke has intentionally imposed a structure. In v. 35b, we read "and your reward will be great"; the term "reward" comes from Q (cf. Mt 5:46-47, and see below), and the phrase is virtually a repetition of v. 23b. This added sentence shows that the promise of v. 35c, "and you will be sons of the Most High," is seen by Luke as a strictly eschatological reward.

The Q-text that Luke used reads:

> 45 and you will be sons of your Father, for he makes his sun rise on the evil and on the good and sends rain on the just and on the unjust. 46 For if you love those who love you, what reward have you? Do not even the tax collectors do the same? 47 And if you salute only your brethren,

what reward have you? Do not even the Gentiles do the same?

In his v. 35, Luke replaced "Father" by "Most High" and summarized the double creative activity of God ("makes his sun rise, sends rain") by "kind," with which he also recalls the three verbs (and particularly "do good") of vv. 32-34. "The ungrateful and the selfish" are also summaries. By *acharistous* ("the ungrateful"), he alludes to a favorite term of his, *charis* ("thank, credit"), which he uses three times in vv. 32-34 to replace "reward" in Q (see vv. 46-47). In v. 33, he writes instead of "and if you salute only your brethren" (Q, v. 47) "if you do good to those who do good to you," which was "for the Greeks a direct link to a widespread ethical doctrine" (Van Unnik, p. 122). Finally, for his Gentile-Christian readers, he replaces the too Jewish-sounding combination of "tax collectors and Gentiles" (Q, vv. 46-47) by the more general "sinners," which is repeated three times in vv. 32-34 (cf. also the "selfish" in v. 35).

Luke has clearly hellenized and generalized this passage. Van Unnik points out how the principle of reciprocity (performing a return service, *charis* for *charis*) dominated ancient Greek society and its ethic. Luke is speaking polemically. To love only those who love us is simply the payment of a debt and in no way qualifies for thanks (*charis*) from God. Luke wants to cut through this Gentile conception, for the Most High is good also to the ungrateful and the selfish. "Luke has here formally hellenized [the text] but at the same time very sharply criticized Greek morality. He has clothed the words in a Greek garment, but thereby not changed the content of Jesus' preaching. On the contrary, he has translated it well, expressed it more pointedly, actualized it, and applied it." (p. 126).

This analysis of vv. 32-35 confirms the findings given above about vv. 27-36. Not only by reordering but also by rewriting and changing the style, Luke has adapted this passage to the needs of his readers on the basis of his own more hellenistic and universalist mentality.

## ACCENTS

I need not repeat here what was said in the second chapter above about the Lucan emphasis in 6:20-26. Luke is, of course, in agreement with the ideas that Jesus presented according to the Q-Sermon on the Mount. His inclusion of this sermon in his gospel proves his concurrence and his desire to transmit the tradition faithfully. We certainly may not lose sight of this. Nevertheless, four Lucan accents in the Sermon on the Plain deserve mention.

a) *Offer no resistance.* Immediately after the fourfold expression of the call to love the enemy in vv. 27-28, the Lucan Jesus in vv. 29-30 gives four tasks that prohibit this resistance. The source text in Q reads:

> 39b If anyone strikes you on the right cheek, turn to him the other also; 40 and if anyone would sue you and take your coat, let him have your cloak as well. 42 Give to him who begs from you, and do not refuse him who would borrow from you.

Lk 6:29a is almost the same as Q: "To him who strikes you on the cheek, offer the other also." In v. 29b, "and from him who takes away your cloak do not withhold your coat as well," Luke changes the coat-cloak order (perhaps ignorant of the Jewish prescription of not keeping the cloak of a poor man as pledge overnight; cf. Ex 22:25-26 and Dt 24:12-13). By the omission of the legal context, he generalizes the saying; the prohibition "do not withhold your coat as well" is an exhortation not to offer resistance. V. 30a "give to every one who begs from you" is also much more general with the addition of "every one" and the use of the present tense *didou* (literally: "keep giving") instead of the aorist *dou* ("give once for good, one time) — the same change as in the Lord's Prayer, Lk 11:3 (see also p. 132 above). V. 30b "and of him who takes away your goods do not ask them again" is the result of a complete rewriting: there is nothing about lending (but see vv. 34-35); there is the repetition of the idea of v. 29b, but the exhortation to allow things to happen and to offer no resistance is even more general. In view of the new stress in vv. 29b and 30b, it seems advisable to read the entirety of vv. 29-30 (including v. 30a) as a call for non-violent submission. Four times, therefore, Luke underlines a far-reaching accommodation to the enemy.

As we have seen pp. 212-213 above), Luke inserted vv. 29-30 between vv. 27-28 (transferred) and vv. 31-36. He considers this renunciation of active opposition as a concretization of the love of the enemy. For Luke, the enemies are probably the persecutors of the Christians, those who "hate" the Christians (cf. v. 27c with v. 22a and with the end of v. 22: "on account of the Son of Man"). The Lucan Jesus recommends an attitude and a spirituality to his humble, powerless, severely persecuted Christians (who are also Luke's readers!) that give us pause.

b) *Love of the poor.* For the readers of the Gospel of Luke and the Acts of the Apostles, this is a well-known theme. I need here only refer to texts such as Lk 5:11, 28; 12:20-21, 33-34; 14,33; 16:19-31; 18:22; and 19:1-10 and Acts 2:44-45 and 4:32-37. With his woes, Luke stresses the poor-rich contrast, and moreover, he is talking about the present situation (cf. the added "now," in this life). Again, Luke is thinking primarily about the poor and persecuted Christians, who are represented by the disciples to whom the beatitudes are addressed. But the call to give, twice in the Sermon on the Plain (v. 30a: "every one", and v. 38, with very strong emphasis) and further throughout the Lucan writings, shows that the horizon is wider. The Lucan Jesus loves all the poor, just as he pities all the rich (cf. the woe of v. 24 with the parable of the rich fool in 12:13-21).

c) *Warning against false teachers?* The Matthean Jesus has the false prophets in mind in 7:15-23. Did the Lucan Jesus in the parallel text about the tree and its fruit (Lk 6:43-45 = Mt 7:16-20) also have leaders, and more specifically false teachers, in mind? According to H. Schürmann and many others the entire text of vv. 39-45 is in fact concerned with them. The verses added by Luke, 39-40, do indeed cause us to think about leaders. Luke would here be warning against a kind of "heretic" about whom Paul speaks in the farewell sermon in Miletus: "I know that after my departure fierce wolves will come in among you, not sparing the flock; and from among your own selves will arise men speaking perverse things, to draw away the disciples after them. Therefore be alert, remembering that for three years I did not cease night or day to admonish every one with tears" (Acts 20:29-31). In this sermon, Paul could also testify that he himself has proclaimed the doctrine in its entirety (cf. 20:20 and 27). Does Luke allude to the integrity and the orthodoxy of Christian doctrine in his Sermon on the Plain with a "a disciple is not above his teacher, but every one when he is fully taught will be like his teacher" (v. 40)? This is not impossible.

Nevertheless, in the entire passage of vv. 37-45, I have the impression that Luke is thinking not so much about those in authority and their false doctrine but about loveless and judgmental Christians. The bad fruit of which the parable speaks is the expressing of unjustified criticism (cf. v. 45c).

d) *Word and deed.* "To do" is a key word in the Sermon on the Plain: see vv. 31, 43, 46, 47, and 49. This was already the case in the Q-sermon. Luke must have very gladly taken over this stress on doing. We are reminded of 3:10-14 (three times: "What then shall we do?"; cf. Acts 2:37: "What shall we do?"); 8:21 ("My mother and my brothers are those who hear the word of God and do it"); 11:28 ("Blessed rather are those who hear the word of God and keep it") and about parables such as that of the faithful and the unfaithful servant (12:42-46) and the pounds (19:12-27). The parable of the Good Samaritan (10:25-37), of course, also comes to mind with v. 25: "Teacher, what shall I do...?", v. 28: "do this," and v. 37: "doing" mercy and the command "Go and do likewise." In this parable, as in the Sermon on the Plain, the subject is love of one's fellow in need (who may be an enemy), and, as in 6:46-49, the distance between theory and practice, i.e., the necessity of "doing."

## ACTUALIZATION

With his emphases, Luke has not only revealed his own insights and convictions. He has also actualized Jesus' message for his fellow believers. For it is on the basis of the concrete situation and in view of the concrete religious-moral needs of his Gentile-Christian community that he has composed his Sermon on the Plain in this way. Like Matthew, Luke also wrote after the time of Jesus and the Q-document and stands in his own era, which was also the time of his first Christian readers. How can we, the later generations, actualize Jesus and the gospels?

Nobody will doubt the need for actualization. A fundamentalist, literal application of the Scriptures is simply wrong, if not pernicious. The times have changed. We need only think about the upheavals in history, the revolution in the social order, the growth of the world economy, the possibilities of communication, and, with daily information about far distant events, the increasing awareness that all people ultimately belong together. Better than ever we understand the differences of culture, race, and religion, but more keenly than ever we yearn for universal brotherhood and sisterhood, disarmament, and peace, because for the first time there is the real danger of total self-destruction by a nuclear war. We are afraid of the continuing tension between the hostile blocs of major powers. Does Jesus' call and that of the evangelists, addressed so directly to the individual or the small group of disciples and Christians, not disappear in this new, vast constellation and the tumult that accompanies it?

Still, the way to a true improvement of the world proceeds from the moral interiority of the individual person. The actuality of the difficult love for every kind of enemy — social, national, religious —, the actuality of the high morality of a properly understood non-violence, the assistance given to the suppressed and impoverished fellow person, the eternal struggle against the dichotomy in the person who acts other than he or she thinks and confesses, the radical motivation of the command to love the other, a motivation that lies in God's concrete love for all of us sinners, manifested in Jesus of Nazareth: who would dispute the urgency of all of this?

Even though one does not follow the command literally and does not offer the left cheek or let the cloak be taken, even though one accepts interest on invested, "loaned" money and stands up for one's rights, even though society punishes criminals and governments demand police, armies, and weapons, still the Sermon on the Mount and the Sermon on the Plain are also intended for Christians who are citizens of this society. There is no doubt that the changed structures and circumstances demand that we live the Sermon in our own, contemporary way. The adaptation will require intelligent consultation and insight into what Jesus meant, but it does not make the fulfillment any easier. The Christian spirit and praxis must be present in the individual, as well as in economic, social, national, and international relations. Otherwise we must suffer the penalty of having betrayed Jesus, the one sent by God and God's ever valid Word.

# Bibliography

See also the general works listed on pp. 41-44.

Lohfink, G., "Der ekklesiale Sitz im Leben der Aufforderung Jesu zum Gewaltverzicht (Mt 5, 39b-42/ Lk 6, 29f)," *Theologische Quartalschrift* 162 (1982) 236-253

Merklein, *Gottesherrschaft* (see p. 79 above), pp. 222-237, 243-346.

Schürmann, H., "Die Warnung des Lukas vor der Falschlehre in der Predigt am Berge Lk 6,20-39," in: Schürmann, *Traditionsgeschichtliche Untersuchungen zu den synoptischen Evangelien*, Düsseldorf, 1968, pp. 290-309.

Topel, L. J., "The Lukan Version of the Lord's Sermon," *Bibl. Theol. Bull.* 11 (1981) 48-53.

Van Unnik, W. C., "Die Motivierung der Feindesliebe in Lukas vi 32-35," in: Van Unnik, *Sparsa collecta I* (Suppl. Nov. Test. 29), Leiden, 1973, pp. 111-126.

Vögtle, *Was ist Frieden?* (see p. 121 above).

Worden, R.D., *A Philological Analysis of Luke 6:20b-49 and Parallels* (Ph.D. diss., Princeton Sem. 1973).

Zeller, *Mahnsprüche* (see p. 121 above).

# *Appendix*

# Synoptic Translation of the Text

The complete text of the Sermon on the Mount and the Sermon on the Plain is printed in this fascicle in a synoptic arrangement. For the parallel texts which were presumably not part of the original Q-sermon (e.g. Mt 5:13 = Lk 14:34-35), see a N.T. edition or the discussion in this book. The numbers of those verses in Lk which are out of order are printed in italics (vv. 21b, *21a*, 22; vv. 29-31, *27-28*, 32-36). For easier identification each verse begins with a new line.

| *Matthew* | *Luke* |
|---|---|
| *Narrative Beginning* (5:1-2) | *Narrative Beginning* (6:20a) |
| 5,1 Seeing the crowds, he [= Jesus] went up on the mountain, and when he sat down his disciples came to him. | |
| 2 And he opened his mouth and taught them saying: | 6:20a And he (= Jesus) lifted up his eyes on his disciples, and said: |
| *INTRODUCTION:* THE BEATITUDES (5:3-16) | *INTRODUCTION:* THE BEATITUDES AND WOES (6:20b-26) |
| 3 Blessed are the poor in spirit, for *theirs* is the Kingdom of heaven. | 20b Blessed are you poor, for your is the Kingdom of God. |
| 4 Blessed are those who mourn, | 21b Blessed are you that weep now, |
| for *they* shall be comforted | for you shall laugh. |

5 Blessed are the meek,
for *they* shall inherit the earth.

6 Blessed are those who hunger and thirst for righteousness, for *they* shall be satisfied.

*21a* Blessed are you that hunger now,
for you shall be satisfied.

7 Blessed are the merciful,
for *they* shall obtain mercy.

8 Blessed are the pure in heart,
for *they* shall see God.

9 Blessed are the peacemakers,
for *they* shall be called sons of God.

10 Blessed are those who are persecuted for righteousness' sake,
for *theirs* is the Kingdom of heaven.

11 Blessed are you when they revile you and persecute you and utter all kinds of evil against you falsely on my account.

22 Blessed are you when people hate you, and when they exclude you and revile you, and cast out your name as evil, on account of the Son of Man!

12 Rejoice and be glad, for your reward is great in heaven, for so they persecuted the prophets before you.

23 Rejoice in that day, and leap for joy, for behold, your reward is great in heaven: for in the same way their fathers did to the prophets.

24 But woe to you that are rich, for you have received your consolation.

25a Woe to you that are full now, for you shall hunger.

25b Woe to you that laugh now, for you shall mourn and weep.

26 Woe to you, when all men speak well of you, for so their fathers did to the false prophets.

13 You are the salt of the earth; but if the salt has lost its taste,

(for Mt 5:13, cf. Lk 14:34-35; Mk 9:50)

how shall its saltness be restored?
It is no longer good for anything
except to be thrown out and
trodden under foot by men.
14 You are the light of the world.
A city on a hill cannot be hid.
15 Nor do men light a lamp and
put it under a bushel, but on a
stand, and it gives light to all in
the house.
16 Let your light so shine before
men, that they may see your good
works and give glory to your
Father who is in heaven.

(for Mt 5:15, cf. Lk 8:16; 11:33;
Mk 4:21)

## MIDDLE PART I:
## THE ANTITHESES (5:17-48)

17 Think not that I have come to
abolish the Law or the Prophets;
I have come not to abolish but
to fulfill them.
18 For truly, I say to you, till
heaven and earth pass away, not
an iota, not a dot, will pass from
the Law until all is accomplished.
19 Whoever then relaxes one of
the least of these commandments
and teaches men so, shall be
called least in the Kingdom of
heaven; but he who does them
and teaches them shall be called
great in the Kingdom of heaven.
20 For I tell you, unless your
righteousness exceeds that of
the scribes and Pharisees, you
will never enter the Kingdom of
heaven.

(for Mt 5:18, cf. Lk 16:17)

(1) *Murder*

21 You have heard that it was said to the men of old, "You shall not kill; and whoever kills shall be liable to judgment."

22 But I say to you that every one who is angry with his brother shall be liable to judgment; whoever insults his brother shall be liable to the council, and whoever says, "You fool!" shall be liable to the hell of fire.

23 So if you are offering your gift at the altar, and there remember something that your brother has against you,

24 leave your gift there before the altar and go; first be reconciled to your brother, and then come and offer your gift.

25 Make friends quickly with your accuser, while you are going with him to court, lest your accuser hand you over to the judge, and the judge to the guard, and you be put in prison;

(for Mt 5:25-26, cf. Lk 12:57-59)

26 truly, I say to you, you will never get out till you have paid the last penny.

(2) *Adultery*

27 You have heard that it was said, "You shall not commit adultery."

28 But I say to you that every one who looks at a woman lustfully has already committed adultery with her in his heart.

29 If your right eye causes you to sin, pluck it out and throw it away; it is better that you lose one of your members than that your whole body be thrown into hell. 30 And if your right hand causes you to sin, cut it off and throw it away; it is better that you lose one of your members than that your whole body go into hell.

(for Mt 5:29-30, cf. Mk 9:43-48)

(3) *Divorce*
31 It was also said, "Whoever divorces his wife, let him give her a certificate of divorce."
32 But I say to you that every one who divorces his wife, except on the ground of unchastity, makes her an adulteress; and whoever marries a divorced woman commits adultery.

(for Mt 5:32, cf. Lk 16:18)

(4) *Swearing*
33 Again you have heard that it was said to the men of old, "You shall not swear falsely, but shall perform to the Lord what you have sworn."
34 But I say to you, Do not swear at all, either by heaven, for it is the throne of God,
35 or by the earth, for it is his footstool, or by Jerusalem, for it is the city of the great king.
36 And do not swear by your head, for you cannot make one hair white or black.
37 Let what you say be simply "Yes, yes" or "No, no"; anything more than this comes from evil.

(5) *Retaliation*

**MIDDLE PART I:**
**LOVE OF ENEMY (6:27-36)**

38 You have heard that it was said, "An eye for an eye and a tooth for a tooth."
39 But I say to you, Do not resist one who is evil.

But if any one strikes you on the right cheek, turn to him the other also;

29 To him who strikes you on cheek, offer the other also;

40 and if any one would sue you and take your coat, let him have your cloak as well;

and from him who takes away you cloak do not withhold your coat as well.

41 and if any one forces you to go one mile, go with him two miles.
42 Give to him who begs from you, and do not refuse him who would borrow from you.

30 Give to every one who begs from you; and of him who takes away your goods do not ask them again.

(7:12 So whatever you wish that men would do to you, do so to them; for this is the Law and the Prophets.)

31 And as you wish that men would do to you, do so to them.

(6) *Love of enemy*

43 You have heard that it was said, "You shall love your neighbor and hate your enemy."
44 But I say to you, Love your enemies

27 But I say to you that hear, Love your enemies, do good to those who hate you,
28 bless those who curse you, pray for those who abuse you.

and pray for those who persecute you,

45 so that you may be sons of your Father who is in heaven; for he makes his sun rise on the evil and on the good, and sends rain on the just and on the unjust.

46 For if you love those who love you, what reward have you? Do not even the tax collectors do the same?

47 And if you salute only your your brethren, what more are you doing than others? Do not even the Gentiles do the same?

32 If you love those who love you, what credit is that to you? For even sinners love those who love them.

33 And if you do good to those who do good to you, what credit is that to you? For even sinners do the same.

34 And if you lend to those from whom you hope to receive, what credit is that to you? Even sinners lend to sinners, to receive as much again.

35 But love your enemies, and do good, and lend, expecting nothing in return; and your reward will be great, and you will be sons of the Most High; for he is kind to the ungrateful and the selfish.

48 You, therefore, must be perfect, as your heavenly Father is perfect.

36 Be merciful, even as your Father is merciful.

## MIDDLE PART II:
## NOT BEFORE MEN (6:1-18)

6:1 Beware of practicing your righteousness before men in order to be seen by them; for then you will have no reward from your Father who is in heaven.

### (1) *Giving alms*

2 Thus when you give alms, sound no trumpet before you, as the hypocrites do in the synagogues and in the streets, that they may be praised by men. Truly, I say to you, they have their reward.

But when you give alms, do
not let your left hand know
what your right hand is doing,
4 So that your alms may be in
secret; and your Father who sees
in secret will reward you.

(2) *Praying*

5 And when you pray, you must
not be like the hypocrites, for
they love to stand and pray in
the synagogues and at the street
corners, that they may be seen by
men. Truly, I say to you, they
have their reward.
6 But when you pray, go into
your room and shut the door and
pray to your Father who sees in
secret; and your Father who sees
in secret will reward you.

7 And in praying do not heap up
empty phrases as the Gentiles
do; for they think that they will
be heard for their many words.
8 Do not be like them, for your
Father knows what you need before you ask him.

9 Pray then like this: Our Father        (for Mt 6:9-13, cf. Lk 11:2-4)
who art in heaven, hallowed be
thy name.
10 thy Kingdom come, thy will be
done, on earth as it is in heaven.
11 Give us this day our daily
bread;
12 and forgive us our debts, as
we have forgiven our debtors;
13 and lead us not into temptation, but deliver us from evil.

14 For if you forgive men their trespasses, your heavenly Father also will forgive you;
15 but if you do not forgive men their trespasses, neither will your Father forgive your trespasses.

(for Mt 6:14-15; cf. Mk 11:25)

### (3) *Fasting*

16 And when you fast, do not look dismal, like the hypocrites, for they disfigure their faces that their fasting may be seen by men. Truly, I say to you, they have their reward.
17 But when you fast, anoint your head and wash your face,
18 that your fasting may not be seen by men but by your Father who is in secret; and your Father who sees in secret will reward you.

## *MIDDLE PART III:* UNCONCERN AND COMMITMENT (6:19-7:12)

### (1) *Earthly concern*

19 Do not lay up for yourselves treasures on earth, where moth and rust consume and where thieves break in and steal,
20 but lay up for yourselves treasures in heaven, where neither moth nor rust consumes and where thieves do not break in and steal.
21 For where your treasure is, there will your heart be also.

(for Mt 6:19-21, cf. Lk 12:33-34)

22 The eye is the lamp of the body. So, if your eye is sound, your whole body will be full of light;

(for Mt 6:22-23, cf. Lk 11:34-36)

23 but if your eye is not sound, your whole body will be full of darkness. If then the light in you is darkness, how great is the darkness!

24 No one can serve two masters; for either he will hate the one and love the other, or he will be devoted to the one and despise the other. You cannot serve God and mammon.

(for Mt 6:24, cf. Lk 16:13)

25 Therefore I tell you, do not be anxious about your life, what you shall eat or what you shall drink, nor about your body, what you shall put on. Is not life more than food, and the body more than clothing?

(for Mt 6:25-34, cf. Lk 12:22-31)

26 Look at the birds of the air; they neither sow nor reap nor gather into barns, and yet your heavenly Father feeds them. Are you not of more value than they?

27 And which of you by being anxious can add one cubit to his span of life?

28 And why are you anxious about clothing? Consider the lilies of the field, how they grow; they neither toil nor spin;

29 yet I tell you, even Solomon in all his glory was not arrayed like one of these.

30 But if God so clothes the grass of the field, which today

is alive and tomorrow is thrown
into the oven, will he not much
more clothe you, O men of little
faith?
31 Therefore do not be anxious,
saying, "What shall we eat?" or
"What shall we wear?"
32 For the Gentiles seek all these
things; and your heavenly Father
knows that you need them all.
33 But seek first his Kingdom and
his righteousness, and all these
things shall be yours as well.
34 Therefore do not be anxious
about tomorrow, for tomorrow
will be anxious for itself. Let the
day's own trouble be sufficient
for the day.

(2) *Not judging*

7:1 Judge not, that you be not
judged
2 For with the judgment you pronounce you will be judged,

and the measure you give will be
the measure you get.
(for Lk 6:39, cf. Mt 15:14)

(for Lk 6:40, cf. Mt 10:24-25)

## MIDDLE PART II: NOT JUDGING (6:37-45)

37 And judge not, and you will
not be judged;

condemn not, and you will not
be condemned; forgive, and you
will be forgiven;
38 give, and it will be given to
you; good measure, pressed
down, shaken together, running
over, will be put into your lap.
For the measure you give will be
the measure you get back.
39 He also told them a parable:
Can a blind man lead a blind
man? Will they not both fall
into a pit?
40 A disciple is not above his

teacher, but every one when he is fully taught will be like his teacher.

3 Why do you see the speck that is in your brother's eye, but do not notice the log that is in your own eye?

41 Why do you see the speck that is in your brother's eye, but do not notice the log that is in your own eye?

4 Or how can you say to your brother, "Let me take the speck out of your eye," when there is the log in your own eye?

42 Or how can you say to your brother, "Brother, let me take out the speck that is in your eye," when you yourself do not see the log that is in your own eye? You hypocrite, first take the log out of your own eye, and then you will see clearly to take out the speck that is in your brother's eye.

5 You hypocrite, first take the log out of your own eye, and then you will see clearly to take the speck out of your brother's eye.

6 Do not give the dogs what is holy, and do not throw pearls before swine, lest they trample them under foot and turn to attack you.

(3) *Prayer*

7 Ask, and it will be given you; seek, and you will find; knock, and it will be opened to you.

(for Mt 7:7-11, cf. Lk 11:9-13)

8 For every one who asks receives, and he who seeks finds, and to him who knocks it will be opened.

9 Or what man of you, if his son asks him for bread, will give him a stone?

10 Or if he asks for a fish, will give him a serpent?

11 If you then, who are bad, know how to give good gifts to your children, how much more will

your Father who is in heaven
give good things to those who
ask him!

12 So whatever you wish that
men would do to you, do so to
them; for this is the Law and the
Prophets.

(6:31 And as you wish that men
would do to you, do so to them.)

## CONCLUSION:
## THE WAY TO LIFE (7:13-27)

### (1) *The Gate and the Way*

13 Enter by the narrow gate; for
the gate is wide and the way is
easy, that leads to destruction,
and those who enter by it are
many.

(for Mt 7:13-14, cf. Lk 13:23-24)

14 How narrow is the gate and
hard the way that leads to life,
and those who find it are few!

### (2) *Tree and Fruit*

15 Beware of false prophets, who
come to you in sheep's clothing
but inwardly are ravenous wolves.
16 You will know them by their
fruits. Are grapes gathered
from thorns, or figs from thistles?
17 So, every good tree bears
beautiful fruits, but the sick
tree bears bad fruits.

18 A good tree cannot bear bad
fruits, nor can a sick tree bear
beautiful fruits.

43 For no good tree bears bad
fruit, nor again does a bad tree
bear good fruit;

19 Every tree that does not bear
beautiful fruits is cut down and
thrown into the fire.
20 Thus you will know them by
their fruits.

44 for each tree is known by its
own fruit. For figs are not gath-

ered from thorns, nor are grapes picked from a bramble bush.

45 The good man out of the good treasure produces good, and the bad man out of his bad treasure produces bad; for out of the abundance of his heart his mouth speaks.

(3) *"Lord, Lord"*

CONCLUSION:
THE HOUSE AND THE STORM (6:46-49)

21 Not every one who says to me "Lord, Lord," shall enter the Kingdom of heaven, but he who does the will of my Father in heaven.

46 Why do you call me "Lord, Lord," and not do what I tell you?

22 On that day, many will say to me, "Lord, Lord, did we not prophesy in your name, and cast out demons in your name, and do many mighty works in your name?"

(for Mt 7:22-23, cf. Lk 13:25-27)

23 And then will I declare to them, "I never knew you; depart from me, you evildoers."

(4) *The House and the Storm*

24 Every one then who hears these words of mine and does them

47 Every one who comes to me and hears my words and does them, I will show you what he is like:

will be like a wise man who built his house upon the rock.

48 he is like a man building a house, who dug deep, and laid the foundation upon rock; and when a flood arose, the stream broke against that house, and could not shake it, because

25 and the rain fell, and the floods came, and the winds blew and beat upon that house, but

it did not fall, because it had been founded on the rock.

it had been well built.

26 And every one who hears these words of mine and does not do them will be like a foolish man who built his house upon the sand;
27 and the rain fell, and the floods came, and the winds blew and beat against that house, and it fell; and great was the fall of it.

49 But he who hears and does not do them is like a man who built a house on the ground without a foundation;

against which the stream broke, and immediately it fell, and the ruin of that house was great.

## Narrative Ending (7:28-29)

28 And when Jesus finished these sayings, the crowds were astonished at his teaching,
29 for he taught them as one who had authority, and not as their scribes.

## Narrative Ending (7:1a)

7:1a After he had ended all his sayings in the hearing of the people....

# I. INDEX OF CITATIONS

## A. OLD TESTAMENT

## B. NEW TESTAMENT

249

**Galatians**
3:1-5    201
4:6    136, 146
5:1—6:10 201
  13—6:10 108
  14    201

**Ephesians**
2:18    146

**Philippians**
2:16-11  146

**1 Timothy**
6:7-10    76-7

**Hebrews**
1:1-3    11
7:25    147

**James**
1:13    142
5:12    97, 98

**1 Peter**
5:7    159

**Revelation**
3:10    142
22:20    146

# II. INDEX OF NAMES

Albright, W. F., 41.
Allen, W. C., 41.
Anselm, 108.
Ashton, J., 149.

Bammel, E., 150.
Banks, R., 118.
Barrett, C. K., 150.
Barth, G., 118.
Beare, F. W., 41.
Best, E., 181.
Betz, H. D., 42, 78, 118, 149, 181, 205.
Black, M., 181.
Bligh, J., 42.
Böckmann, A., 78.
Boff, L., 149.
Bomans, G., 216.
Bonhoeffer, D., 182, 198. 204.
Bonnard, P., 41, 149.
Bornkamm, G., 42, 101, 118, 149, 155-64, 165, 176, 181.
Bossuyt, J., 42.
Brocke, M., 150.
Broer, I., 99, 118.
Brown, R. E., 74, 149.

Caird, G. B., 42.
Calvin, 23.
Campbell, K. M., 78.
Carmignac, J., 133, 139, 143, 149.

Carson, D. A., 42.
Catchpole, D., 42, 181.
Chrysostom, 20.
Conzelmann, H., 121, 139.
Crossan, J. D., 118.

Danker, E. W., 42.
Daube, D., 150.
Dautzenberg, G., 97, 99, 118.
Davies, W. D., 42, 150.
De Fraine, J., 78, 149.
Delobel, J., 205.
Denaux, A., 183, 196, 205.
Derrett, J. D. M., 205.
Descamps, A.-L., 43, 67, 118.
De Vriese, J., 86-7, 119.
Dibelius, M., 42.
Dietzfelbinger, C., 119.
Doberstein, J. W., 44.
Dodd, C. H., 78.
Dorneich, M., 149.
Dumbrell, W. J., 78, 119.
Ducey, W. M., 150.
Dupont, J., 43, 48, 56, 57, 61, 65, 71, 78, 88, 119, 137, 149.

Ebeling, G., 118.
Edmonds, P., 149.
Eid, V., 78.
Ellis, E. E., 42, 150.